Truth Betrayed

W.J. West

Duckworth

First published in 1987
Gerald Duckworth & Co. Ltd.
The Old Piano Factory
43 Gloucester Crescent, London NW1

ISBN 0 7156 2182 3

British Library Cataloguing in Publication Data

West, W.J. (William John)
Truth betrayed.
1. Radio broadcasting—Political aspects
—Europe   2. Radio broadcasting—Europe—
History
I. Title
384.54′094   HE8699.E85

ISBN 0-7156-2182-3

Photoset in North Wales by
Derek Doyle & Associates, Mold, Clwyd
Printed in Great Britain by
Redwood Burn Limited, Trowbridge

Contents

In memory of
Charles Melhuish
and his forebears at Washfield

Plates

The National Photographic Record is held at the National Portrait Gallery and contains portraits of all leading figures in national life from 1919 until 1970 when, unhappily, it was temporarily suspended for administrative reasons. The National Gallery also holds the Howard Coster photograph collection (nos. 25 & 31 above). For a catalogue see Terence Pepper, *Howard Coster's Celebrity Portraits* (1985). It should be noted that the BBC Hulton Picture Library is quite distinct from the BBC's own photograph collection (photos described above as BBC photograph) and that the two collections are also housed separately.

Preface

The original research on which this book is based has been carried out largely in the Public Record Office and the BBC's Written Archives Centre. The BBC's Archives, although not held with the papers of the great Departments of State at the Public Record Office, are at least as important for the study of recent history and contain, proportionately, a far greater number of original letters, papers and memoranda; furthermore they remain intact without any thoroughgoing 'weeding' of sensitive material. It is difficult to believe, for example, that the material by Guy Burgess quoted here would have reached the Public Record Office from the Foreign Office or, if it had, that it would have been made available for study before the next century.

The theme of this book is radio and politics. The great importance of radio and the fact that the BBC was a Government-funded body, although not strictly controlled by the Government, means that a vital part of the material needed to understand the political events of the mid-twentieth century is to be found in the BBC's Archives. Material in the Foreign Office files of the Public Record Office cannot properly be understood without reference to correlate files in the BBC and vice-versa. Much that is new in this book stems from such considerations. Also, the general nature of the theme of radio and politics means that many events are linked here which might seem at first sight to have no relevant connection. The activities of Guy Burgess and Sir Oswald Mosley might appear to have little in common. But Mosley's efforts to establish a radio station were very similar to those of Burgess and his colleagues in MI6; at times, in Liechtenstein for example, the two were actually fighting for the same broadcasting concession. There were numerous connections of this kind, as we shall see, all resulting from the inestimable impact of the first new medium of communication since the advent of printing.

In view of the central importance of the BBC in the narrative that follows it should be made absolutely clear that the comments about the BBC made by diplomats and civil servants, and the struggles of the BBC with the Foreign Office, relate to the BBC of fifty years and more ago. Much time, and a world war, have intervened, and the BBC of today bears little resemblance to the BBC of those times. Nothing said of the BBC in this book refers to the present BBC or its staff in any way whatsoever.

In working on this book I have had the assistance of a great many people whose kindness in the face of often urgent queries and requests has been greatly appreciated. In particular I should like to thank Mrs Jacqueline Kavanagh and Mr Jeffrey Walden at the BBC Written Archives Centre; Dr Meryl Foster and the staff at the Public Record Office, Kew; Mr Jonathan Vickers at the National Sound Archives; the staff at Exeter University Library, and in particular Dr John Stirling, the librarian, for making the facilities of the Library available to me; and the staffs of Bristol City Library, Oxford City Library and Westminster City Library. I should also like to thank Professor Peter Pulzer, Professor Ivan Roots, Dr Anthony Glees, Dr Richard Hitchcock, Dr Jeremy Noakes and Dr Patrick Pollak for their opinions on a number of points; Lord Houghton of Sowerby, Mrs I.D. Benzie-Morley, Mrs Le Grand, Mr David Armstrong, Mr Leonard Miall and Mr Michael Wigan for their help; and Mr David Slade, Mr Len Kelly, Mr Dominic Winter and Mrs Rachel Lee for making available to me various printed and other sources to which I would not otherwise have been able to obtain access. Finally, I am grateful once again to the staff at my publishers, Gerald Duckworth, and my editor and publisher Colin Haycraft with whom discussions have been invaluable. The opinions and conclusions contained in this book are mine entirely.

Exeter   W.J.W.
July 1987

Introduction

Politics in the twentieth century has been influenced by technological advance in communications more than in any previous time since the invention of printing. Radio was the first, and arguably ti.e most important. In barely a decade it came to affect the lives of people in every country of the world. Just as printing enabled books to spread rapidly and a book printed, say, in Rome could be obtained in London bookshops without delay, so radio enabled people in one country to listen in to programmes from many others. From the first genuinely world-wide broadcast in 1930,[1] the radio listener before the war could turn the tuning dial of his set to broadcasts on a myriad of wavelengths from every country in the world,[2] often in his own language. Important concerts taking place in Vienna or Berlin, Paris or Rome were listed in the national press alongside those recorded by the BBC, together with the wavelengths of the stations broadcasting them. The listener could spend his evening with a choice of programmes from the best the world had to offer, in a way which would be the envy of the television viewer today, who is confined to the channels of his national networks. The implications for politics of this wide international choice were even greater, for fierce propaganda wars were being waged over the air waves.

Many of these were carried on by secret radio stations run by people who were, in effect, a new kind of espionage agent. It was no accident that one of the most notorious spies in modern English history, Guy Burgess, was actually a skilled radio producer, trained at the BBC, which he also infiltrated, and later engaged in secret operations abroad. He and his colleagues affected international affairs directly and often more significantly that the more conventional

[1] George V made the first world-wide broadcast at noon on 21 January 1930 from the Royal Gallery at the House of Lords welcoming the delegates to the Five Power Naval Conference. Although it was in the early hours of the morning in America countless people there, from President Hoover downwards, listened to the broadcast. There are references to the conference below, see Index.

[2] It was not until the mid-thirties that sets began to appear with station names on their dials rather than frequencies which had to be looked up in tables that were often changed. This fact alone increased curiosity about other nations' broadcasts.

propaganda wars that described and misdescribed the political
happenings of the inter-war years.

The purpose of this book is to examine these events as they
appeared to the listening public, and as they were affected by the
existence of radio and radio propaganda. The 'listening public' at the
beginning of the period was already the greatest audience available
through any medium. Far more people listened to the radio than read
newspapers, and the broadcaster who was politically conscious knew
that he was addressing people, both illiterate and educated, who
formed the closest approach to pure democracy so far known.
Although it was the totalitarian states who first made great use of this
fact,[3] the BBC and the British Government were fully conscious of its
importance. An election in New Zealand had been won through the
intervention of broadcasting on behalf of the Labour Party and the
folly of a Conservative Party caught in attempts to jam the
broadcasts.[4] Many events – for example, the banning in Britain of the
Duke of Windsor's broadcast from Verdun in May 1939 appealing for
World Peace, which was heard by hundreds of millions of people all
over the world;[5] or Britain's rejection out of hand, in complete
secrecy, of the Anglo-German Cultural Agreement proposed by
Germany early in 1939[6] which had agreements on broadcasting as one
of its main objects – show clearly that Britain's earlier high intentions
for radio's impartiality had been forgotten in the face of the power of
peace-time propaganda over the new mass audience.

In the study of broadcasts and their effects it is an unfortunate fact
that the most important elements of the picture, the broadcasts
themselves, are relatively few.[7] The technical advances which made
world-wide broadcasts possible were not matched by advances in
recording. The modern tape-recorder did not exist, and a programme

[3] Not surprisingly Russia was the first: see below, p.22.

[4] The broadcasts were by a politically-conscious vicar, the Reverend C.
Scrimgeour, affectionately known as 'Scrim'. There is an account of the affair in Les
Edwards, *Scrim, Radio Rebel in Retrospect* (1971).

[5] It was the habit at the time to ascribe audiences of hundreds of millions to all
sensational broadcasts made on a world-wide link-up, as it was called, and some
commentators have been sceptical of such claims. However, subsequent experience
with television broadcasts of Royal occasions suggests that the world-wide audience
was real and did indeed reach these proportions. For a full account of the broadcast,
see below, p.161f.

[6] See below, p.147f.

[7] In the texts that follow reference is made to surviving broadcasts which can be
heard in the National Sound Archives, London. In some cases actual recordings
mentioned survive; in others individuals mentioned in the text can be heard talking on
other subjects. All these recordings help to provide an historical perspective of a kind
unique to the twentieth century.

was only recorded where its importance was seen at the time to merit a special disc recording. Often these discs were transcribed and the text appeared in the daily press shortly afterwards, providing direct evidence both of what was said and of what was thought at the time to be important. But most of the countless hours the listening public spent by their receivers were filled with material, light and serious, of which no record of any sort survives.[8] The content and feeling of these programmes are almost as lost to us as the spoken folk-lore of a primitive tribe, or the legends of the ancient world. In mainland Europe, for example, the German propaganda broadcasts to the Saar at the time of the plebiscite,[9] or Russia's German-language broadcasts to her German minorities – which could also be heard, only accidentally of course, in Germany itself – or the similar Czechoslovakian broadcasts in German to their Sudeten German minorities which so infuriated Hitler and the Nazis, exist only in the briefest extracts, if at all. Later the numerous German English-language broadcasts to Britain during the 'phoney war', which were attributed by a brilliant counter-propaganda campaign to a fictional 'Lord Haw-Haw', exist only on a few 78 rpm records and some selective monitors' reports.

Enough material survives, however, for a broad description to be attempted. As always, information becomes available when a system goes wrong. Clumsy censorship by the British Government of the BBC's programmes showed how the Government began controlling the supposedly independent BBC as war approached, totally after war broke out. Papers in the BBC's Written Archives enable the picture to be completed. Foreign Office files released in the Public Record Office contain many comments on the subject known originally as 'Wireless Telephony', and these are particularly informative when they deal with broadcasts from Berlin or concern British affairs.[10] There is also record of a full discussion in Cabinet of how Britain herself came to carry out foreign-language broadcasts both openly and through extensive secret means fully approved by the Prime Minister of the

---

[8] The BBC Written Archives contain the programmes and scripts of a large proportion of programmes in Britain. The BBC Sound Archives, which are open only to fee-paying researchers, enable some idea to be gained of these.

[9] See below, p.67f.

[10] Wireless telephony was preceded by wireless telegraphy, which was used during World War I for the dissemination of news. For this reason, no doubt, both categories were usually placed in the 'Press' sequence of files, normally the Foreign Office 395 (FO 395) files in the Public Record Office. Anyone interested in getting a complete picture of the thirties should read this series in parallel with the normal FO 371 series. The importance of radio at the time meant that many important matters, which would normally be looked for in the latter sequence, were placed in FO 395.

day, Neville Chamberlain, and carried out by Guy Burgess and his colleagues.

Newspaper reports are frequently a good guide both to broadcasts which took place and to matters connected with broadcasting which were often considered to be news in themselves. The discovery of secret broadcasting stations, whether in India, run by Congress Party supporters or in Europe, run by the Comintern to control political strikes, were worth an article, if not a headline.[11] There was also an increasing tendency as the decade wore on for important announcements and speeches to be made first over the radio and only later in the press or as an official announcement. Hitler first announced the Anschluss over the air from his home town of Linz, apparently without any previous intention of doing so, making his listeners, as he said at the time, witnesses to his actions. The people of Britain were told by their Prime Minister that they were at war with Germany before he went down to the House of Commons to tell their representatives assembled in Parliament. It could almost be said that the broadcast itself was the declaration of war; there are many references in memoirs of the period to where the writer was when he heard the broadcast, just as people remembered where they were when they heard, over the media again, that President Kennedy had been assassinated.

Direct political broadcasting in Britain itself was confined to occasional talks by the parties who had seats in the Commons and was fixed on a rota system arranged privately between the BBC dominated effectively by Reith and the party Whips.[12] The views of the active politician, whether of the extreme right or left, were banned from the air in this way, but so were those of many senior figures in Parliament. Privy Councillors and former Cabinet Ministers, Churchill prominent among them, complained in vain that they were banned from the air when, for the first time in history, an almost perfect democracy was possible. The result from the point of view of British mass audiences was disastrous. Although they were sheltered from the propaganda battles waged over the air on the continent – the first cold wars – they were also kept from the truth. A senior BBC official, writing after the Munich Crisis of September 1938,[13] spoke of

[11] For further details of these, see below, Chapter 6.

[12] There are extensive files on this question in the BBC's Written Archives Centre, both in the policy files and in relevant sections of the contributors' files of politicians who actually broadcast. See also, for example, below, p.13f.

[13] The memorandum 'The BBC and National Defence', written by John Coatman, may be found in BBC Written Archives Centre R34/600/10. It is referred to in greater detail below, p.41f. Coatman wrote an autobiography while at the BBC,

a 'conspiracy of silence' in which he and his colleagues had taken part and which had prevented the British public from obtaining any genuine understanding of the events that were shortly to plunge the country into war.

Whether a conspiracy to avoid unwelcome reality is a greater betrayal of truth than outright lies of the kind that filled the air abroad on all sides is a difficult question. Suppression of the truth can only lead to attempts to get round the ban: on the left Burgess and his circle infiltrated their views on the BBC. A right-wing party, on the other hand, attempted to set up its own broadcasting system abroad which led, as we shall see, to the suppression of a political party in Britain for the first time in her history.[14]

which became a *cause célèbre* when he was told that he could not publish it as long as he worked for the Corporation. See Governors' Minutes for 3 May 1945, no. 82. Coatman remained with the BBC and did not publish his book.

[14] This was the British Union run by Sir Oswald Mosley.

'Nation shall speak Peace unto Nation'
Motto of the British Broadcasting Corporation

PART ONE

1. Churchill, Mosley and the BBC

Among those listening to King George V as he broadcast his opening remarks at the Five Power Naval Conference in 1930[1] were two men who were to have important, but starkly contrasted, careers over the next decade. One, Sir Oswald Mosley,[2] was a junior Minister in the Government of the day; the other, Winston Churchill,[3] was seen as a figure with a great past but uncertain future, isolated from the main stream of his party's political thought. By the end of the decade Mosley had become the leader of a party of his own creation, the British Union, and was fighting a rear-guard action to bring about peace before the 'phoney war'[4] that followed Germany's occupation of

[1] The King's speech was followed by other broadcast speeches by all the main delegates, which were fully reported in the press at the time, no doubt for this reason as much as for their importance. Excerpts from Ramsay MacDonald's speech are printed below, pp.81-2.

[2] Sir Oswald Mosley (1896-1980). There is now an extensive literature on Mosley and the movement which he founded before the war, referred to in this book in its final form, 'British Union'. Mosley wrote an autobiography, *My Life* (1968). His son, Nicholas Mosley, has published two volumes – *Rules of the Game: Sir Oswald Mosley and Lady Cynthia Mosley, 1896-1933* (1982) and *Beyond the Pale: Sir Oswald Mosley and Family, 1933-80* (1983). The appearance of a biography of Mosley by Robert Skidelsky (*Oswald Mosley*, 1975; revised edition 1981) for the first time made discussion of Mosley in a serious context acceptable. A shrewd comment on him written in the thirties by a colleague, Oliver Baldwin, has stood the test of time: 'I think a great deal about him because he has guts and intelligence ... Had he stayed on the left he would have been Socialist Prime Minister; having gone to the right he will die on some self-erected barricade' (Oliver Baldwin, *Oasis*, 1936, p.313).

[3] Sir Winston Churchill (1874-1965). Of the even more extensive literature on Churchill it perhaps suffices to mention here the biography commenced by his son Randolph S. Churchill, *Winston S. Churchill*, vols 1-2 (1966-7), and continued by Martin Gilbert up to the present day in exhaustive volumes, with supplementary volumes of documents, *Winston S. Churchill*, vols 3- (1971-). Of relevance to the later part of this book are Warren F. Kimball (ed.), *Churchill and Roosevelt: The Complete Correspondence* (3 vols 1984) and Arrigo Pettacco, *Dear Benito, Caro Winston: verità e misteri del carteggio Churchill-Mussolini* (1985).

[4] The first use of this phrase I have come across is in the *New York Daily News* for 23 October 1939, when a report from Washington that the war was not living up to expectations was headlined 'The War is Phoney'. Cited in *Action*, no. 129, 2, November 1939.

Poland had a chance to deteriorate into a greater conflict. Churchill, on the other hand, was a member of the War Cabinet and as actively engaged in the nation's affairs as he had been in the First World War. A few months later Churchill was to authorize the detention of people considered a threat to the safety of the realm. One of the principal people affected was Mosley, who was detained without trial, his party abolished and its senior members interned with him.

In the intervening years both men sought to gain an active part in the political discussions of the time from the outside. Mosley had resigned from the Labour Party after it showed itself insufficiently determined for his liking on the question of unemployment;[5] he had gone on to form a New Party, which failed, and then the British Union, which was much more successful. The most obvious way he could gain an audience was through the new communication medium of radio, run as a state monopoly in Britain by a quasi-non-Governmental body, the British Broadcasting Corporation. His officers approached the Corporation throughout the decade, to no avail. His views were too extreme, his party not represented in Parliament; he had no Whip. The left were more successful, using Burgess and others to infiltrate the BBC secretly. Astonishingly to us now, Churchill found himself in much the same position as Mosley. His career followed the more normal course of a rebel outside his party; there was never a question of his forming a new party or of departing from the great traditions of British public life as he saw them. But he too was told by the BBC, in unambiguous terms, that he could not be heard by the British public. Being one of the senior Privy Councillors, he felt the exclusion more keenly than Mosley, and saw it in different terms.

The position from the BBC's viewpoint was, in 1930, still very much a matter of experiment. Until two years before, all political talks had been forbidden. Then the regulations had been relaxed and simple political talks had been allowed at election times and on matters of great importance. The Party Whips had become involved in ensuring that each party had an equivalent time on the air. The matter was

[5] Sir Oswald Mosley and five of his fellow members of the Labour Party, Lady Mosley, John Strachey, W.J. Brown, Dr Robert Forgan and Oliver Baldwin, decided to resign on 20 February 1931. However, they did so on successive days and, by the time Mosley's turn came – he was to be the last – the Labour Party had expelled him. Mosley inaugurated his New Party on 28 February 1931 and announced its closure at a meeting on 5 April. The British Union of Fascists, later to become the British Union, was launched on 1 October 1932.

raised clearly by the Labour Prime Minister Ramsay MacDonald:[6]

> I wish to minute this for the record. The Government has no desire to interfere with the BBC programmes, but it cannot be disinterested regarding the political use made by it of its opportunities. Just as it supplies Jazz rubbish (not even good Jazz) for popular consumption so, if it is not careful with its politics, it will have to supply Jazz politics. Mr Beckett created great interest by his mace escapade,[7] and thousands of BBC subscribers wish to hear Mr Beckett. The only way the BBC can protect itself is by planning its political broadcasting in close cooperation with the parties. That cooperation has not been sought with any degree of businesslike capacity in this case, and final steps have been taken without proper consideration and upon palpable misunderstanding, certainly without a conclusion of negotiations having first of all been reached. There I leave it until I have seen the Chief Whip.[8]

A few years later the Conservative Stanley Baldwin,[9] alarmed by the rise of extremist politics, made a broadcast appealing to the younger members of the community:

> I know quite well when one is young one is always in a hurry, and it may well be today that these two alien plants, for they neither have their roots in England – Communism and Fascism – may appeal to many of you. This is a free country. You can support either creed and you can support it in safety, but I want to put this to you. If there be one thing certain to my mind it is this, that if people of this country in great numbers were to become adherents of either Communism or Fascism there could only be one end to it. And that one end would be

---

[6] Ramsay MacDonald (1866-1937), Prime Minister. For an account of MacDonald's life see the entry in the *Dictionary of National Biography* by Lord Elton, who had earlier written *The Life of James Ramsay MacDonald* (1939). For later accounts, see for example David Marquand, *Ramsay MacDonald* (1977).

[7] Nowadays rowdiness is a commonplace, almost the norm, in the House of Commons, as anyone listening to the daily radio reports when the House is sitting will be aware. MacDonald is here alluding to an early example of this tendency in 1929 when the mace was seized and carried off by John Beckett (1894-1964). Beckett was later involved with William Joyce, and subsequently with the Duke of Bedford's British People's Party. For further references see Index.

[8] BBC Written Archives Centre: R34/563/1, Political Broadcasting 1928-32.

[9] Stanley Baldwin (1867-1947), Prime Minister and one of the earliest masters of the political broadcast in Britain, who was as successful in his way as President Roosevelt and his 'fireside chats'. Baldwin was notoriously uninterested in foreign affairs. Despite later apologists, blame for political developments in the thirties in this sphere often borne by his successor, Neville Chamberlain, properly belongs on Baldwin's shoulders. The broadcast quoted here shows his grasp of the political creeds of his time, but in a purely domestic sense.

civil war, and that is, I was going to say, latent in both these creeds – I would say it is not only latent but blatant – and for this reason. They both alike believe in force as the means by which they can get their way and set up their dictatorship; and they further believe, as you have seen on the continent, that, having got into power – and it does not matter for the argument whether it be Communist or Fascist – by force, all free opinion, all opinion that does not agree with them, must be suppressed by force – in other words, kill everything that has been a growth in our people for the last eight hundred or a thousand years. No. Freedom is not dead yet. Nor is Democracy.[10]

The BBC had to find a path through this political minefield. Inevitably it came down on the side of Parliamentary democracy in the form of the united opinions of the Whips of the two major parties. Although Baldwin talked about the advantages of freedom, and the dangers of Fascism and Communism for free speech, he did so over the radio, where these ideas no longer applied. He may not have been fully conscious of it, but his words would have sounded nothing but the most blatant hypocrisy to a large number of people on all sides of the House of Commons and from many more outside it. Churchill in particular, by 1934, when Baldwin spoke, had learnt the truth. Further he had put the case for just the same Democracy that Baldwin claimed to be defending. Writing to John Whitley, the Chairman of the BBC's Board of Governors,[11] on behalf of the three senior Privy Councillors – himself, Lloyd George[12] and Sir Austen Chamberlain[13] – he said:

[10] As published in Stanley Baldwin, *This Torch of Freedom* (1937 ed.), p.31f.

[11] John Henry Whitley (1866-1935), Speaker of the House of Commons from 1920 to 1928 and Chairman of the Governors of the BBC from 1930 to 1935, a post to which he was appointed by Ramsay MacDonald. He has become best known to posterity as the founder of the 'Whitley Committees', joint consultative committees between employers and employees set up as a result of recommendations of a committee he chaired in 1917-18. His entry in the *Dictionary of National Biography* was written by Horace Wilson, and there is a recorded tribute to him by Lord Reith in the National Sound Archives: NSA.LP441.b.2.

[12] David Lloyd George (1863-1945), Prime Minister. For the entire period dealt with in this book Lloyd George was away from the levers of power. However, his influence was considerable and usually seen as sympathetic towards Germany, particularly after the publication of his massive two-volume work *The Truth About the Peace Treaties* (1938). His talks and speeches were among those most frequently quoted by German radio in the early years of the war. For current views, see for example W.R.P. George, *Lloyd George Backbencher* (1983) and Kenneth O. Morgan, *David Lloyd George* (1981).

[13] Austen Chamberlain (1863-1937). The last of the formidable trio whose power

We have considered with attention the programme of broadcast political speeches which is proposed for the Autumn. Surely it introduces an entirely new principle of discrimination in British public life, namely the elimination and silencing of any Members of Parliament who are not nominated by the Party Leaders or Whips. As a former distinguished Speaker of the House of Commons, you will no doubt realise how foreign this is to the whole spirit of our Parliamentary practice. Such a principle if applied in Parliament would reduce its debates to mere regimentations of machine-controlled opinion and would deny fair expression to independent and non-official views. The Post Master General assured the house earlier in the year that 'Minorities should have their place, and individuals, perhaps not at the moment attached or perhaps only very lightly attached to any party should be chosen if they have any useful contribution to make'. It would seem therefore not at all out of harmony with the wishes of the Government if a few additional speakers could be added to the lists chosen by the Party Whips. As we are the three senior Privy Councillors in the House of Commons and have also some experience of public affairs, we venture to ask you to take the matter into consideration and add some independent speakers to the series of political talks.[14]

This letter, which was referred to Reith, failed completely in its intention. For all Baldwin's pleading for Democracy in his broadcast, barely six months after this powerful letter on behalf of the most eminent men in public life at the time, the BBC had stuck firmly to the line laid down for it by the Whips. None of the three were allowed to speak on anything other than unimportant occasions, almost always as one of a series of speakers on topics arranged half a year earlier without reference to them beforehand. The refusal, which came to them from the Chairman of the Board of Governors, was not allowed to pass without reply:

---

was seen to be non-existent in the face of the BBC and the Party Whips acting together. Of the three, Chamberlain had the closest connection to power through his brother. There has been frequent comment on the role played by his, and later his widow's, views on Italian affairs immediately before the war. There is a recent study by David Dutton, *Austen Chamberlain: Gentleman in Politics* (1985).

[14] BBC Written Archives Centre. Contributor files for those involved, the file on the incident, and related files: R34/563/2. The Churchill letters are thus to be found either in Churchill's contributor file or in R34/563/2.

Dear Mr Whitley,
    We regret to receive your refusal of our request that representatives
of independent or unofficial opinions should be included in the series of
political broadcasts arranged for this autumn. We are obliged to you
for stating that you do not desire by this suppression to establish a
precedent. In fact, however, a precedent is established and the effective
exclusion from the broadcast [radio] of all persons not nominated by
party leaders or the Party Whips has been enforced.[15]

This extremely serious matter was treated with little short of outright
laughter within the BBC. The correspondence was published and,
when the BBC asked how it had been received in the House of
Commons, their lobby man wrote:

If there are any points you would like us to watch in connection with
the political talks and the controversy thereover, no doubt you will let
us know. I think you have on the whole a very good press, and really if
everybody who thinks he ought to be allowed to broadcast is given the
opportunity there never would be any real recreation at all, and we
should confine all our listening to talks. P.S. I would like to see Whitley
show a little more bite and tell these politicians they suffer from swelled
heads and the public doesn't want to hear them.[16]

It has been said that Reith was responsible for shielding the public
from the reality of inter-war politics; this letter, and the whole topic,
shows that he was in fact simply reflecting the universal corruption
and cynicism of public life at the time, based on a total
misunderstanding of how serious matters were and how weak Britain
had become in European terms. At the time of the 1930 Naval
Conference Churchill, as an ex-Lord of the Admiralty, had wished to
speak on the radio. The BBC refused to allow him to do so.[17] The
public heard nothing that in anyway departed from the bland image
of public affairs that they and the Government wished to project.

[15] Ibid.
[16] BBC Written Archives Centre: R34/563/2. The lobby agents were Watney and
Powell.
[17] Ibid., Churchill file. It was this incident which seems to have originated
Churchill's deep feelings on the question. Matters have greatly improved today in this
aspect. It would be inconceivable for the BBC, or any of the other channels, to refuse
comment in such circumstances.

The international aspect of politics in the thirties played a much more direct part in Sir Oswald Mosley's case. He too wished to get to the microphone, but he had even less luck than Churchill. His first party, the New Party, had a number of members in the House of Commons, including the well-known radio personality Harold Nicolson, who later went on to do some highly controversial broadcasting for Guy Burgess, a close friend of his.[18] It might have been expected that some provision for the party be made, especially as Mosley had until recently been a member of the Cabinet. He was soon disabused, and had even less luck with his next departure, the British Union. Baldwin's references to Fascism quoted above without doubt reflected his worries about Mosley getting a hearing in Britain.

After some years had passed, Mosley's case for a broadcast became more pressing. It was clearly absurd that the political philosophy which had been adopted by one of Britain's allies during World War I could not be discussed in any way in Britain.[19] Mosley repeatedly made his case either in person, or through his officers, until finally he made an impression on one person in the BBC who was not unsympathetic to his cause, his fellow veteran of the Royal Flying Corps, Gladstone Murray.[20] In December 1934 Murray had visited the British Union headquarters in the Kings Road and held formal discussions with Mosley on the possibility of a broadcast. Murray's report on the meeting paved the way for some definite agreement:

I made it clear at the beginning that there was no present possibility of Fascism receiving the same microphone facilities as any of the established parties. I reminded him of the conversation when he lunched with myself and Lord Reith about two years ago. It was made

[18] For a full discussion of the relationship between Burgess and Nicolson as it affected the latter's broadcasts, see below, p.53f.

[19] This philosophy was, of course, Fascism. The most common layman's introduction to the subject at the time was a volume in the Home University Library series: James Strachey Barnes, *Fascism* (1931). Barnes was an important figure among British Fascists (see below, p.48n10) and it is a measure of the work still to be done on the subject that there is no mention of him, for example, in the index of Richard Thurlow, *Fascism in Britain: A History, 1918-1985* (1987).

[20] William Ewart Gladstone Murray (1893-1970). An Oxford Rhodes Scholar in 1913-14, Gladstone Murray joined the Royal Flying Corps, where he logged 2,000 hours of combative flying time. After the war he acted as publicity manager for one of the private radio companies before joining the BBC, where he was Director of Public Relations, Information and Publications from 1924 to 1935. In 1935 he became briefly Controller of Programmes, before going to Canada, where he became General Manager of the Canadian Broadcasting Corporation. He published a number of pamphlets in Canada including, for example, *Canada's Place in Civilisation* (1946).

clear then that our attitude to new political parties would be governed at least partly by representation in Parliament, and by the attitude of the Speaker in the House of Commons. Sir Oswald said he disagreed but he saw our difficulties ... I said we would be prepared to consider some form of discussion in which the more extreme proposals for constitutional reconstruction would be debated either separately ... or in direct opposition. We could hold out no promise of a specific date when this could be arranged, but if the idea appealed to him we would be prepared to examine it.[21]

It has to be observed that, compared with the freedom of the press, the position in broadcasting was an echo of an earlier age. Lord Reith and Gladstone Murray occupied no recognizable position within the democracy and yet they were deciding the exact nature of the debate which the British public were to be allowed to hear. The tone of Murray's report is very much *de haut en bas*, of a senior official wondering if some very unimportant person might be allowed some peripheral liberties, as offensive in its way as the sarcastic humour of the BBC's lobby correspondent at the expense of the three most distinguished public figures of their day. *Faute de mieux* Mosley was obliged to accept Murray's offer, and later the following year, Murray again contacted Mosley and told him that a talk would be possible in the autumn, reporting back to his controller.

This communication has given Sir Oswald great satisfaction and should keep him quiet over the summer and autumn. I do hope, however, that the plan succeeds this time.

The plan, as he called it, almost did succeed but was foiled at the last moment by the direct intervention of the Foreign Office who, not for the last time, as we shall see, had decided that enough was enough and that the BBC had to be brought to heel. Mosley had found the idea a desirable alternative to the more normal political broadcast because it provided an opportunity for solid proselytization. There were to be twelve broadcasts, and the series was to be of an educational kind, with a pamphlet to be issued beforehand and study groups arranged all over the country, just as is now done with the Open University.[22] Hitler's National Socialists had set up just such groups all over Germany before he came to power and they were the

[21] BBC Written Archives Centre: Mosley contributor file.

[22] The idea of a Radio University was even then in the air and was finally brought into being in Italy by Mussolini. For an example of the extent and thoroughness of the BBC's publications for this kind of series, see those for *The Changing World: A Broadcast Symposium* and in particular John A. Hobson, *The Modern State* (1931).

most effective 'underground' means of spreading a political doctrine at the time. The Foreign Office News Department had been consulted when the series, called 'The Citizen and his Government' was being arranged, but because it was in the adult educational series not much attention was paid to it. The list of speakers had alerted them, especially when one, Harry Pollitt,[23] appeared on Moscow radio, speaking as leader of the Communist Party of Great Britain, and mention was made in London that he was to continue his campaign in Britain when he returned. Furthermore extensive rumours began to spread through Mosley's organization that some British Union talks by Mosley were planned. The time for action had obviously come. But what kind of action was open to the Foreign Office? Here was an educational programme of great scope already past the contract stage for which all the preliminary work had been done. The central worry was Mosley and the use he might make of the opportunity, and it was he who bore the brunt of the Government's attack.

Vansittart, the Permanent Head of the Foreign Office,[24] first called in two senior BBC officials, Cecil Graves[25] and Colonel Dawnay.[26] They duly acknowledged his request, getting the backing of the BBC's Board of Governors, who made a formal statement of their opinion. They had decided that it might be possible to cancel the series if

the possibility that a situation might arise between now and 19 November would make it desirable to cancel the whole series owing to

[23] By a strange coincidence Harry Pollitt returned from Russia on the same boat as Anthony Blunt and his friends, in the late summer of 1935. Others of the party included Nancy Cunard.

[24] Lord Vansittart (1881-1957), at this time Sir Robert Vansittart, Permanent Head of the Foreign Office and later Chief Diplomatic Advisor to the Government. Vansittart features extensively in the pages that follow. In the years leading up to the war he had a great reputation with Churchill and others for his knowledge of German affairs. However, the private secret service through which he obtained much of his information was infiltrated by the Communist Party (see below, p.196) and his view became confused. After the failure of the Venlo Incident (see below, p.190f.) he became almost incoherent, as the BBC producers of his series of broadcasts, published as *Black Record: Germans Past and Present* (1941) discovered. His views at this time gave rise to the term 'Vansittartism'. For a recent biography, see Norman Rose, *Vansittart: Study of a Diplomat* (1978).

[25] Sir Cecil Graves (1892-1957). At school at Gresham's School, Holt (also attended by Lord Reith); General Staff War Office (Intelligence Branch) 1919-25; joined the BBC in 1926; Assistant Director of Programmes 1929-32; Empire Service Director 1932-35; Deputy Director General 1938-42; Joint Director General 1942-43.

[26] Alan Geoffrey Charles Dawnay (1888-1938). Commander, First Battalion Coldstream Guards 1928-30; General Staff Officer, War Office 1930-32; Controller Programmes BBC 1933-35; Officer Commanding, Irish Guards Regiment 1935-36.

the International situation having developed in such a manner as to make a talk on Fascism inopportune.

They stated further that

> in the event of this not being applicable there did not seem to be any valid reason why a balanced series of talks which included one by a Communist leader should not be given. Furthermore publicity had been given to the series, contracts had been issued to the speakers and a pamphlet in connection with the series had been prepared.[27]

When Graves and Dawnay read out these observations at a meeting on 27 September Vansittart would have none of them. He remarked, according to the BBC minute of the talk,

> that he saw very little possibility of the International situation developing in such a way that a talk by Sir Oswald Mosley would be innocuous. In his opinion it would be absolutely impossible for such a talk to be given in the event of economic sanctions being imposed by the League.[28] Sir Oswald Mosley must be looked upon as an agent of Italian Fascism taking his orders from Italy.[29]

On the question of a Communist broadcast Vansittart pointed out that he had been taking great pains to make it clear to the Russians that Communist propaganda in Britain was getting out of hand; at a crucial moment the BBC were going to give the leader of the Communist Party in Britain 'the maximum facilities for spreading Communist propaganda by means of a talk in the National programme'. Vansittart became more conscious of the leftward drift in the BBC as time went on, although he never identified the full Soviet penetration that actually took place. But his main concern now was with Mosley. The report continued:

[27] BBC Written Archives Centre. Programme file for 'The Citizen and his Government'.

[28] Limited sanctions were imposed, but not on oil, a crucial commodity. For an interesting discussion of the question of League of Nations sanctions, see S. Engel, *League Reform: An Analysis of Official Proposals and Discussions 1936-39* (1940), pp.135-91. This was published by the Geneva Research Centre as nos. 3-4 of Volume XI of *Geneva Studies* and gives great insight into the League and its methods, which continued throughout the war and provide, indeed, an almost uninterrupted bridge with the proceedings and methods of the post-war United Nations.

[29] BBC Written Archives Centre. Programme file for 'The Citizen and his Government'.

Sir Robert hoped that the question would resolve itself into the undesirability of Sir Oswald Mosley speaking. Should it be decided that Mosley should not speak then there would be no need to inform the public that it was because of Mosley, but merely to say that, owing to the present situation, it was not considered desirable to go forward with this particular series of talks; it should be left to listeners to form their own conclusion as to why the series had been dropped, but probably 90 per cent would assume it was the Mosley issue ...[30]

Matters did not end there, however. The series was at first simply postponed; there was no great public attention paid to this since a general election intervened and such a series would obviously have been difficult.[31] Early in the following year the BBC returned to the charge and was again told that the broadcast was impossible. It was ordered to cancel the series entirely and at first given permission, if it wished, to say that it did so at Government request. But, while a harassed BBC official was actually dictating the report of the meeting with Lord Stanhope, Under Secretary at the Foreign Office, when this verdict had been given, he was called to the telephone with a stern *volte face* by the Government. He turned back to dictating his report, ending:

Since dictating the above Lord Stanhope rang me to say that he had spoken to Mr Eden, who would infinitely prefer that we did not in the first instance state that we were not giving the talks because they would embarrass the Government. He would like us to say that we were postponing them indefinitely owing to the International situation. Lord Stanhope stated, however, that if we could not do this we could in the last resort, fall back upon the Government, as he and Mr Eden were prepared to stand for this; going on to say that he would require notice if this was done.[32]

Finally, on 13 February, the Postmaster General, who was ultimately responsible for the BBC, saw the Chairman of the Governors of the BBC, Ronald Norman,[33] and gave the Government's final opinion. In a memorandum of the talks submitted to the BBC, Norman is recorded as saying:

[30] Ibid.

[31] A General Election was held on 14 November 1935.

[32] BBC Written Archives Centre. Programme file for 'The Citizen and his Government'.

[33] Ronald Collet Norman (1873-1963), Chairman of the BBC's Board of Governors 1935-39. During the war he served as the first Chairman of the Central Citizens' Advice Bureaux Committee. His brother was the Governor of the Bank of England, Sir Montague Norman.

The Postmaster General said that the Government was of the opinion that any announcement of the Corporation's decision to cancel the talks should contain no reference to any intervention on the part of the Government. After some discussion Mr Norman agreed that the Corporation would state that it had followed the usual practice of consulting the Foreign Office and that, in view of the information received as to the bad effects which the proposed talks would have had abroad and the aggravation of the position by recent international developments, the Corporation had decided to cancel the talks.[34]

And this was indeed the version of the facts which was given to the public. Mosley was kept off the air and the myth of the BBC's independence was preserved intact. The effect in Italy was serious. Despite Eden's attempts to conceal his and the Government's role all the facts would have been known to Mussolini through Ian Hope Dundas,[35] Mosley's Chief of Staff, who was soon to broadcast directly to England from Italy.

From the point of view of domestic politics, had the proposed series taken place, with the full range of discussion groups all over the country addressed by Mosley's supporters, as was no doubt planned, then to a very considerable extent the focus of attention and of political change, or the need for it, would have shifted from Parliament to the medium of radio itself. The constitutional significance of this, apart from the practical results, could not have been faced by the authorities at the time. Far better Baldwin's hypocrisy, the banning of political extremists in secret while proclaiming loudly that free speech and democracy existed and must be preserved. It was not without significance that it was at this time that the BBC was advised by the security services to take steps to

[34] BBC Written Archives Centre. Programme file for 'The Citzen and his Government'.

[35] Ian Hope Dundas was the scion of a great British family, a Dundas of Dundas, whose line, beginning in the twelfth century, may be examined in his entry in *Burke's Peerage*. At the time he occupied a prominent place in Fascist affairs; see for example the account of his wedding at St. Michael's Church, Chester Square, conducted in full uniform with Sir Oswald Mosley as best man, in *The Fascist News*, 23 December 1933, vol.1, no.27, p.10. His main purpose in visiting Italy was to establish a connection with Mussolini, which appears to have included arrangements for the transfer of funds to the embryo British Union. The money was transferred to a British bank account held jointly in the names of Dundas, W.E.D. Allen and Allen's secretary. Allen appears to have been working for the British Security Services, although, hardly surprisingly, the question is shrouded in mystery. For further discussion of this important matter, including the original funding of Mussolini by British Military Intelligence during World War I, see below, p.84n.14.

protect its premises from being taken over in what were euphemistically called 'civil disturbances'.[36] The precautions recommended, and taken, were no more than the usual barbed-wire topped fences around 'sensitive' transmitting stations and the securing of premises, but they were a first small step along the road which ended with the wartime total security under armed guard. And it was Mosley and Italy which brought the threats of the totalitarian world to the new medium still seen by some as a possible aid to the maintenance of world peace.[37] *E70722*

Churchill did manage to get access to the microphone on a number of occasions, but he could find little to say within the constraints placed upon him. Talking to Guy Burgess visiting him to discuss a possible broadcast in 1938 he complained bitterly of the way the BBC had treated him.[38] Indeed it was a great tragedy that the BBC and the Government could not have evolved some way whereby people of the calibre of Churchill, Lloyd George and Austen Chamberlain could be allowed some say on world affairs, even if the out-and-out extremists of the right were restricted to the street corner and the left to their secret underground infiltrations – particularly as the BBC's programmes from Germany and relating to foreign affairs in general were seriously flawed, as we shall see in the next chapter.

[36] This was an obvious allusion to the increasingly violent scenes at political meetings in the country, when the behaviour of stewards at Mosley's meetings at Olympia and elsewhere created great anger on the left. It is of interest that Mosley's British Union by no means always came off best in these encounters and was usually greatly outnumbered by 'Reds', who pioneered many techniques attributed to Mosley's men. Tommy Moran, a Mosley supporter, writing to John Beckett, remarked: 'Hull last Sunday was a revelation, ten thousand reds throwing stones, bottles, using iron bars, pieces of lead, one rat had a sickle with the handle painted red, women were using hat pins [! a period note], in fact the reds did everything that was filthy' (private archive; letter 17 July 1936). Inspection of the police reports in the Public Record Office bears out this account. Mosley's behaviour under such circumstances played a large part in creating his devoted following. In the same letter Moran wrote: 'The Leader was superb, if we loved him in the past his courage last Sunday made us his for life.' These events formed the true background to events such as Olympia. Unlike the bitter fights in industrial disputes today, the 'civil disturbances' mentioned here genuinely were signs of a revolutionary situation and justified the precautions taken.

[37] Prominent among these was Arthur Henderson, who broadcast from the World Disarmament Conference at Geneva and wrote a moving article in the independent radio magazine *Radio Pictorial*, 'Broadcasting Will End War!', in which he remarked: 'One of the developments to which I personally look – in the near future – is an expansion of broadcasting arrangements for the fuller discussion of international affairs ... particular interest attaches to the League of Nations Wireless station near Geneva [Radio Nations, see Index] ... I hope it will be more extensively used.' *Radio Pictorial*, vol. 2, no. 2, 19 January 1934.

[38] See below, p.57.

2. The BBC and the Foreign Office

The first world broadcast from the Naval Conference in 1930 had been the result of co-operation from broadcasting organizations and stations all round the world. It did not mark the inauguration of any equivalent regular service by the BBC,[1] but the need for such a service and the need to pay attention to the international implications of broadcasts that could be heard abroad became obvious. There were programmes from Milan heard by Willert in the Foreign Office in 1929, but these were local stations whose signals were carrying much further than the broadcasters realized.[2] More propaganda-conscious countries were already taking advantage of this effect by the middle of the year. A member of the public writing to Hugh Dalton at the Foreign Office in May 1930 first directed official attention to the problem of broadcasts by Russia to England:

> ...on last Wednesday night, the 14th instant, soon after 1 p.m. I tuned in my wireless receiving set to what was a wavelength indicating Leningrad or Moscow.
> I heard what apparently was the voice of an Englishman speaking in English and urging Revolution repeatedly ... Evidently the object is to disseminate Revolutionary ideas amongst British Sailors and others, probably in India and other of our dominions.[3]

Dalton remarked:

> Propaganda by wireless may, of course, be just as objectionable as propaganda by any other method, possibly more so. It would, therefore, be interesting if we could discover what Moscow Communists are committing to the ether for the consumption of their comrades here;

[1] The closest approach to this was the Empire Service, an English-language programme inaugurated on 19 December 1932. There was always an element of chauvinism in the service, since clearly it was open to anyone in the world who understood English to listen to it, not merely citizens of the Empire. For an account, see Gerard Mansell, *Let Truth Be Told* (1982), ch.2, 'Empire Service'.

[2] For Willert and the Italian broadcasts overheard by him, see below, pp.80-1.

[3] Public Record Office: FO 371/14893/33/38.

and it has occurred to us that the Post Office might be in a position to take down what is said.[4]

This observation lead to trial monitoring by no fewer than three separate groups, the Special Branch, the Post Office and the BBC. The development of monitoring was tortuous,[5] but the acute need to be aware of the possible propaganda significance of broadcasts from the BBC on questions relating to Russia was then a matter very much in the public domain and made it a necessity. As important as the desire not to give offence was the desire not to echo the Russian propaganda about itself or revolution.

Reith was fully conscious of this at the time and, initially, was prepared to co-operate fully with the Foreign Office on matters concerning broadcasts on Russia. He soon went on to the broader question of relations with the Foreign Office generally, writing to Vansittart:

> The Russian business, as you doubtless know, seems more or less in shape now, so I am writing about the general question of liaison between the Foreign Office and the BBC. This exists with considerable definition with most other Government departments. What would you think of there being some arrangements between us so that you may be in touch with what we propose doing in general with regard to Foreign Affairs, and so that we may have proper advice?[6]

There must have been many occasions over the following years when Reith wished he had never written this letter, and when the Foreign Office news department dearly wished they had been able to fix some such arrangement definitely. However, at the time they themselves did not see the full need for what Reith had proposed. He had earlier asked Sir Lancelot Oliphant[7] whether some unofficial 'advice' might be given but Oliphant had shown very great reluctance for the Foreign Office to be involved. Reith remarked to Vansittart:

---

[4] Ibid.

[5] For a full account of the early history of monitoring in Britain, see Olive Renier and Vladimir Rubinstein, *Assigned to Listen* (1986).

[6] Public Record Office: FO 395/453; P418/39/150.

[7] Sir Lancelot Oliphant (1881-1965). When the image of a 'Foreign Office mandarin' is conjured up, it is such figures as Oliphant that are meant. A man of great authority, he entered the Foreign Office in 1903, serving initially in Constantinople and Tehran, and visiting the Kahnates of Central Asia in 1911. He was Assistant Under-Secretary of State for Foreign Affairs from 1936 to 1939. On the outbreak of war he was Ambassador to Belgium and suffered the unusual fate for a diplomat in those days, before the rise of Islamic Fundamentalism, of being held in internment for over a year. He wrote *Ambassador in Bonds* (1946).

I gather he thought that the most that could be done would be for us to submit any doubtful passages in the manuscripts. This, of course, we shall do.[8]

Although this was to form the model of what later came to be the relationship between the Foreign Office and the BBC it was only reached after a lengthy chronicle of mistakes and disagreements. The first serious incident affected Reith personally, to his considerable embarrassment, and may have been one which sent him off on an increasingly independent path. It concerned a broadcast on 31 December 1932 featuring link-ups with reporters all over Europe. When the speaker in Poland came on the air he made a speech lacking in seasonal spirit; Poland was severely criticized for spending a third of its budget on armaments. The Polish Ambassador in London heard the broadcast and immediately went to the Foreign Office with a formal complaint. Reith was then obliged to apologize in person to the Ambassador, assuring him that such an incident would not occur again.[9] Reith seems to have taken this in good part initially, but the resulting controversy, with all the panoply of letters to *The Times* and questions in the House of Commons, did nothing to dampen his feeling of being the person in sole control of what should be an independent broadcasting system. It also reinforced the idea in people's minds abroad that the BBC was a Government department. Reith was apologizing as a result of a diplomatic protest made from one Government to another, and clearly was a man of great authority in the Government circles that dealt with broadcasting. As we shall see, he himself took this view of his own position to extraordinary lengths notably in his dealings with the Austrian-German radio war in 1934.[10]

The next serious clash with the Government came over a broadcast by Vernon Bartlett[11] on Germany's withdrawal from the League of Nations. The response had been immediate both at home and abroad. R.F. Wigram[12] of the Foreign Office minuted:

---

[8] Public Record Office: FO 395/453; P418/39/150.

[9] For Reith's account, see *Into the Wind* (1949), p.171.

[10] See below, pp.32-3.

[11] Vernon Bartlett (1894-1963), journalist, broadcaster and politician, who first caught the public eye with *The Brighter Side of Chaos* (1925). He went on to become a successful broadcaster and the BBC's chief spokesman on foreign affairs until the incidents now being described. As Independent MP for Bridgewater, he was one of the first men to enter the House of Commons purely on the strength of his reputation as a broadcaster. He held the seat from 1938 to 1950.

[12] Ralph Follet Wigram (1890-1936). First Secretary, British Embassy, Paris 1924-33; Counsellor in the Foreign Office from 1934.

It is only necessary to read Berlin telegramme No 227 to see the unfortunate effect of last Saturday's BBC broadcasts on our relations with Germany. The effects were undoubtedly bad also in France (the French Ambassador mentioned it to me yesterday) and no doubt in other countries. There is further the effect on our own (ie the British public's) opinion to be considered.

We *must* prevent recurrence of this kind of thing ...[13]

Rex Leeper[14] made his feelings on the BBC plain, not for the last time:

The BBC cannot be regarded as an independent institution and views broadcast by the Corporation either anonymously or by a salaried member of the staff like Mr Bartlett are inevitably associated with HMG both here and in the foreign countries. The responsibility rests not with Mr Bartlett but with the BBC on the ground that Mr Bartlett as a salaried official acts according to instructions ...

going on to propose:

The BBC should appoint two or three members of their staff to deal with Foreign affairs either anonymously or in the way Mr Bartlett deals with them, then they should be obliged to discuss in advance the

[13] Public Record Office. FO 395/484; P2484/96/150.
[14] Sir Reginald ('Rex') Wilding Allen Leeper (1888-1968), a figure of the greatest importance in the Foreign Office, whose name will occur frequently here. During World War I he served in the Intelligence Department of the Department of Information, and then entered the Diplomatic service, serving at Warsaw, Riga and Constantinople. In 1929 he went to the Foreign Office, where he embarked on the most important part of his career under Sir Robert Vansittart, becoming a Counsellor in 1933 and Assistant Secretary in 1940. His time as a war propagandist at the head of the secret propaganda organisation at Woburn Abbey was an unhappy one. Violently anti-German, Leeper was also anti-Communist and clashed repeatedly with Dalton and his protégés, including R.H.S Crossman. His treatment was disgraceful and reflects badly on those responsible, notably Dalton. In 1943 he became Ambassador to the Court of the King of the Hellenes, going on to become Ambassador to the Argentine 1946-48. He wrote only one book, *When Greek Meets Greek* (1950), but his extensive writings within the Foreign Office and occasionally for learned journals are of the profoundest significance for an understanding of the history of the period. His part in the setting up of the British Council, the Travel Association, the Vansittart Committee and the Ministry of Information was of central importance. On a more mundane level his interest in radio propaganda lead to the discovery that, until 1937, British embassies abroad had no radio sets of any kind on their premises, but relied on gossip from journalists to find out what was being said! (see Public Record Office: FO 395/502; P2433/2431/150 et al.). The expense caused by remedying such defects made him bitter enemies; on one legendary occasion a recommendation for his promotion was minuted by Sir Warren Fisher at the Treasury: 'I would be prepared to pay Leeper more – as a pension.' One of the most significant and influential men of his day, it is astonishing that no biography of him has been written.

subjects they propose to treat and that they should accept the ruling of
the Foreign Office both as regards the nature of the comment and the
advisability of any comment at all at a particular moment.[15]

Another major incident was perhaps not one which even this rigorous
counsel of perfection on its own would have been able to stop. It
concerned the BBC main news coverage of one of the talks on the
perennial inter-war problem of reparations and debt repayment. As
arrangements for dealing with Germany's loan repayments were
changed over the years, public opinion came to be more and more in
favour of the German view of them. The German Propaganda ministry
under Goebbels seems to have become aware of this. They also
noticed that the BBC news programmes frequently took material
directly from the wire news services, and they appear to have evolved a
plan for getting their view of the 1934 economic discussions put over
on the BBC.[16] The Allied authorities in Germany soon complained
about the content of the BBC's main news programme dealing with
the conference, and the Foreign Office rapidly got advice on its
content:

> Mr Perowne's analysis of this BBC news bulletin regarding the
> conference at Berlin between the representatives of the Reichsbank and
> representatives of Germany's long and medium term foreign creditors
> show that it entirely misrepresented the circumstances out of which the
> necessity for the conference had arisen, and did so in a manner highly
> prejudicial to the creditors' [i.e. Britain, the USA and France] case.[17]

The first objection to this produced the defence from the BBC that the
material had appeared on Reuters' tapes.[18] The Foreign Office
pointed out that this was no excuse and seems then to have realized
what had happened:

[15] Public Record Office: FO 395/484; P2484/96/150.
[16] The BBC had no news service of its own at the time. Indeed it was not allowed to
establish such a service, a situation arising from the vigorously expressed anxieties of
the press barons in the early days of broadcasting. Their lack of experience in the field
made them vulnerable, as in the present instance. For further attempts to get the BBC
to take Foreign Office advice as a supplement to their limited experience in dealing
with live political issues, particularly those with international overtones, see below,
pp.102-3.
[17] Public Record Office: FO 395/515; P1531/196/150.
[18] For an account of Reuters, see John Lawrenson and Lionel Barber, *The Price of
Truth* (1985; revised ed.1986). The British Government took highly secret action to
gain control of Reuters, no doubt as a result of this and similar instances. They
succeeded. For an account of the covert control exercised, see Lawrenson & Barber,
pp.53 ff.

...Had the Corporation maintained with the News Department of the FO the sort of contact which all the more responsible newspapers regularly maintain they would have been in possession of accurate information ... It is moreover well known among press correspondents that Reuters' intimate association with the Deutsches Nachrichtenbüro makes it desirable to treat Reuter messages from Berlin with particular care.[19]

In fact Goebbels' text had been broadcast over the BBC's main news programme! Vansittart fully endorsed the anger of his staff at the News Department:

The knowledge of these subjects is available here. The BBC appears to have gone really wrong on this important topic from failure to utilize that knowledge.

It was hoped that there would be improved daily contact between the BBC and the Foreign Office, but again this did not transpire. The next incident that came to the attention of the Cabinet was a broadcast from Berlin at the time of the notorious 'Night of the Long Knives' when Hitler ordered a strike against Roehm and large numbers of people were murdered in a general settling of scores. To the horror of the British authorities, the BBC put out a broadcast by R.H.S. Crossman[20] which appeared to endorse what Hitler had done. On this occasion the complaint came, not from one of Britain's embassies abroad or a foreign legation, but from the Secretary of State himself, Sir John Simon:[21]

I have heard from several quarters complaints of the broadcast by the BBC from Berlin after the weekend events in Germany. It seems to have been couched in a vein of exultant approval of everything Hitler had

---

[19] Public Record Office: FO 395/515; P1531/196/150. 7 May 1934.

[20] Richard Howard Stafford Crossman (1907-1974). Crossman had first become interested in broadcasting through contacts with Willi Münzenburg (see below, p.109). At this time he was acting as a freelance broadcaster for the BBC in Germany. Like Guy Burgess, also a friend of Münzenburg's, Crossman gained access to the authorities in Germany by feigning an ardent interest in Hitler and National Socialism. He wrote a graphic account to the BBC explaining that the suspicions of the SS officer dealing with the matter had been aroused but that he had got round him by saying that in Britain he was regarded as so pro-Nazi that even his best friends wouldn't speak to him! During the war Crossman specialized in inventing lies for broadcasting to Germany from the secret radio station at Woburn and by other means. In later life he became a politician of some notoriety.

[21] John Allsebrook Simon, First Viscount (1873-1954), Secretary of State for Foreign Affairs 1931-35; Secretary of State for Home Affairs 1935-37; Chancellor of the Exchequer 1937-40; Lord Chancellor 1940-50.

done ... This is clearly within the realm of Foreign Affairs and I understood that we had an informal arrangement with the BBC to secure that they did not without our knowledge issue unduly tendentious or ill-informed statements which affect international relations.[22]

In view of the long-standing confrontation between the BBC and the FO and the fact that the arrangements referred to by Simon were indeed supposed to be in place, Orme Sargent[23] at the FO decided to attempt to stick by Dawnay and the BBC. Orme Sargent's minute infuriated Vansittart even more than a mere defence from the BBC would have done, and he peppered it with sarcastic and pointed comments in the margins:

Col. Dawnay told me that, although Crossman himself was violently anti-Nazi, the talk would be entirely factual and objective and I think that a perusal of the talk bears this out ...[24] The complaints which have reached the S[ecretary] of S[tate] [Sir John Simon] however are not because the talk was not sufficiently objective but because it was altogether too objective. The very fact that Mr Crossman expressed no criticism seemed to suggest that he was actually approving the Hitler murders. In fact what the critics wanted was a wholesale condemnation of the way the purge was carried out. But it was obviously impossible for the BBC to give them this. [*Vansittart: Then they had much better keep quiet.*] In the first place it is contrary to their rule to set themselves up in judgement in such a matter and I think it is in our interest to encourage this rule as far as foreign affairs are concerned. Secondly the BBC system of getting eye-witness accounts from foreign capitals has this fundamental weakness, [*Vansittart: of course it has and therefore I object to it. It is not the business of the BBC to gabble about everything.*] that inasmuch as the speaker is dependent on the hospitality of the broadcasting organization of the country in which he is speaking he can only be either objective and dull or laudatory and tendentious. He can in no case be critical or condemnatory.

    As regards the present case, I have discussed the matter with Col. Dawnay and on my telling him that certain criticisms had reached the

---

[22] Public Record Office: FO 395/515; P2201/196/150.

[23] Sir Orme Sargent (1884-1962), a Foreign Office 'mandarin' who adopted an even lower profile than Sir Lancelot Oliphant. He entered the Foreign Office in 1906 and was Permanent Under-Secretary 1946-49. His frequent minuting of a wide variety of papers show his great influence and authority. His clash here with Vansittart is unusual.

[24] The text of the talk is in the BBC Written Archives Centre, and in the related Public Record Office files mentioned in note 22 above.

Secretary of State he expressed considerable surprise. [*Vansittart: It must take little to surprise Col. Dawnay.*][25]

Vansittart then launched into his own detailed and typically savage statement which, even today, it is difficult to disagree with:

I am afraid I do not agree with Mr Sargent's estimate of the broadcast. It gives – and was bound to give – a general impression of condonation. Indeed it could not be otherwise, though no doubt the condonation was not fully intended. The fundamental vice is that the BBC should feel obliged to fly to the microphone about everything under the sun and without a moment's reflection. This is what happened in the case of Mr Bartlett in October. Now it has happened again in a more vicious form. One moment's reflection would have shown anybody with any sense that any broadcast from *Berlin* on such a topic could only be couched in terms that were bound to be interpreted *here* as favourable. If Mr Crossman had taken any other tone but this – which is to me rather sickening and not at all objective – he would either have been thrown out or shut up.

There are two obvious paths of wisdom. Either to maintain a dignified silence on such revolting butchery, or to broadcast from London and to say what almost every decent man in this country feels.

I have no sympathy whatever with this go-getter, sensation-mongering Hearstliness, man-on-the-spot red-hot stuff, especially when it leads to such inevitable errors. I submit that it is *not* the function of the BBC, and that if they persist in it their activities will have to be revised.[26]

Students of the period might be forgiven for thinking that this all sounds like a classic inter-departmental feud which may or may not have had real significance in the wider political world outside the corridors of Westminster and Portland Place. Perhaps the soundest evidence for the direct relationship seen by politicians between the radio and international affairs is the fact that matters did get taken to the highest level. The first of the broadcasts referred to by Vansittart above was seen in an even more serious light by Ramsay MacDonald himself who, as we have seen, had early shown himself to be very conscious of the effects of radio within Britain. His attack on the BBC is every bit as intense as Vansittart's:

[25] Public Record Office: FO 395/515; P2201/196/150.
[26] Ibid. For Hearstliness see below, p. 145.

10, Downing Street, Whitehall   16 October 1933
My dear Whitley,
    I am very sorry to have to put in rather a serious complaint about the
way the German situation has been handled by the British
Broadcasting Corporation. We have been trying to suppress all sorts of
panic and serious concern about the action of Germany, and have been
with-holding any judgement on the position until we have had
opportunities of discussing it amongst ourselves, after receiving Sir
John Simon's views and exchanging ideas with some foreign
Governments. A propaganda in favour of Germany is certainly the most
dangerous thing that can be started at present, especially by people
who know nothing about what has been going on before this last stage.
    On Saturday there was broadcast by Vernon Bartlett an estimate of
the situation which was simply absurd in its ignorance of the latest
phases and its one-sidedness as a report of what had taken place before.
One statement which he made – that if we had been in the same
position as Germany we would have done likewise – would be
repudiated by every one of us who knows the position and the true
nature of the Hitlerite claims. Last night, I am told, the comments
when the news was broadcast were even worse in tone and in spirit, and
today I am hearing all round of the effect of the two broadcasts.
    I know your difficulties, especially in dealing with political news and
observations, but surely at a very critical moment like this, when a false
statement or an observation which completely misjudges the situation
may upset international negotiations and the handling of the
Government, the British Broadcasting Corporation should be
particularly careful and should ask for some advice before it puts its
foot into it, as you did on Saturday and Sunday. It was very easy to
have asked either the Foreign Office or myself how matters stood and
what might be the effect if the broadcasting went on one line or
another.
    I can assure you you have caused me a very great deal of
embarrassment and have contributed largely to a continuing deadlock,
should that be unfortunately what is going to happen.

                              Yours very sincerely, Ramsay MacDonald[27]

There is no record of an assessment by MacDonald or the BBC about
whether the broadcast had the effect that MacDonald feared; but it is
certain that the letter had no effect on the BBC, as Vansittart's
comments on the Crossman incident show. MacDonald was coming
to the end of his career, but the sensitivity which he showed on
broadcasting matters and the effects they would have on people such
as Hitler and Mussolini, totalitarian leaders who depended on the
relationship with their peoples established through the new media at

[27] BBC Written Archives Centre: MacDonald contributor file.

least as much as the old ones of press and public meetings, indicate that his judgement was thoroughly sound. Indeed, whereas MacDonald immediately noticed this pro-German right-wing sentiment, the later infiltration of the BBC by Burgess and his speakers seems to have passed almost unnoticed by Neville Chamberlain or his *eminence grise* Sir Horace Wilson. MacDonald saw matters more directly, and it was perhaps a sign of his growing weakness that, having written such a stern letter, he was unable to get the BBC to alter its ways, or reach them through the force of his argument.

The BBC was not alone in its difficulties over international affairs. There were serious cases in Europe itself of radio as a source of international disagreement flaring into open hostility. In the twenties there had been some conflict between the Eiffel Tower radio station and a German station over the occupation of the Ruhr, but radio was still in its infancy and it was not taken entirely seriously by either party, it seems; certainly no rigorous action was taken of the sort seen in the Polish-German dispute of 1930. German broadcasts from the border radio station of Gleiwitz aimed at the German-speaking minority in Poland had produced a fierce counterblast from Polish Stations and, for a time, it seemed as though an actual conflict might result. But then an extraordinary thing happened. The German and Polish broadcasting authorities, introduced to each other through the International Broadcasting Union,[28] agreed to call a halt to the war and, after consultation with their respective Governments, signed a treaty that banned all contentious broadcasting from either country addressed to the inhabitants of their neighbour. This was the first such agreement. Unfortunately it was not followed by anything quite as specific again. Shortly after the treaty was signed Poland approached the League of Nations with a proposal that a multi-lateral treaty be drawn up which all nations could be invited to sign.

Preliminary work on the treaty took a great deal of time and the draft document was not available until 1936. In the meantime there had been numerous further examples of what might be called local cold wars. Nearly all of these involved Germany, particularly after

[28] The International Broadcasting Union (IBU) or, as it was sometimes known, the Union Internationale de Radiophonie (UIR), had been set up in 1925, largely at Reith's instigation, to regulate the chaos caused by unlimited broadcasting on the myriad of wavelengths. By a convenient arrangement its offices were in London, and its President was Vice-Admiral Sir Charles Douglas Carpendale (1874-1968), who filled the post while working for the BBC as Controller of Administration. He was later Deputy Director General of the BBC (1935-38). The IBU none the less did have a genuine international existence, as its success in the present case shows.

Hitler came to power in 1933. Russian broadcasts in German, ostensibly to their German-speaking minorities in the Volga Republic, soon came to be of such strength that they could be heard all over Germany and were particularly resented. No agreement about them was possible, and the first of the laws making listening illegal was passed in Germany as the only possible remedy when the Russian programmes descended to vulgar abuse of the Nazi leaders.[29] To the south of Germany, in the years leading up to the Anschluss, there was a series of broadcasts put out by the Austrian Nazi leader Habicht from Munich. These had an interesting consequence for Britain which showed the need for the League of Nations Agreement and somewhat amusingly the role which Reith saw for himself in the wider context of European broadcasting.

The Austrian Government, having appealed to the Germans for some modification, if not cessation, of the Austrian Nazi broadcasts from Munich, decided to act on the precedent of the Polish-German dispute in 1930 and approached the International Broadcasting Union with a request for help. Admiral Carpendale in turn mentioned the matter to Reith, whose diary entry carries on the story:

> It occurred to me that I, as the sort of broadcasting doyen of Europe, might make a personal request to the German Ambassador to have it stopped, not hopeful of any result and not expecting he would have any influence in Berlin. To my surprise Carpendale welcomed this and still more to my surprise Vansittart, of the FO, not only had no objection but was delighted with the idea and wanted to give it publicity. I saw the Ambassador this morning and was very civilly received, leaving an aide-memoire with him and then went with a copy to Vansittart.[30]

It is hardly surprising that the BBC, with Reith at its head, was

[29] The position in Britain is somewhat surprising, for it had always been illegal for British people to listen to unauthorized broadcasts, a condition which was printed on the licences that all owners of radio sets were obliged to have. Condition No. 5 read: 'The only messages received by means of the station [i.e. the radio set] shall be those intended for receipt thereby or sent by a duly authorised broadcasting station for general reception. If any other message is unintentionally received the Licensee [the listener] shall not make known or allow to be made known its contents, its existence, or the fact of its receipt to any person (other than a duly authorised Officer of his Majesty's Government or a competent legal tribunal) ...' Similarly, by Condition No. 7, the Government reserved the right to withdraw the Licence and prohibit the use of all radio sets in the country. The existence of these laws in Britain did not prevent a public outcry against Nazi totalitarianism when they were introduced into Germany. During World War II these laws were enforced in Britain and a number of people were imprisoned for infringing them; see below, pp.180-1.

[30] Lord Reith's Diary, 26 July 1933.

universally seen in Europe as a Government Department. The results Reith hoped for were not forthcoming. He was visited a fortnight later by the Secretary to the German Embassy and Reith's next diary entry provides an interesting coda to the incident:

> He [the Secretary to the German Embassy] tried to make out that the Munich broadcasts against Austria had been done because Vienna was broadcasting stuff against Germany, but I said that this was not so ... I asked him what he had to say about the further anti-Austrian broadcast from Munich the night before and he said that the instructions could not have got through in time. It is all quite unsatisfactory. If I had seen Hitler himself I believe I could have got the thing stopped.[31]

The last paragraph is particularly revealing about Reith's state of mind, and of the extraordinary way in which Hitler's reputation had spread through Europe. Had Reith reflected, he would surely have seen how singular his proposal was. Hitler was the head of a totalitarian state; Reith was merely the Director-General of an organization which repeatedly declared that it was independent of the British Government. Those in the Foreign Office and the press who criticized Reith for running, effectively, his own fiefdom within the state do not appear to have been far wrong.

On the French-German border there was also a continual radio war, although it seems that the French programmes sent out from a powerful transmitter at Strasbourg, were on a far more regular basis than the German, which were confined to the short wave. The Foreign Office in London were kept informed of these transmissions; for example a report to them in February 1936 raised all the most obvious points:

> In the news transmission [from Strasbourg] at 9.00 p.m. on 13 February 1936 the transmitters gave out the speeches made by Chancellor Hitler and Minister Goering. In the course of the review the announcer used these words: 'One does not know whether one has to deal with lunatics or cynics who want to make fools of us'. Such an insulting description of the leading German statesmen in the German language by a French radio station can only give rise to the greatest indignation and the deepest concern for peaceful intentions.[32]

In 1935 the Spanish Civil War broke out and soon gave further examples of the impact of radio war as it moved from its 'cold' phase

[31] Ibid., 9 August 1933.
[32] Public Record Office: FO 371/19894; C2025.

to actual conflict. The phrase 'Fifth Column' was used for the first time in a Nationalist broadcast. Franco's Generals frequently broadcast, and one even became known as the 'Radio General'.[33] Republican stations broadcast in Italian to Italy, and, only incidentally of course, to Italian troops fighting with Franco, even developing clandestine stations purporting to be revolutionary Communist stations in Italy itself. Italy appears to have returned the compliment and broadcast in Spanish a programme supposedly in Spain urging support for Franco.[34] Towards the end of the Civil War the Republican Government actually issued one of the sternest edicts ever delivered against radio, forbidding its citizens to listen to the radio at all.[35]

In Europe generally there was a plethora of small underground Communist stations that broadcast much as small local stations do now, becoming actively involved in fomenting strikes and acting as centres of information and propaganda. Occasionally these were found, but no satisfactory answer on the question of the nature of their activities seems to have been forthcoming from Moscow. Rather they vigorously encouraged their agents and fostered the activities of people such as Burgess and Münzenburg.

Finally, after much deliberation on the original Polish proposals, the League of Nations distributed a draft agreement and called a conference at Geneva in September 1936. The agreement was called: International Convention concerning the Use of Broadcasting in the Cause of Peace. As soon as the Foreign Office read it, serious difficulties for Britain became apparent to them. For example the actual wording of Article 4 of the convention was as follows:

> The High Contracting Parties mutually undertake to ensure, especially in times of crisis, that stations within their respective territories shall broadcast information concerning international relations the accuracy of which shall have been verified – and that by all means within their power – by the persons responsible for broadcasting the information.[36]

Leeper commented:

[33] General Quiepe de Llano.

[34] For an account of this radio warfare, see Harwood L. Childs and John B. Whitton, *Propaganda by Short Wave* (1943), p.26.

[35] For a valuable study of this and other aspects of political broadcasting before the war, see Thomas Grandin, *The Political Use of Radio* (1939) published by *Geneva Studies*.

[36] Grandin discusses the Convention in *The Political Use of Radio* (1939) and the quotations are taken from there. They also appear in the Public Record Office in the files cited in note 37 below.

This would raise a very big question with the BBC ... The Foreign Office has to walk very warily in seeming to censor news. It has taken a long time to establish our present friendly relations with them, and we are most careful not to dictate or control them in any way. When I gave evidence before the Ullswater Committee Major Attlee cross-examined me very closely on this point and I think he was satisfied. If some control were established over the BBC news the Government would have to consider this aspect very carefully.[37]

There was an amusing prelude to the actual talks in Geneva when the London press got hold of the fact that the BBC's delegate was to be a woman, Miss I.D. Benzie.[38] The account published suggested that she would even be the person signing the agreement on behalf of the British Government. Clearly there had been a leak of some kind from within the BBC, and Vansittart wrote a stern letter to Reith asking him to ensure that the staff sent to the conference by the BBC would be people who would be capable of understanding that they would be bound by exactly the same regulations as the Government officials who went on such trips, and that no talking with the press was allowed. Reith sent him a reply which seemed of a key with his usual lofty view of the world:

I enquired into the *Evening Standard* article to which you refer. Our people envy you in knowing less than they do of the capacity for invention of the author thereof and others of his kidney. They say they have long since learned to sigh and pass on. I spare myself even this amount of trouble by not reading such things.

Anyhow you are quite right in feeling sure that there could be no misunderstanding. Anyone who we would entrust with work of this kind would be incapable of the slightest impropriety.[39]

Vansittart was satisfied with this reply, though he might have been less pleased had he known that Reith's actual response to his letter had been to hand it directly to Miss Benzie. It was she who wrote the reply, returning it to Reith, who duly signed it and sent it off. The discussions carried on at Geneva were protracted and the agreement was not finally signed by Britain until 1 May 1937. All the clauses which had seemed likely to cause difficulty were in the final agreement in essentially unmodified form. Germany and Italy had not been involved in the negotiations, and as Russia, who did sign, was not in

[37] Public Record Office: FO 371/20487; W11390/550/98.
[38] I.D. Benzie joined the BBC from Oxford in 1927 becoming Foreign Director in 1934. She married Royston Morley, the novelist and pioneer television producer.
[39] Public Record Office: FO 371/20487; W11390/550/98.

reality amenable to any pressure should she depart from the terms of the agreement, the Convention has usually been regarded as a dead letter. However, it is clear that the Government signed the agreement knowing that the question of the BBC's broadcasts would now become one of considerable seriousness; indeed infringements rendered the Government liable to subsequent action on detection or complaint. The exact wording was:

> They further mutually undertake to ensure that any transmission likely to harm good international understanding by incorrect statements shall be rectified at the earliest possible moment by the most effective means, even if the incorrectness has become apparent only after the broadcast has taken place.[40]

The position within the BBC had been improved, as far as talks went, by the appointment of Sir Richard Maconachie[41] as Director of Talks. He had been a diplomat in Afghanistan, the British Minister in Kabul from 1930-36, and was fully aware of the problems that broadcasts could cause in the international sphere. As we shall see in Chapter 5 on Britain's first radio war, another ex-Diplomat was appointed to the Foreign Language News Department in 1937. However, there were still problems which caused Vansittart considerable worries. In March 1937, just before the signing of the Convention, he asked a representative of the BBC to call on him at the Foreign Office. His first concern was a proposed talk on Russia by John Hilton.[42] The BBC's report on the meeting was, as usual, detailed and thorough:

[40] See note 36 above.

[41] Sir Richard Maconachie (1885-1962). Beginning life in the Indian Civil Service in 1909, he pursued a conventional career in India. He served briefly as Counsellor in Kabul in the twenties, returning there as Ambassador to Afghanistan 1930-36. On retirement he began an entirely new career, joining the BBC with responsibility for talks and going on to become Controller Home Division 1941-45. He was highly regarded by all those who worked for him at the BBC.

[42] John Hilton (1880-1943), Professor of Industrial Relations at Cambridge from 1931. He was the first occupant of the chair and was always said to be the first man to occupy a chair at Cambridge without having passed any examinations of the usual kind. He had started life as an apprentice mill mechanic in Bolton and risen through his own abilities to become Assistant Secretary and Director of Statistics at the Ministry of Labour 1919-31. Hilton was in the forefront of political broadcasting in the thirties and his series on Unemployment is still regarded as a classic of its kind, not without significance for the present day. He was a close friend of Sir George Barnes (see below, p.45n1) and the group which gathered around him at Cambridge. When he died Barnes wrote a moving tribute to his family, recounting his attendance at Hilton's first lecture. Hilton's broadcasts no doubt sprang from this connection (his

He [Vansittart] said that the Foreign Office was very worried about the Hilton talk on Russia, and also about some Nazi propaganda which I could not recognize. He said that he did not feel that the European situation was any better and that we were still on the edge of a crisis etc. He said that there was no doubt that chronologically Germany is a greater danger than Russia, but that although at the moment British foreign policy is linking the country to some extent to Russia, Communism and Nazism were equaly abhorrent.

He said that the Hilton talk would quite likely be quoted against him when he was protesting against some Communist activity and assured me that nothing whatever will persuade foreign countries generally that *The Times* and the BBC are not both Government controlled. He repeated, you will see, some of the arguments used in connection with 'The Citizen and his Government' series last year. He said he and others in the Foreign Office had read the Hilton talk and that they had no hesitation at all in saying that it was definitely Communist propaganda ...

What he would like is for us to keep off Communism and Nazi-ism and Fascism for the next year or two, and if, for any reason, we were unable or unwilling to do so, he asked that there might be good liasion between his people in order that the ground might be properly prepared and such talks as were given not open to misunderstanding and, above all, not be liable to cause trouble in the Foreign Office in the delicate state of affairs existing and likely to continue to exist ...

I cannot tell how serious the position is, nor whether he is exaggerating: if so to what extent. There is no doubt, however, of the urgency of his plea to us.[43]

The terms of the last paragraph make it quite clear that the accepted view within the BBC was still one of general cynicism about the Foreign Office's worries connected with the seemingly inevitable general European war. Had Leeper been able to see this minute he would no doubt have echoed his observation on another paper.

---

early contributor files at the BBC have unfortunately been lost, probably destroyed in the blitz, so that the exact connection cannot be known for sure). For further reference to this circle, see below, p.45f. There was a biography written after his death by a close friend, Edna Nixon: *John Hilton: The Story of His Life* (1946). For a brief period at the beginning of the war Hilton was Director of Home Publicity at the Ministry of Information, but he soon returned to broadcasting, doing invaluable work for Guy Burgess and Norman Luker, his producers. He died suddenly after an exhausting tour to the Middle East. He has frequently been confused with another John Hilton, a schoolfriend of Anthony Blunt's.
[43] BBC Written Archives Centre: R34/44, 9 March 1937.

One would think from the BBC attitude that there was no international crisis at all, that the halcyon days of the post-war period had come to stay forever, that no other country was threatening our interests seriously.[44]

The BBC submitted a memorandum on 26 April which attempted to come to terms with their difficulties in dealing with foreign affairs. They claimed the right to broadcast talks and discussions on all questions regarding foreign affairs which were freely discussed within the Press. They saw themselves as 'confined to exposition rather than persuasion and the proper method would be scientific and factual ...'. Charles Peake at the Foreign Office News Department shrewdly commented that this was a counsel of perfection:

> Few indeed are the speakers qualified both by experience and temperament to treat a political subject in this ideal manner ...

and he went on to draw attention to the BBC's production of Hilton's broadcast on Russia

> which professed to have been an impartial survey but which was in fact biased to a degree.[45]

As we shall see shortly, there was a dawning realization within the Foreign Office that the BBC, known to be sympathetic towards the left, might be actively proselytizing from a Communist standpoint. With hindsight, these first attempts at understanding what was in fact a classic case of 'infiltration' seem extremely weak. But it must be remembered that the conflicts taking place, particularly in Spain,

---

[44] See below, p.95, with a fuller quotation.

[45] Sir Charles Peake (1897-1958). He entered the Diplomatic Service 1922. In 1939 he became head of the Foreign Office News Department in succession to Rex Leeper. He was always spoken of as having a special connection with Lord Halifax and, in 1941, went to Washington as Halifax's Personal Assistant. He ended his career as Ambassador at Athens, again a post previously occupied by Leeper. The quotations are from the Public Record Office: FO 395/547; P2120/20/150.

were seen as the focus of action within Britain, with volunteers going to fight for the Republic in large numbers; action by ideologically committed Marxists such as Burgess nearer to home could only have been conceived of with the greatest difficulty.[46] Leeper described the origins of the BBC's memorandum:

> This memorandum arose out of a conversation which I had some time ago with Mr Graves and Sir R. Maconachie. On that occasion they tried to tie me down to what could or could not be said about Spain or what we wanted to do about other countries. I told them I thought this a profitless discussion over the luncheon table and suggested they should state their case on paper.[47]

The Spanish question had been dealt with by Vansittart in his meeting with Graves on 9 March and he had made his views abundantly clear, but they had obviously not gone down at all well with the BBC. Reading them now it is easy to see why:

> With regard to Spanish news, [Vansittart] says there is now little doubt that Franco will be in Madrid and in due course in control of Spain. He says that Franco feels that the BBC and *The Times* are against him and therefore the Government must be against him too. He says this is deplorable, since it will send Franco more into the arms of Italy and Germany than ever. The Foreign Office are very anxious to prevent the establishment of a new Fascist state in Spain which would, of course, put France in a nice position, and the British Government is the only power that can prevent this happening. He quite honestly feels that our Spanish news will make a considerable difference to the future in this respect.
>
> He would be very grateful if we could at least put out no more Government [i.e. Republican] news, irrespective of the amount that comes in, than insurgent [i.e. Franco or Nationalist] news. It is quite obvious, in fact, that he would be glad if we could become sufficiently obviously pro-Insurgent to convince Franco that we, and therefore the Government, are not anti-Franco. He would, in addition, be very pleased if we could see our way to dropping the term 'insurgent', which apparently is resented on that side, adopting perhaps

---

[46] How some of the most privileged members of our society could behave as they did is incomprehensible to many even today. For a full account of Burgess's activities in the BBC, see below, Chapter 3.

[47] Public Record Office: FO 395/547; P2120/20/150.

'Nationalists'[48] ... I think we can without inconvenience do what he wants with regard to Spanish news, but I don't think we can adopt the new term. We might, however, drop the old one.[49]

In fact the Foreign Office policy was successful, and in carrying it through under the flag of his 'appeasement' policy Chamberlain without doubt contributed largely to Spain's decision to remain neutral in the world war which was shortly to break out. At the time it would have been impossible for the left in Britain to see Franco as anything but a fascist – indeed they could not do so to this very day. So great was the Communist propaganda campaign during the Civil War that fascism became a general term of abuse to be applied indiscriminately by the left to anyone not avowing their cause.[50] The truth was very different, as Hitler was to find out. The BBC and its staff, in common with most of the British intelligentsia, took an essentially Communist line at the time, the reason of course why the more sinister activities of Burgess and his circle remained unremarked. Vansittart saw this very clearly; when Leeper suggested that there should be a meeting to discuss the BBC's memorandum he replied:

> I concur. But I must add that I think the BBC will need a lot of guiding, and I do not think they will really take the guidance, anyhow not kindly. There is a very widespread impression that the BBC is biased towards the left and there seems to be good grounds for the belief. If the BBC is to be really fit to do what it evidently thinks itself capable of doing – personally I doubt it – it will have to divest itself of all bias of any kind whatever and get the best people for the job and exclude some of its former lecturers.[51]

The state of affairs in the BBC's news departments was different and more open; controversial matters had regularly to be dealt with, especially in reports of proceedings in Parliament. MPs were particularly vocal in their insistence that coverage by the BBC was

[48] The BBC in fact decided to adopt this practice after discussion at boardroom level.

[49] BBC Written Archives Centre: R34/44, 9 March 1937.

[50] The process had begun much earlier with, for example, the Plebs League publication *Fascism: Its History and Significance* (1924), whose detailed analysis of Mussolini's movement reflected the bitterness with which the Communists viewed their defeat in Italy and their particular fear that Fascism would be seen as supporting the proletariat and moving towards a Guild Socialist state. The Spanish Civil War reinforced the tendency for the word to be used as a general term of abuse; at the same time it was of course true that Italian soldiers were fighting in Spain.

[51] Public Record Office: FO 395/547; P2120/20/150.

impartial and the BBC over the years seems to have developed a defence mechanism which served them well. All complaints were dealt with by analysing the number of minutes given to each contribution to a debate and this was then compared with the number of column inches given to the same speakers in the reports in *The Times*. Even over a brief period the comparison showed that the BBC had been as unprejudiced as the press; what more could be asked of it than that was then the query raised. The actual question of political bias in the BBC talks programmes, personnel and structure were never dealt with; the news departments alone had to bear the brunt of any public scrutiny, and the result was a bland neutrality. In a highly controversial report written in the wake of the Munich crisis a Chief News Editor revealed the truth of what had been happening:

> I say, with a full sense of responsibility and, since I was for over three years Chief News Editor, with a certain authority, that in the past we have not played the part which our duty to the people of this country called upon us to play. We have, in fact, taken part in a conspiracy of silence. I am not saying that we did this willingly or even knowingly, and most certainly there is not a word of accusation against any individual in what I am saying. In view of our history and our peculiar relationship to the Government, and also of the very short time, comparatively speaking, during which we have been at work, I think even the sternest critic can hardly have expected us to behave differently. But now things have changed. The position of this country is infinitely more dangerous than it has been in modern times, and the past few weeks ... have invested the BBC with a new importance, given it a more vital role in the national life and have, therefore, laid a new responsibility on us who are its servants.[52]

His reference to a 'conspiracy of silence' had been explained earlier when he remarked that the people of Britain and the Empire were ignorant of many of the facts which would have enabled them to make a proper judgement of what was happening, adding: 'Even now they know very little of what they ought to know.'[53] The fact that these difficulties stemmed from real problems of foreign policy which could not be solved merely by a statement of facts, albeit of their own biased selection, however much the BBC's news reporters would like to be able to see them in those terms, was equally clear to him:

> I am not for a moment suggesting that the BBC should have a rival Foreign Policy to that of the Government. In any case that is

[52] BBC Written Archives Centre: R34/600/10.
[53] Ibid.

impossible, and even if it were not impossible it would still be grossly improper and irresponsible.[54]

The author of this confidential memorandum had already moved from the News Department and probably did not know that much of what he said, having been the over-riding concern of the Foreign Office News Department and many in other places in Whitehall, had already been dealt with.

The essential difficulty was that the BBC, already a problem, was going to be more of one if war came. There was also bound up with this the perception that, if a final attempt at appeasement was to be made, the BBC and others associated with Foreign Affairs might well be dealt with in a way which would show to totalitarian powers that there was no inherent hostility in key British institutions.

The first move along these lines was the startling one of removing Vansittart from his post as Permanent Head of the Foreign Office to a newly created post of Chief Diplomatic Advisor to the Government. This was seen at the time, and later, as a classic case of someone being 'kicked upstairs'. Vansittart himself knew that his violently anti-German and, in effect, anti-Government attitudes had become known through Churchill's open visits to him at the Foreign Office; in his memoirs he specifically blamed Churchill for his troubles at this time.[55] But the picture was in fact more complicated. Vansittart remained in his old rooms at the Foreign Office. They were those always occupied by the Permanent Head, and that he kept them was an indication to those observers who knew their Whitehall that he was not being removed far from the levers of power. His duties in his new post were taken from those normally carried out by the Permanent Head and included representing the Foreign Secretary at meetings of the Committee of Imperial Defence. He was also to deal with all matters regarding propaganda. In fact the Foreign Office had been split in two. Vansittart was to deal with matters relating to war, Cadogan with other matters, essentially the normal running of the Foreign Office. Hitler would see Vansittart removed, apparently, from the seat of power; in fact he was devoting his attentions exclusively to matters concerned with war should it break out. Cadogan represented an appeasing view of the Foreign Office.

[54] Ibid.

[55] See Lord Vansittart, *The Mist Procession* (1958), p.497: 'He [Churchill] became an embarrassing ally. At first he only telephoned to my house in Park Street to test parts of a speech on me. Then he would come there after hours and that was all right too. It was not all right when he took to striding into my room at the Foreign Office and turned our connivance into an open secret. He cost me more than he knew.'

Vansittart's powers on questions of propaganda were soon greatly increased with the creation of the 'Vansittart Committee', or the Committee for the Co-ordination of British Publicity Abroad. One modern commentator has remarked:

> The committee ... was the first serious attempt to combine the activities of the various official and semi-official organizations engaged in the projection of Britain abroad with an effective utilization of the available media.[56]

It was largely the creation of Leeper, and Vansittart's role as Chairman was no doubt part of the original conception. Vansittart now found himself directly concerned with the BBC's foreign programmes and lost no time in writing to Reith to inform him of what he was doing.[57]

Taylor remarks that Leeper had expressed himself as strongly opposed to the setting up of a Ministry of Information in peace time and that his ideas for the Vansittart Committee may have evolved from considerations along those lines. The question of the Ministry of Information may well have been much closer than that. The embryo Ministry had been set up under Leeper's guidance, and its Director-General designate had been Stephen Tallents.[58] Tallents worked for the BBC as a Public Relations expert and was very close to Reith, who had himself been considered for the MOI post but then nominated Tallents. With such a set-up there was a real danger that the BBC might end up actually running the Ministry. And this might even have seemed desirable in some quarters, for the BBC was undoubtedly expert in the field of radio, which was vital, and one area which was not represented in any way in the Ministry of Information as it was during World War I.[59] Anyone knowing the inside story of the Foreign Office's struggles with the BBC would have seen that

[56] Philip M. Taylor, *The Projection of Britain* (1981), p.216.

[57] BBC Written Archives Centre: R44/85. Vansittart wrote, on 11 February 1938: '... I am most anxious to have your cooperation and much hope that you will yourself as often as possible represent the BBC at meetings of the Committee.' Almost nothing came of this approach and, as we shall see, Reith was soon to be gently eased from the position he had occupied for so long.

[58] Sir Stephen Tallents (1884-1958), author of *The Projection of England* (1932), which made him famous, and an autobiography of his early years, *Man and Boy* (1943). After Working for the Empire Marketing Board he went to the BBC, where he became Controller of Public Relations 1935-40 and Controller of Overseas Services 1940-41.

[59] Wireless telegraphy, as opposed to Wireless telephony or radio, was used in World War I. See Campbell Stuart, *Secrets of Crewe House* (1920), pp.17, 103. Observation planes at the front communicated with their guns by morse sets, in flight.

such a result could only lead to disaster. Apart from lack of staff and limited experience, there was also the question of its political leanings, which Vansittart had noticed, and above all else the question of the role of Reith.

By the time of Munich there was an almost entirely new situation. Reith had gone, manoeuvred into resignation from the organization he had created and placed in charge of another Government corporation, Imperial Airways, at the personal insistence of the Prime Minister. The foreign news broadcasts of the BBC were largely written, or in any event controlled in the closest way, by the Foreign Office News Department.[60] The anxiety of the BBC's news editor about the BBC having a foreign policy of its own had thus already been dealt with before he entered his report, although, with the intense secrecy surrounding these changes, it is unlikely that he knew. The only bastion of independent political views was the talks department, and Burgess's encouragement of Nicolson and others soon brought that to an end. Vansittart's Committee was seen by some as itself an alternative model for a future Ministry of Information. In the event it was replaced by a committee under Lord Perth, but the germ of truth in the idea is seen in the fact that *that* committee, and Lord Perth, were cast in the roles of shadow Ministry, and Perth became the first Director-General of the Ministry of Information. It was an ironic comment on the inter-departmental fighting of those few years that Reith himself occupied the post of Minister of Information for a brief period, but the BBC, although resisting Churchill's attempts to take complete control of it, never again directly affected foreign policy in the way Leeper and Vansittart feared it would.[61]

---

[60] For the development of Foreign Office control, with examples, see below, p.101f.

[61] For Churchill's attempt to get the BBC under Government control, see below, pp.241-2.

3. Guy Burgess and His Circle at the BBC

When Vansittart commented on the left-wing bias of the BBC's 'former lecturers' he was making a shrewd thrust. While it was John Hilton and the broadcast he made praising Soviet Russia that had first caught Vansittart's attention, many other speakers on the BBC were drawn from the extreme left. The explanation of this, the existence within the BBC of Guy Burgess, an undisguised Communist, also most probably a Comintern agent, and his circle will be examined in this chapter.

Few of the BBC's programmes had any political content. Politics was confined almost exclusively to news broadcasts and to talks, and the department of the Corporation responsible for the arrangement of who was to speak, and on what subject, was the appropriately named Talks Department. As we have seen, a retired diplomat, Sir Richard Maconachie, had been put in to head the department, but most of the day-to-day running devolved to his deputy, George Barnes.[1] The real power, however, rested largely with the producers who assembled the programmes. Radio producers, responsible for the production, literally, of what the public was to hear, in what was still a new highly sophisticated world requiring rare skills, could insist on who they wanted round them to do the necessary work. If, in bureaucratic theory, the head of the Talks Department was responsible for what went out, in practice it was his Talks Producer who actually chose the speakers and monitored their texts.

[1] Sir George Barnes (1904-1960), younger son of Sir Hugh Shakespeare Barnes KCSI, KCVO. Educated at Dartmouth, he returned there to teach (1927-30) after graduating at Cambridge. In 1930 he became Assistant Secretary to the Cambridge University Press where his position brought him into contact with many famous literary and academic figures (see below, p.48). In 1935 he moved to the BBC; he was apparently recruited personally by Reith when Reith visited the University Press in connection with BBC publications. After a brilliant career at the BBC, which ended with his being knighted at the BBC itself for his services in connection with televising the Coronation, he went on to become Principal of Keele University, a post previously occupied by A.D. Lindsay. He died at an early age after a brief tenure, but the University Library is indebted to him for the acquisition of the Sarolea collection, an immense private library which Barnes himself assisted in sorting and cataloguing.

One of the most successful of the pre-war radio producers was Guy Burgess. The BBC was his first important job after leaving Cambridge and it was one of the most desirable posts then available. As we shall see, his authority among his contemporaries at Cambridge and the patronage he found in his hands stemmed from his position and the success he made of it. Burgess's circle of broadcasters, those he chose to come to the microphone, included Harold Nicolson, Roger Fulford, Lord Elton,[2] Anthony Blunt, David Footman, E.H. Carr and John Hilton. Nicolson[3] was already a famous broadcaster whom Burgess knew socially: Roger Fulford[4] and Anthony Blunt[5] were also people who formed part of the social world in which Burgess flourished. It is clear from his quite open correspondence with them that they were both broadcasters and friends. Of the others there were some whom he got to know at Cambridge who were as much friends of George

[2] Lord Elton (1892-1973), broadcaster and biographer of Ramsay MacDonald. His broadcast talks, which made him a household name, were published as *It Occurs to Me* (1938). Unfortunately his early contributor files are among the few that were lost in the bombing. It has not therefore been possible to establish more than that Burgess produced a number of his programmes. Throughout the period here discussed he was a Fellow of Queen's College, Oxford and a University Lecturer in Modern History.

[3] Harold Nicolson (1886-1968). He entered the Foreign Office in 1909 and rose rapidly, serving on the British Delegation to the Paris Peace Conference in 1919. He left the Diplomatic Service in 1929 to become a journalist for Lord Beaverbrook's *Evening Standard* at a time when Beaverbrook was actively involved in fringe politics and starting his Empire Free Trade Party. Nicolson also soon became involved in politics (see index). He began broadcasting in 1930, presumably through an invitation from Hilda Matheson at BBC Talks whom both he and his wife, Vita Sackville-West, knew well. His later career may be followed in outline through his diaries, which were published in three volumes (1966-68). They contain much interesting material and are among the most quoted sources for the period which they cover. It must be said, however, that neither of the two episodes mentioned in this book, the bitter row over the censoring of his talk at the time of Munich, or the banning by Churchill of a wartime discussion with Sir Frederick Whyte, are mentioned in the diaries as published. The talk took place on 5 September 1938 and the published version contains no entry at all for that date. The diaries should therefore be treated with caution.

[4] Sir Roger Thomas Baldwin Fulford (1902-1983). President of the Oxford Union 1927; joined the editorial staff of *The Times* 1933; became a part-time lecturer in English at King's College London 1937-48. An Assistant Censor from 1939 to 1940, he worked in MI5 from 1940 to 1942 (describing this period in his *Who's Who* entry as 'Civil Assistant War Office') and spent the rest of the war as Assistant Private Secretary to the Secretary of State for Air. He published numerous books, many on Royal subjects, including George IV, the Prince Consort and Queen Victoria. He edited the *Greville Memoirs* with Lytton Strachey.

[5] Anthony Frederick Blunt (1907-1983), art historian, sometime Surveyor of the Queen's Pictures, and Director of the Courtauld Institute 1947-73.

Barnes as his. Such was John Hilton.[6] Others, like E.H. Carr,[7] came
to him through BBC connections or were already doing talks for other
producers which Burgess agreed to take over. The relevance of this
analysis of Burgess's contributors' connections with him is more than
the obvious one of establishing how Burgess's links with the London
literary and political world were forged. Fulford, for example, was a
key man in MI5 during the war; David Footman was at the time a
serving officer of MI6 and the man who gave Burgess his entrée into
the security services.[8] It is not clear when Burgess first met Fulford
but he would certainly have got to know him in his brief spell on *The
Times* where Fulford was already working. As we shall see later,
Burgess contacted Footman in an entirely different way, through a
literary agent, and with a persistence that was very uncommon and in
stark contrast to the casual operation of the 'old boy' network with his
other speakers.

Burgess joined the BBC in 1936. There is a well-known account of
how he got his job there. A senior member of his old Cambridge
College is said to have rung up an official of the BBC and put in a
word for him after he had failed to get a fellowship at a College.[9] This
story has been generally accepted, but seems extremely unlikely; even
in the heyday of Reith's nepotism it would not have been possible for a
don, however eminent, merely to telephone the BBC and obtain a job
for one of his graduates, however brilliant and promising. Such a
telephone call may well have taken place, but it is more likely to have
been in order to supply a reference for an application already made.
The BBC's staff records are closed for seventy-five years, but the most
probable explanation of Burgess's appointment is the connection he
made at Cambridge with George Barnes, in whose house he lived for a
while when Barnes was working for the Cambridge University Press.
Burgess shared with Barnes a common background. Both had been
destined for the navy and had begun their education at Dartmouth,
and then been found for various reasons not to be suitable for a naval
career. Burgess had gone to Eton and Cambridge; Barnes had also
gone to Cambridge. A few years later he had moved to his post at the
BBC. It is clear from their internal correspondence within the BBC

[6] See above, p.37.

[7] E.H. Carr (1892-1984), historian of Russia.

[8] See below, p.62f.

[9] The story of G.M. Trevelyan's phone call appears in Tom Driberg, *Guy Burgess: A
Portrait with Background* (1956), p.33. It is repeated in many other subsequent
accounts, most recently in Barrie Penrose and Simon Freeman, *Conspiracy of Silence:
The Secret Life of Anthony Blunt* (1986), p.194. The same source also quotes John Green
as warning Barnes about Burgess; but it is clear that Green did not know of the
prior connection between Barnes and Burgess.

that Barnes and Burgess occupied exactly the same social circle and shared largely the same views. However, on the question of politics Barnes never expressed the same obviously Communist view as Burgess. Indeed it would be difficult to establish what his political opinions were. Some commentators have thought that he was right-wing, basing their feelings on Barnes's impeccable appearance and society background (Lord Curzon was his godfather). But there was another side to the Barnes family, represented by his elder half-brother James Strachey Barnes,[10] whom we shall meet later. This brother was acutely politically conscious. He was an extreme right-wing professional politician who lived most of his life in Italy, where he was one of Mussolini's closest supporters and also, for a while, a broadcaster. George Barnes might therefore have been himself very politically conscious. His position at the University Press was one of great social influence. The fact that he was not at the University itself probably explains how he has escaped the attentions of the 'mole-hunters' over the years. But he was none the less near the centre of a left-wing social group and was closely attached to John Hilton, as well as to Keynes, E.M. Forster[11] and other well-known Cambridge figures.

With Burgess once established at the BBC, Barnes supported him on every occasion. Therefore, just as Talks Producers chose their speakers, so it seems likely that Barnes had requested Burgess for his

[10] James Strachey Barnes (1890-1955), son of Sir Hugh Shakespeare Barnes KCSI, KCVO and elder half-brother of Sir George Barnes. Born in India, Barnes was largely brought up in Italy at the house of his grandparents, Sir John and Lady Strachey. He studied briefly at Cambridge, reading Arabic and lodging with his cousin Monsignor A.S. Barnes, Catholic Chaplain to the University. In World War I he served in the Royal Flying Corps, taking an active part in the Battle of the Somme and the Third Battle of Ypres, where he was seriously injured. His first volume of autobiography, *Half a Life* (1933), contains a valuable account of his experiences. After the war he served under Harold Nicolson as an expert on Albania and subsequently went to live there. He formed a close friendship with Mussolini and became actively involved in Fascist politics, as we shall see below, p.91f. He occasionally visited England at this time; Harold Nicolson writes of a lunch with Barnes and T.S. Eliot to discuss the start of a Fascist periodical in England (see H. Nicolson, *Diaries and Letters, 1930-39* (1966) p.111). An anonymous obituarist wrote of his later years: '... his brave old world, so lovingly fashioned from mediaeval materials, collapsed with the fall of Mussolini.' The Home Office have declined to release his papers, presumably because of his knowledge of the early support given to Mussolini by the British authorities. See below, p.84n14.

[11] It is interesting to notice that, whereas Barnes got on well with Forster, Burgess did not. During the war Forster declined a request for a talk from Burgess saying that he preferred working for the Indian service, where his producer was George Orwell. See correspondence printed in W.J. West (ed.), *Orwell: The War Broadcasts* (1985), p.275.

assistant. After the usual brief period of training, Burgess spent three months doing routine production of the more simple programmes that Barnes or one of his colleagues had set up. His political inclinations and his interest in Russia were both evident even at this early stage. Discussing the need for programmes which would interest ordinary people he remarked to Barnes:

> This Dr Barron question and the talks of 'popular industry' ... I am convinced that this type of subject and talk appeals to a class of listener for whom we do not ordinarily cater sufficiently, that is, the class that can only be called the 'technician' class, the large number of people who read Darwin, attend night classes and are interested in popular science and industry. From this point of view I would rather like to have the talks ... the question is: is Saturday morning an impossible time for such talks? Or does the factory whistle blow at noon?[12]

Barnes curbed this youthful enthusiasm for proletarian topics by the normal procedure of accepting the principle while denying the particular case:

> I agree that talks on this subject are desirable, and that we probably do too little for the 'technician' class. But I remain convinced that these talks [by Dr Harry Barron on plastics and rubber] are not suitable for our programmes and that better talks on this subject could be obtained.[13]

Burgess's interest in Russia, which had actually taken him there in 1934, lead him to commission talks such as 'A schoolmaster in Russia', a simple account by a midland schoolmaster, J.E. Whittaker, of his tours in Russia in 1930 and 1936 and the contrast he found on the two visits. There is nothing in the BBC files to indicate how Burgess met Whittaker, but Blunt had also been on the 1936 tour and it was probably he who made the introduction. Another example was a talk 'Tramping through the White Sea' by H.S. Marchant.[14] Burgess did not seem to find him a congenial companion in the studio,

[12] BBC Written Archives Centre. Harry Barron contributor file.
[13] Ibid.
[14] Sir Herbert Stanley Marchant (b. 1906). After leaving St. John's College, Cambridge, Marchant went straight to Harrow school where he was an Assistant Master 1928-39. After the war he entered the Diplomatic Service and became Ambassador to Cuba 1960-63 and Ambassador to Tunisia 1963-66. He was the United Kingdom representative on the United Nations Committee for the elimination of Racial Discrimination 1969-73.

and though Marchant went on to do more programmes it was for other producers.

In April Burgess submitted a report of his first three months' work[15] and, as countless new producers have done before and since, bemoaned the fact that he had not been given a series – that is, a group of talks around a theme which would involve broader planning and approaches to a wider range of speakers. Eventually his plea was answered, and he set about making a group of six programmes on 'Forgotten Anniversaries' to be broadcast fortnightly.

Among the first speakers he brought to the microphone was Anthony Blunt, his closest Cambridge friend. A number of possible subjects for Blunt were canvassed, some of which seemed to be above the average BBC listeners' heads. Burgess being ill briefly, Barnes, who knew Blunt almost as well as Burgess, wrote:

> I am a little fearful of Guy's note on the Florentine subject, and, confirmed low-brow as you know me to be, I would prefer something as well known as, for example, the stealing of the Mona Lisa or the starting of the Sistine Chapel roof.[16]

Blunt replied with a brief note:

> I am going away to Paris tonight. If you want to write anything more about this my address will be: Hotel Recamier, Place St Sulpice, Paris 6. I may meet Guy there in which case of course I will talk it over with him.[17]

In the end it was agreed that a programme should be done on the event suggested by Barnes, the anniversary of the starting of the Sistine Chapel roof. This talk, before the days of the Third Programme which Barnes was later to set up,[18] was perhaps the earliest of its kind, certainly the first talk about such matters treated at the highest level over the air. It was the forerunner of a number of talks by Blunt which, together, throw a light on his personality and character. The world in which Burgess and Blunt lived before the war centred on their two London addresses, Blunt at Palace Court, Burgess at Chester Square; on the BBC and the newly founded Courtauld Institute, where Blunt worked, and a number of London

---

[15] To be found, for reasons that are not clear, in the Harry Barron contributor file at the BBC Written Archives Centre.

[16] BBC Written Archives Centre: Anthony Blunt contributor file.

[17] Ibid.

[18] For the origins of the Third Programme, see C.S. Whitehead. *A Literary History of the Third Programme 1946-70*, DPhil. thesis, Oxford 1985; to be published in 1988.

clubs which they came to in the normal way, through Harold Nicolson, or Keynes, or other older members of their Cambridge and London circle. There was no possibility in this milieu of clandestine activity and, although the situation in Europe was menacing, with Civil War in Spain, war in Britain itself seemed a long way off and the idea of 'espionage' of any real value in such a war only a remote possibility. But the connections established at this time provide the key to a great deal, if not all, that has mystified the mole-hunters of recent years. Burgess was closest to the real world of politics, through the BBC, and the espionage world, through Footman and later Fulford. Blunt, by contrast, carried on his scholarly work.

Perhaps the most influential of Blunt's broadcasts at the time was a series of three talks that Burgess invited him to do on Modern Art, followed by a discussion on Modern Art with William Coldstream, about whose work Blunt was then enthusiastic.[19] The series showed Blunt in a new light and made him an authority on Modern Art as well as the more classical themes. So much so that when the BBC were contemplating a full series on Modern Art and Sculpture in 1939 it was he who was called upon to give advice. In an interview with Barnes at Broadcasting House Blunt laid down the essentials of any successful treatment of the subject. He insisted that an interview with the young sculptor Henry Moore was essential: so also was another with William Coldstream. Interestingly enough a political element entered into the discussion, with Blunt's recommendation that Tom Harrison, with the help of his Mass Observation team, should be asked to investigate the influence of Modern Art in Preston and among miners. This was a reflection of Blunt's political interests at Cambridge. Harrison had been set off on his search for what the British public actually thought and did by a suggestion of John Hilton's.[20] An alert listener who knew the background would have been able to discern from Blunt's recommendation where his political sympathies lay. In another broadcast announced as on the seemingly apolitical subject of 'Spanish Painting' Blunt gave a brief account of one of the little known facets of the Spanish Civil War:

> The pictures in the Prado are now on their last journey to safety. First they were put into the cellars of the Prado itself, but when that was

---

[19] The original scripts of these talks (except for the second of the series of three, which in error was not recorded) and related correspondence may be found in the BBC Written Archives Centre, either in the Blunt contributor file or on the scripts microfilm.

[20] This is clearly established from material in the Hilton and Harrison contributor files at the BBC Written Archives Centre.

found to be too unsafe they were moved first to Valencia and then to Barcelona and finally, now even that has fallen, they're over the border into France on their way to Geneva ... I think we can imagine the Ghost of Goya watching with approval the saving of this work – these two works [Goya's paintings the 2nd and 3rd of May] perhaps above all others from the dangers that now threaten them.[21]

Much later, during the war, Burgess was able to get for Blunt a further talk on a very similar subject, the Allies' rescue of works of art as the war drew to its close. Blunt unquestioningly associated the Nazi and Fascist powers with philistinism, even iconoclasm, as he had earlier done with Franco's forces, without perceiving the simple truth that the self-avowed home of iconoclasm in the twentieth century was Soviet Russia. Through Burgess's introduction of Blunt to broadcasting and the resulting broadcasts and letters, we are given an insight into a man who was without doubt one of the most puzzling figures in recent British public life. The biography of Blunt which has recently appeared makes no proper reference to his broadcasts, despite a close analysis of Blunt's connection with Burgess. Had it done so, Blunt's profoundly intellectual study of works of art would have been seen to have been linked with his as profoundly naïve view of the modern world, in art and politics, which developed largely as a result of his connection with Burgess. Broadcasting for Burgess removed Blunt from the quiet world of the Courtauld to a world of *Realpolitik* and struggle in which he was later to play a suitably refined and complex part.

Roger Fulford was already established in a successful career, being at this time, as has been mentioned, an editorial writer on *The Times*. Although Burgess was only on *The Times* for a few weeks there is no doubt from their correspondence that they knew each other well. The first broadcast Fulford did for Burgess was based on his book on the Coronation of George IV. In an early letter Fulford profoundly apologized to Burgess for doing a piece in *The Times* on the same subject and hoped that this would not mean the cancellation of the broadcast or any embarrassment for Burgess with his talks director. Burgess was in fact not the least bothered and replied asking for a complete series from him:

I am still looking for someone to do the series of about five talks called 'They came to England' describing the experience of travellers such as Erasmus and Julius Caesar on first setting foot on this wretched island

[21] BBC Written Archives Centre: scripts microfilm for Anthony Blunt.

and I still think you might do it, or know someone who would.[22]

Had Burgess possessed the gift of foresight and known that he was to end his days in political exile in Russia he would not, perhaps, have been so blasé about his own country, but the phrase 'wretched island' is interesting in showing a typical upper-middle-class view of England at the time, of a piece with casual weekends in Paris, but strangely at odds with a professed concern with the need for more talks for the 'technician' class.

The significance of Burgess's connection with Fulford from the point of view of Burgess's subsequent involvement with spying is considerable. It has been pointed out by Anthony Glees that Fulford worked during the war for MI5 and that he was asked to join by Roger Hollis.[23] Glees has described in detail the background to this appointment and to Fulford's knowledge of Hollis. However the connection between Burgess and his world and Fulford has not been known till now. Hollis approached Fulford for a job on *The Times* before joining MI5, and it is clear that he knew him well at the same time as Fulford knew Burgess. I have not been able to establish whether these two parts of Fulford's world merely overlapped or whether they were, indeed, identical. In either case the possibility of a clandestine connection between Burgess, Fulford and Hollis can be seen to be of great importance. First, Fulford worked for 'F' division of MI5 with Hollis and was actually responsible for supervising the activities of known Communist sympathizers in Britain. Secondly, even more important, it is at least possible that Fulford was the famous mole first referred to by the would-be defector Volkov as 'the acting head of a section of the British Counter-Intelligence' that sent the mole-hunters on their quest.[24] As Glees has pointed out, Roger Fulford had become 'acting head' of 'F' division when Hollis was ill with tuberculosis from March to October 1942. Clearly these matters are outside the timespan of this book, but the vital significance of Burgess's close connection with Fulford, originating in Fulford's broadcasts, which may well have amounted to an infiltration in depth of MI5, can be seen. We shall examine later Burgess's connection with MI6 where infiltration did unquestionably take place, again through the agency of the BBC.

Harold Nicolson produced many programmes for the BBC and was also part of Burgess's circle; his letters to him at the BBC, and

[22] Ibid.: Roger Fulford contributor file.
[23] Anthony Glees, *The Secrets of the Service: British Intelligence and Communist Subversion 1939-51* (1987), p.329.
[24] Ibid., p.308f.

Burgess's replies, are singularly indiscreet in some matters, in a way which only goes to confirm Glees's identification of Burgess as a close friend.[25] Burgess greatly valued Nicolson as a contributor and succeeded in getting for him a remarkable weekly series 'The Past Week'. This series was extremely important, not least because it became acutely controversial and enables us to see exactly how the Government controlled the BBC's home political programmes at the time.

The controversy occurred over an episode that Nicolson wrote at the time of the Czechoslovakia troubles in September 1938. A full account of the incident is given in a later chapter.[26] It is sufficient to say here that the contents of Nicolson's programmes were seen at Cabinet level to be a directly significant intrusion into the conduct of the country's affairs. The question naturally arises: how far did what Nicolson say stem from Burgess's interests, and was Burgess even influencing the talks in a way essentially sympathetic to his Russian advisors? The answer is seen clearly in a letter written by Burgess to Nicolson a few days after the incident:

> ... from now onwards, since Parliament has stopped sitting the only talks we are having on world affairs are, in fact, yours and I am thus able to encourage you to do (what I know you would like to do) – to discuss rather seriously and for most of the talk the various political events of the past week – i.e. to do exactly what you did in your talk about Czechoslovakia ten days ago. I hope we may meet on Monday.
>
> Incidentally, you may remember what you said to me about Hitler making a great peace speech? From one or two comments that I have heard this does seem portentously likely, even going to the extent of coupling it with demands for a conference of the allied powers (?excluding Russia) to make a new settlement to take the place of the Treaty of Versailles for the whole of Southern and Eastern Europe as well as the colonies. What do you think? I only mention this as I heard it on quite good (semi-confidential) authority, but it is only a guess (inspired).[27]

What can have possessed Burgess to write such an open letter is unclear. Normally he would have spoken about such matters over the telephone or in person. But the evidence of this one letter is clear enough and damning. Nicolson's talks were indeed the only political talks emanating from the BBC at this critically important time, and it is obvious that Burgess was supervising them in the closest way. It can

[25] Ibid., p.149.
[26] See below, p.138f.
[27] BBC Written Archives Centre: Harold Nicolson contributor file.

only be surmised who the 'semi-confidential' authority might have been, but the reference to Russia's possible exclusion from the talks, and the tenor of the line Burgess proposed to Nicolson, point to a deliberate Russian propaganda ploy. Nicolson was much more of a littérateur than a politician, though he had yet to understand this himself. His ability to make sound judgments on political matters had already been called into question by his support of Oswald Mosley's New Party, and subsequently when he put forward his own political line under the 'National Labour' slogan.[28] None the less his talks would have had immense authority with the British listening public. Being able to control them directly was a major coup for those giving Burgess his instructions.

Burgess's last series was on the Mediterranean, a vital area since the Spanish Civil War was at its height and Mussolini's submarines were roaming the high seas sinking Russian and other ships. He does not seem to have commissioned the original series himself, but he soon took over the major share of the work for what was one of the most ambitious and politically sensitive series put out by the BBC at the time. The 'interlocutor' – anchorman or interviewer as he should now call him – for the series was the academic E.H. Carr. Burgess got on well with Carr, which was essential for the construction of this kind of series, for what was involved was one of the most complex of editing problems. Although each interview appeared to the unsophisticated listener to be a spontaneous discussion, it was in fact fully scripted. The method used to get this result was as follows. The contributor first wrote a brief essay on the subject to be dealt with. This was sent to the interviewer, who wrote out a trial dialogue in question-and-answer or 'discussion' form. The programme's producer then edited this and returned it to the writer for comment and final alterations.[29] Some contributors objected to the whole procedure and objected to finding themselves saying in a supposedly spontaneous discussion things which they had not written and which they did not entirely agree with. If the producer and interviewer saw eye-to-eye, the process was greatly simplified. For example Burgess wrote about one talk:

> Miss Munro suggests that you should begin by taking up her last sentence and saying 'You can't count on those reserves for Europe, as France might have to fight the next war on North African fronts as

[28] Nicolson put forward his position in a pamphlet published at the time: *Politics in the Train* (1936).
[29] As long as there were only two contributors the system was reasonably workable. More complex programmes could involve a tour-de-force of editorial skills; see for

well.' And you answer, 'Yes, that is the fright she has got over the
Spanish War. A neutral Spain and a friendly Italy is just as important
to her as to Great Britain.'[30]

Acceptable perhaps, but Burgess could be more intrusive and take
control of the scripts:

> I am becoming rather impressed about the importance of saying
> something about Portugal in the modern half of the talk and am
> contemplating introducing a five-minute talk by Hugh Gosschalk[31] of
> *The Economist* on the subject of Portugal. I should dovetail that into the
> script myself if I decided to do so.[32]

At times Burgess's and Carr's similar views about a topic and a
speaker give us an insight into the more deliberate manipulation of
speakers' opinions which even today is extremely controversial.
Talking of Hugh Seton-Watson,[33] another contributor, Burgess
remarked to Carr:

> The real trouble has been that Seton-Watson found himself very
> unwilling to talk about the point you raised as to the choice for
> Yugoslavia between Germany and Italy, and England and France. He
> feels this question involves a lot of very controversial history which is in
> the making at the present moment and, between you and me, I think he
> himself feels so deeply about it and is so deeply involved that he is
> unwilling to speak ...

Burgess always had the last word, and this for the severely practical
reason that the series was one of those which only went out after being
vetted by the Foreign Office. As we shall see for overseas broadcasts,[34]
the BBC's alleged independence from Government supervision was a
myth − widely propagated and, indeed, firmly believed in by many
employees at all levels in the BBC from that day to this, but a myth
none the less. Returning a script to Carr after his last scrutiny,
Burgess wrote:

---

example a poetry magazine on the air produced by George Orwell in *Orwell: The War
Broadcasts* (1985) p.80f.

[30] BBC Written Archives Centre: E.H. Carr contributor file.

[31] Unidentified.

[32] BBC Written Archives Centre: E.H. Carr contributor file.

[33] Hugh Seton-Watson (1916-1984), Professor of Russian History, University of
London, author of *Eastern Europe Between the Wars* (1945) and *The Pattern of Communist
Revolution* (1953).

[34] See below, p.101f.

Here is the script. You will see I have made two minute alterations one on p 3 and one on p 12. The first one is to remove the impression that we have talked about nothing else but Anglo-Italian rivalry [as indeed they had] in order to please the Foreign Office. The alteration I have made does not I think in any way alter the sense. The second one is along the lines that I spoke to you over the telephone and it is only a suggestion but I do feel that so much depends on what one means by the work of 'intervention'. In one sense, after all, propaganda is intervention and the Third International (though not, I suppose, strictly the Soviet Government) was, I think, pretty busy in Spain before the Civil War.[35]

Besides the discreet allusion to Foreign Office control, Burgess's remarks about the activity of the Comintern were no doubt a subtle attempt to plant in Carr's mind the idea that he, Burgess, was not himself a Communist Party supporter, though of course a man of the left. It is possible that the remark may have represented some residual doubt in Burgess's mind about the Comintern's position and responsibility for the Spanish disaster. The question is worth raising because it was à propos of this series that Burgess made his famous visit to see Churchill in an attempt to get him to broadcast (Burgess subsequently became a keen supporter of Churchill's). The circumstances which led to the visit were that Churchill had at first agreed to do a talk for the Mediterranean series, quite independently of E.H. Carr of course, but had suddenly cancelled giving the international situation as his reason. Burgess went to see him to persuade him to change his mind, receiving a typically Churchillian riposte for his trouble, as his report on the visit makes clear:

Mr Churchill complained that he had been very badly treated in the matter of political broadcasts and that he was always muzzled by the BBC. I said I was not myself in possession of the facts and, in any case, had nothing to do with such matters since I believed that the allotment of space was settled by arrangement and discussion between the BBC and the parties. I imagine that he was referring to a past controversy that I believe (though I didn't say so) there was over India and the election time.

He went on to say that he imagined that he would be even more muzzled in the future since the work at the BBC seemed to have passed under the control of the Government. I said that this was not, in fact, the case, though just at the moment we were, as a matter of courtesy, allowing the Foreign Office to see scripts on political subjects.[36]

[35] BBC Written Archives Centre: E.H. Carr contributor file.
[36] Ibid.: W.S. Churchill contributor file.

Their meeting ended on an amicable note and Churchill willingly signed for Burgess a copy of one of his books, which Burgess later came to regard as one of his most prized possessions. Many stories have been written about the book and its inscription, without any understanding of how Burgess might actually have come by it, or of what Burgess's job actually entailed or of the circles in which he found himself moving.[37]

After Burgess finished this series, his position at the BBC changed. He was reported later as claiming that he resigned from the BBC because he was not given sufficient latitude. Similar sources quote him as saying that he had arranged for some left-wing broadcasts on Spain 'From Both Sides of the Line'. It seems he produced no such talks, although he may have recommended J.B.S. Haldane as a speaker for a news broadcast with the same title. But the general inaccuracy of these popular accounts is shown by such simple errors of fact as the date of his leaving, mentioned by all as 1938, when in fact he left in 1939. He most probably left because he was offered a far better job, one which might even have been created for him – that of producer for the Government's highly secret broadcasting section of the Joint Broadcasting Committee, set up by Laurence Grand of MI6's 'D' section.[38]

Overshadowing all Burgess's work with the BBC was his interest in Russia, and, as we now know, his secret allegiance to the Communist Government of Russia, though perhaps through the Comintern rather than the Soviet secret service itself. Neither he nor George Barnes were able to arrange for any talks directly about Russia before the war. This was largely due to Vansittart and the Foreign Office's difficulties over the activities of the Comintern. Any broadcast that seemed to show direct recognition of Russia and International Communism in any form would have resulted in great difficulties for the Government when they came to protest against the Comintern's activities.[39] However, after war had been declared and Russia later invaded by Germany there was a rapid change in the Government's attitude. Those who wished for exact information on the extent of Burgess's knowledge of, and interest in, Russia then had their curiosity satisfied,

[37] Anthony Glees, *Secrets of the Service* (1987), p.50, citing Stephen Spender as an example.

[38] The evidence that Burgess worked for the Joint Broadcasting Committee is extensive; at the most mundane level his name appears on lists of those attending regular meetings of the JBC, for example on 24 July 1939 at 71 Chester Square, to be found in file E2/374/2 at the BBC Written Archives Centre. Other sources will become apparent. I am also indebted for information from former employees of the JBC.

[39] See below, p.37.

for Burgess was the first to submit recommendations on possible Russian broadcasts, and his views were clearly authoritative:

Draft Suggestion for Talks on Russia

The suggestions which follow are put down hastily, as the problem is urgent.

I have had several informal conversations with John Strachey[40] and Professor Bernal[41] and one or two people at the M of I and the Foreign Office, but what follows is not intended to be in any sense a worked-out scheme:

(1) Literature: Not much to be said here. We should all probably agree on what must be done from the Russian classics. the suggestion has arisen that War and Peace,[42] if intelligently handled, could be both an illustration of great Russian literature and topical, the crossing of Beresina, Kudenov, Borodin, the burning of Moscow, etc., all the instances about which the public is reading in the press.

There is also the famous hunting scene which is probably the most beautiful description of old Russia and which was Lenin's favourite passage in Tolstoy, and one which he is said to have been reading, and to have referred to during the hunt that took place on the day of his death.

Modern literature: The obvious name here is Zoschenko. This man's satires are extremely popular in Russia today. They are translated and are well known over here. They have the advantages of painting a picture of contemporary Soviet Russia, of being humorous, of not being Bolshevist propaganda, and of being the sort of thing that could not be published by the Nazi régime in Germany. There are also young Soviet writers, such as Nicholai Tikhonov and Ilya Ehrenburg who are translated.

(2) Science: Professor Bernal will advise, but he is on Government work and is not often available in London. He has suggested J.G. Crowther[43] (who has spoken for us – badly), but who is in touch and would know who to go to. Haldane, if the ban is lifted, would obviously be an

[40] John Strachey (1901-1963). Strachey had at one time been closely associated with Mosley but moved left writing, inter alia, *The Menace of Fascism* (1933). He formed a close association with Burgess at this time and did many broadcasts as 'Wing Commander Strachey' that gained him considerable fame.

[41] John Desmond Bernal (1901-1971), Professor of Physics at Birkbeck College, University of London 1937-63; Lenin Peace Prize 1953. Author of *Marx and Science* (1952).

[42] Tolstoy's *War and Peace* was produced by the BBC; E.M. Forster collaborated and wrote an accompanying pamphlet.

[43] J.G. Crowther did a talk for the BBC Indian Service on 'Science and the Soviet Union'. See W.J. West (ed.), *Orwell: The War Broadcasts*, pp.29-30 etc.

excellent man. Bernal says that he would be prepared, if asked, to arrange a very friendly approach for me to Haldane, whom he says, is now more difficult than ever.

(3) Culture: There is possibly something to be done both in history and the arts. Dr Klingender, Dr Blunt are possible speakers on Art – neither are Communists. Christopher Hill[44] (a Fellow of All Souls) is a Communist but is also probably the best authority in England on Russian historical studies. Ballet and Music are probably easily covered.

On wider topics for 9.20 talks audience, the problems are greater. Three themes are suggested as being of interest and contemporary importance and capable of being covered without any too great tendenciousness.

(i) A concept of economic planning: The Soviet Union were the pioneers in economic planning, which is now a fairly 'safe' subject, or at least one which is frequently talked about in our programmes. It is suggested that Barbara Wootton,[45] whose book on Planning has a high reputation generally in academic circles (it is also fairly simple) as a speaker here. I don't know what her broadcasting is like. On town and civic planning Sir Ernest Simon is an authority, both in general and on the work done by the Russians.

(ii) The Soviet Union treated as a federation of States. It is suggested that though the political and economic independence of the nationalities of the Soviet Union is purely fictional, there is never the less here a topic of general importance and interest, and one in which the Soviet Union has done some interesting experiments.[46]

It seems probable that the Turkomans, the Uzbeks, have had – at any rate among the youth – an impression of national life and vitality, at least on the cultural side. There is probably material in the work that has been done in producing written languages and fostering contemporary culture of the Argine people in Central Asia, Trans-Caucasia, etc.

[44] For the significance of this identification of Hill as a Communist, see below, pp.61-2.

[45] Barbara Frances Wootton (b.1897), Baroness Wootton of Abinger, author of *Plan or No Plan* (1934), *End Social Inequality* (1941) and *Freedom Under Planning* (1945), and Governor of the BBC 1950-56.

[46] It is still true today that the existence of the Soviet Union as a totalitarian block obscures the very identity of the constituent States. When Afghanistan appeared in the news in recent years most people in the West would have had no trouble in placing it, whereas they would never have heard of Tadjikistan, on Afghanistan's borders.

John Lehmann[47] has written a certain amount of interesting stuff on Trans-Caucasia for the Geographical Magazine and should be safe on this topic. Ella Myatt and C[ontroller] H[ome] [i.e. Sir Richard Maconachie] would probably have something to say on Central Asia. There must be others.

(iii) Carefully handled there should be room for an objective talk on the foreign policy of the Soviet Union. Its peasant and agrarian policy which, though tendencious for other countries, can probably safely be tackled for the home audience here.[48]

Apart from the very broad knowledge of Russian literature and politics shown here, there are some points of particular interest about those whom Burgess recommends as speakers. The deception involved in recommending Blunt and denying specifically that he was a Communist is interesting, as is the clear statement that Christopher Hill was a member of the party. Anthony Glees goes to some lengths to establish whether it was known to MI5 at the time that Hill was a Communist.[49] The evidence given here, in Burgess's recommendation, that they did is conclusive for the following reasons. During the war *all* who appeared before BBC microphones had to be given MI5 clearance. None of the standard accounts of MI5 refer to this essential part of their activities, so it is not clear exactly how the system worked. It is sufficient to say that it did, and that it was reliable. When recommending speakers for programmes talks producers were obliged to indicate whether the person concerned had been cleared by MI5 or not. In this case when Burgess refers to Haldane as being 'banned' he is pointing to the fact that Haldane was someone who had previously broadcast but who had subsequently failed to get MI5 clearance.[50]

[47] John Lehmann (1907-1987), literary editor and publisher. At this time he knew Burgess quite well. However, as he was at the time at the height of his literary fame and editor of the vastly successful *Penguin New Writing* and knew all of literary London, this almost certainly would not imply that he was part of Burgess's circle.

[48] BBC Written Archives Centre: R51/520/1, 15 July 1941.

[49] Anthony Glees, *The Secrets of the Service* (1987) p.279f.

[50] The question of why Haldane was banned was the subject of much discussion during the war at the BBC. A possible answer is to be found in files in the Public Record Office which establish that Haldane broadcast for the Republic in Spain during the Spanish Civil War. The matter came to light when an English amateur radio enthusiast, G.M. Whitehouse, who had heard his broadcasts, wrote to the Foreign Office to complain. In the enquiry that followed the paper for which Haldane had claimed to be writing when applying for his travel documents immediately disowned him. It is always said that the Russian spy acting as a correspondent in Spain must have been Philby, who was then working for *The Times*. Haldane also fits this description. The file may be found at the Public Record Office: FO 371/21369; W7794/37/41.

Hill had not broadcast before, and therefore Burgess had to say that he was known as a Communist. His statement that Hill was a party member meant that MI5 would have identified him as such. Had the BBC Talks Director still wanted Hill on a programme, he could have raised the matter with MI5. It may be that, since Burgess knew Fulford at MI5, he had prior knowledge that Hill would be acceptable, but of Hill's being a Communist and MI5's being in full knowledge of it there cannot have been any doubt. By the same token it is clear that MI5 did *not* then know of Blunt's involvement with the party despite his now working for MI5. Had Burgess deceived his Talks Director about this it would have been immediately obvious, unless Burgess could have been absolutely sure that any query would go to Blunt himself or someone over whom he had direct influence in MI5 – a risky business. The use of Blunt for a broadcast without further reference would have exposed Burgess's deception when the talk took place, or when MI5 saw it announced, and therefore Burgess had no option but to tell the truth as told to him when he made his routine enquiry through the MI5 liaison officer in the BBC. Had Blunt himself heard of the query, he would no doubt have been amused.

We have seen above how Burgess brought his political interests into his broadcasting directly, even influencing the contents of talks of such well-known people as Harold Nicolson. As has often been recorded, he also throughout this period carried out espionage activities for MI6. How this connection was made has not until now been known, although it was understood on the clear evidence of friends of Burgess who also became peripherally involved that David Footman was the person employing him.[51]

Burgess's approach to Footman, then a well-known author, was through his literary agents Christie and Moore:

> I have just read your book *Balkan Holiday* with great pleasure and ask myself whether you might not be just the person to give some travel talks of a rather personal nature in the style of – though of course not out of – your book. I wonder if this prospect interests you? The possibility would of course depend on various factors such as the suitability of your voice, and space in our programmes; but if you would enjoy doing anything along these lines I should very much like to meet you to talk it over. Perhaps you would like to write or ring me up and let me know if this is possible.[52]

[51] David Footman (1895-1983). Entered Colonial Service 1919; Levant Consular Service 1919-29; Foreign Office 1935-53; author of the successful novel *Pig and Pepper*. Fellow of St Anthony's College, Oxford 1953-63.

[52] BBC Written Archives Centre. David Footman contributor file.

This form of approach was unusual for the BBC, where speakers were more often drawn from a circle of acquaintances and accepted broadcasters; certainly Burgess never approached anyone else on this basis. Did Burgess know that Footman was an MI6 officer? It seems that this is the most likely explanation for his use of this distant, formal and hence, for the BBC, unconventional approach. He had to make the approach as certain as possible. Footman's reply was in fact very guarded. He did not follow Burgess's suggestion that he telephone or write but answered through his agents by return in terms which show him to have been a civil servant cast very much in the twentieth-century mould. He wrote to his agents:

> What sort of fee does the BBC pay and, even more important, how can I find out how much time it would be likely to take me to prepare what they want? As you know at the moment what little leisure time I have is pretty well taken up with NASH'S and 'terrorism'. I am willing to take a little trouble for a little cash, but not a lot of trouble for a little cash, even with publicity thrown in. That is how I feel about it. If you think it is worthwhile going on I shall be pleased to meet Mr Burgess.[53]

After several such exchanges Footman agreed to do some talks, usually sending one of the small pieces he was doing for journals which could be readily adapted by Burgess. They were a success, and more followed; and, in the course of his regular visits to Broadcasting House, Footman seems to have decided that Burgess was worth introducing to MI6. It has been suggested that Footman was himself a Russian agent. If this were the case, it could provide an alternative explanation of the formal initial approach which would prevent any possible prior link between them being made by outsiders. However, this seems to be unlikely. Footman made no secret of his interest in Russian revolutionary politics. Indeed he wrote a book on the subject during the war, *Red Prelude* (1944)[54] – this, no doubt, being the book he referred to indirectly in his letter as 'terrorism'. It seems far more likely that Footman had been identified to Burgess as someone in MI6 whose public identity as an author would make him vulnerable to an approach, as indeed he was. The connection was doubly useful. Not only did it lead directly to Burgess's employment in MI6, but it also enabled Burgess's fellow-spy Kim Philby to enter through the same gate, for it was Burgess who introduced Philby to Footman, in what is

[53] Ibid. 'NASH'S' refers presumably to *Nash's Magazine*.
[54] Furthermore he included the information in the biographical details that he supplied to the BBC in later years. The full title of his book was *Red Prelude: The Life of the Russian Terrorist Zhelyabov* (1944). It contained also 'A Revolutionary Who's Who'.

surely one of the most successful gambits in the history of spying. Other possible links have been made between Philby and MI6, including a connection through his father. But this introduction by Burgess via Footman is here established as a fact.

The question, often asked, of why Burgess was so important needs no further answer than this brilliant feat, one which moreover would have been impossible had it not been for his position in the BBC.

PART TWO

4. The Saar, the Olympics and the Anschluss

The first international political event in which radio was seen to have played an important, even crucial role was the campaign leading up to the plebiscite in the Saar. Under League of Nations supervision since the end of World War I, provision had been made for there to be a plebiscite fifteen years later to determine whether the country should remain under its existing administration, or be joined to France or re-united with Germany. This eventually happened in 1935. One of the first authoritative accounts of radio propaganda contained a description of the campaign for the Saar plebiscite under the heading 'Nazis and the Saar: The First Hitler Victory by Ether Waves'. It gave a convincing description of the campaign but, inevitably, as it was written in 1942, while America was at war with Germany, the conviction stemmed from a belief in the cause she was defending. The authors remarked:

> ... the Saar plebiscite demonstrates how, with the aid of radio, an unscrupulous party can attain a *de facto* monopoly of opinion.[1]

This sounds straightforward, but the actual situation was far more complex.

In an era of rapid growth of radio, and radio propaganda, the Saar was unusual in having no radio transmitting station of its own. All attempts at setting up a system under the administrative powers had failed. As a consequence, much as the British took to listening to Radio Luxembourg and other continental stations when dissatisfied with the fare at home, so the Saarlanders had taken to listening to programmes put out by their neighbouring countries. But, whereas the British listener had a choice, the man buying or making a receiving set in the Saar had none. Most of the population of the Saar spoke German, and the German broadcasting stations' programmes for

---

[1] Harwood L. Childs and John B. Whitton, *Propaganda by Short Wave* (1943), p.12.

Germany were readily heard throughout the Saar. As the time for the plebiscite approached, Goebbels did indeed launch a through-going propaganda campaign. However, this was very far from being a '*de facto* monopoly of opinion'. The French broadcasts in French were heard in the Saar with ease and those they put out in German were heard even better. The problem was that, in the propaganda war with the stations broadcasting from Germany, the French-German stations lost hands down. Their programmes aimed at the Saarlanders and the Germans as a whole were regarded as almost as bad as those aimed at Germany from Russia. It was said to be impossible for a German with even mildly patriotic feelings to listen to them without anger. The result of the war by 'Ether Waves' was indeed helped on by the radio propaganda from Germany, but it was the help given by the exposure of an issue as a stark one between patriotism and sophistry. And there was one crucial element missing in the scenario of a completely manipulated 'radio' election. This was in the conduct of the election process itself.

After the occupation of the Baltic States in 1940 Russia held a number of plebiscites which also produced a massive 99 per cent majority with the aid of radio propaganda; there, however, the elections were a fraud. The method was simple: voting was made compulsory, the issue of rationing cards being made conditional on the casting of a vote in the election, and there was no choice of candidate or issue. The radio merely made it impossible even for an illiterate peasant not to know what he had to do, or what the consequences of failing would be. In the Saar plebiscite matters were quite different. The election was conducted under the closest scrutiny by the world's press. A large armed contingent, in which thousands of British troops were joined by similar numbers from other nations, supervised the actual voting process itself. The officer in charge of the entire administration was also British. Those who voted had a choice between three options which they could exercise in complete freedom in a secret ballot. They chose to be re-united with Germany, despite the existence of the National Socialist regime, whose totalitarian nature was becoming every day more obvious. There were Germans in the Saar who campaigned vigorously against the union with Germany and for maintenance of the status quo; these were members of the Social Democratic and far-left parties who had been driven from Germany, or who were native to the Saar and held those views. It was obvious to all Jewish people in the Saar that absorption into Germany would be a disaster for them. Some of these proved to be long-term opponents of the Nazi regime who ended up in Britain during

World War II.[2] All fled when the election results were announced.

There was considerable interest in the election at the time and, despite the fact that there was no broadcasting system in the Saar, broadcasters did manage to report what was happening, sending their signals out over land-lines to transmitters in neighbouring countries. The American broadcaster César Saerchinger has left a memorable account of the principal broadcasts sent out.[3] Having got permission for the broadcasts from Colonel Knox who was responsible for the administration of the Saar, he obtained agreements from the French authorities for a telephone land-line to be installed. This arrangement immediately fell through, however, and equipment smuggled into the Saar through France was only set up at the last minute.

> The broadcast had been arranged to take place at an improvised studio – the furnished flat of the American member of the plebiscite committee, Miss Sarah Wambaugh ... her presence was our greatest piece of luck and saved the whole enterprise. The BBC, who also wanted to broadcast from the region but had no facilities of their own, made common cause with us, and that increased our staff by two.[4]

Until the very last minute there were difficulties but at last two telephone linesmen arrived to connect up the 'studio':

> I had the greatest misgivings, but somehow the technicians of different nations soon found the magic key of understanding. By mid afternoon the studio had been rigged and our British engineer was calling gadgets by their German names, pronounced as in Bromley or Bow.[5]

Saerchinger was emphatic about the propriety with which the polls were conducted:

> Absolute order was maintained; the voting machinery was as perfect and fraud-proof as anything can be. Englishmen, Dutchmen, Americans – solid citizens of all neutral countries – acted as watchers and tellers, the most complete example of international collaboration in a critical task I had ever seen ... The result was a forgone conclusion. but the extent of Hitler's victory was a surprise; and the story full of human interest. The snowclad, spired city astride the lovely river made

[2] For example Max Braun, leader of the anti-Hitler front in the Saar, worked on the secret British radio stations at Woburn Abbey. See Sefton Delmer, *Black Boomerang* (1962), p.50 and elsewhere.

[3] César Saerchinger, *Hello America! Radio Adventures in Europe* (1938) ch.15, 'German is the Saar', p.207f.

[4] Ibid., p.209.

[5] Ibid., p.211.

a fascinating picture. Frederick Voigt,[6] the Diplomatic correspondent of the *Manchester Guardian*, described it for the English, I for the American audience; Miss Wambaugh, world authority on plebiscites, explained the technical procedure. Both broadcasts were successful. Elated we went forth to gather more atmosphere for the next day's stint.[7]

At the end of their broadcasting they obtained an early example of 'actuality' when a group of people celebrating the victory went past their windows:

> We shouted down to them to sing the Saarland song, opened our windows wide and placed a microphone on the windowsill. And so we gave American – and England – an earful of patriotic singing and '*heiling*' as background to the plebiscite returns.[8] When it was all over we too felt like celebrating, for we had transmitted the first plebiscite ever broadcast and the first programme from a place that had never been on the air [i.e. there was no station before then in the Saar].[9]

The complete contrast between this account and the subsequent version provided by Childs and Whitton, written only four years later, shows how, even in the academic world, truth can be betrayed under the stress of total war. What was unquestionably true was that radio had been of great importance; Saerchinger's broadcast may have been the first-ever of a plebiscite; it was not to be the last, and the German propagandists would not always find themselves under the closest supervision of an international body, directed by a Scot of the calibre of Colonel Knox.

The next major propaganda exercise set up by Goebbels was the 1936 Olympics.[10] There is a mistaken tendency to remove purely

---

[6] Voigt also ended up broadcasting to Germany, but for the 'white' propaganda station run by the BBC, rather than the secret 'black' station at Woburn. He was at first destined for the latter, but Sir Campbell Stuart at Electra House sent him to the BBC. There they were worried about his accent and got involved in a curious row over the matter. No Germans were allowed to broadcast over the BBC since nearly all exiled Germans were Jewish and, by a curious projection of British snobbery, it was held that Germans would be able to tell from his accent that it was a Jewish person speaking. Voigt was British by birth and after a short period was accepted as a suitable broadcaster. See Gerard Mansell, *Let Truth be Told* (1982), pp.107 and 151. There may well have been political overtones also, as Voigt was of the right rather than the left.

[7] Saerchinger, op.cit., pp.211-12.

[8] See the recordings made at the time in the National Sound Archives: NSA 9661, Ralph Murray, the Saar celebrations; NSA LP.64.b.1, F.A. Voigt, the Saar Plebiscite.

[9] Saerchinger, op.cit., p.215.

[10] For a detailed account, see Richard D. Mandell, *The Nazi Olympics* (1971.)

sporting events from the standard narrative of events of the inter-war years which are deemed to be 'political'. This is particularly true of the greatest event of all, the modern revival of the Olympics. Perhaps this was because in 1936 it was not normal to think of sport in political terms. This did not stop Hitler and Goebbels from making as great a propaganda success out of the Games as possible, and radio provided a completely new way of bringing the events to the world. In order to ensure that as many foreign countries as possible would be reached, an enormous expansion of the short-wave transmitting stations at Zeesen, just outside Berlin, was carried through with great speed.[11] By the time the winter Olympics began at Garmisch-Partenkirchen all the new systems were fully operational. The channels from the eight transmitters, the most powerful in the world, were made available to all the foreign correspondents who wished to use them, and the results exceeded all expectations. Day after day broadcasts went out to the world with an increasing note of euphoria. Speaking of the final ceremony, Saerchinger described the slow descent of eight skiers from the mountainside holding the Olympic flag between them, highlighted by a spotlight:

> To the playing of the Olympic Hymn, the tolling of bells and the gradual dying down of the Olympic fire, the immense crowd stood, electrified. That was one of the most beautiful spectacles it has been my fortune to see from a broadcasting booth or anywhere else.[12]

But Saerchinger was also becoming more aware of the political implications.

> Radio provided not only the instrument for news-distribution and the gingering up of morale, but for the marshalling of crowds. This regimentation by means of the ubiquitous loudspeaker – especially in Garmisch, where arc-light standards and flagpoles were endowed with a mechanical voice – give one the idea of the uses to which this new gift to man might be put in time of war.[13]

---

[11] A brief publication about the new station was published at the time: Franz Ludwig Habel, *'Hello Everybody!': A Voice of Friendship: Short Waves over the World* (1936). No copy of this has been located in the British Library, or any other major library, but there is a copy in the BBC Written Archives Centre: E1/760/1.

[12] Saerchinger, op.cit., p.188.

[13] Ibid., p.187. Speakers in columns on street corners exerted a fascination at the time and formed an essential part of the later vision of an Orwellian totalitarian state. Plans were made to introduce them into Britain, but they got no further than the affixing of speakers to lamp posts and other suitable objects in times of emergency.

The undoubted success that Germany made of the winter Olympics gave her a new presence in the world. The summer Olympics were eagerly looked forward to by all the competing nations of the world whose training teams had already arrived and whose publicity and transport arrangements were being brought to final perfection. Germany anticipated with particular satisfaction the repetition of the triumphs of Garmisch at Berlin, for many still remembered that the cancelled 1916 Olympics had originally been scheduled to take place in Berlin. In the wake of this public euphoria Hitler took an astonishing step. Worried by the signing of a Franco-Soviet pact[14] he decided to occupy the Rhineland with a token force of German troops. Although he had announced the resumption of conscription the previous year the German army was in no state to act against the French troops who were on the border of the de-militarized zone; the Officers of the Wehrmacht were, by all accounts, acutely worried. Knowing the facts now, we can see that it really amounted to a propaganda exercise on a grand scale rather than a military action. The arrangements for it were similar to a great apolitical event such as the Olympics, which had just ended. Many have spoken of it as a gamble; Hitler himself is said to have agreed that the troops would be pulled back if there was the slightest show of resistance. But he need not have worried. The troops marched under the radio commentator's eye, with the cheering crowds being broadcast all over Germany and later, in recordings, all over the world.

Nothing happened; there was no response from France, and no response from Britain, who had the previous year made an arms agreement with Hitler in breach of the Stressa Front.[15] It was indeed as if another event such as the Olympics had been successfully completed. What is certain, if this confusion of the use of armed force with that of sporting enthusiasm seems far fetched, is that had Britain and France acted and invaded the Rhineland once again the Berlin Olympics would not have taken place. The effects of the world-wide enthusiasm for the Olympics produced by live radio broadcasts must have been a major factor for all at the time in their consideration of what action, if any, they should take.

The success of the Rhineland occupation was not allowed to pass without some direct political affirmation by the people of Germany. And this time the developing skills of radio crowd-martialling, experimented with in the Saar, were used in Germany itself. A ballot

[14] The Franco-Soviet Pact of Mutual Assistance was initialled in Moscow on 2 May 1935 and signed on 27 March 1936. The occupation of the Rhineland took place on 7 March 1936.

[15] This was the Anglo-German Naval Agreement of May 1935.

was arranged for 29 March 1936, and in the campaign leading up to it the fullest use was made of the radio, culminating in formal instruction all over Germany for people to listen to Hitler's speech broadcast from the Krupp armament works at Essen. The extent of his audience can be gauged by the announcements which habitually appeared in the German press throughout the country:

> Attention! The Führer is speaking on the radio. On Wednesday 21 March the Führer is speaking on all German radio stations from 11.00 to 11.50 am. According to a regulation of the Gau headquarters, the district Party headquarters has ordered that all factory owners, department stores, offices, shops, pubs, and blocks of flats put up loudspeakers an hour before the broadcast of the Führer's speech so that the whole work force and all national comrades can participate fully in the broadcast. The district headquarters expects this order to be obeyed without exception so that the Führer's wish to speak to his people can be implemented.[16]

The result was a 98.79 per cent vote in favour of Hitler; but here, unlike the Saar, there was more than a hint of totalitarianism. The ballot papers had only one space for a vote; voting was effectively compulsory, and there was no supervision other than by employees of the ruling party. An American news broadcaster remarked succinctly:

> March 30 1936 – The German election has aroused a new case of the jitters. After 99 per cent of the voters have endorsed Hitler's policies, he will be spurred on to fresh aggression.[17]

The next major adventure that Hitler created for his country was another step in the destruction of the Versailles treaty. Radio played a vital role in the chain of events which, at the end, occurred in a matter of hours. This was not merely a question of long-term radio propaganda sent across the border, but one in which broadcasts and the threat of broadcasts revealed the way events were unfolding and themselves brought about a premature crisis, unexpected either by the Austrian Government, headed by Schuschnigg, or by Hitler.

Popular English accounts to this day refer to Austria's absorption into a greater Germany, the Anschluss, or Union, as the 'rape of Austria'. Anschluss is talked of as if it were a private scheme of Hitler's, Austrian born and bred, that was forced upon a startled Austrian and German people. The reality was very different.

---

[16] Quoted in J. Noakes and G. Pridham (eds), *Nazism 1919-1945:* vol.2, *State Economy and Society 1933-39* (Exeter University, 1984), p.386.
[17] Lowell Thomas, *History As You Heard It* (1957), p.77.

Anschluss had been proposed at the time of Versailles. It had been rejected by the victorious powers despite almost universal support within Austria and Germany. Anschluss was from that moment on a cornerstone of the policy of many parties in Austria. For most it remained so until Hitler brought it about, but, with Hitler's advent to power in Germany in 1933, there had been a rapid polarization of opinion in Austria. For the first time there were parties, usually of the left, who were prepared to talk about Austria's independence. In a rapid sequence of events the far-left parties had been suppressed in a bloody attack by troops on workers' flats in Vienna, events in which Burgess's fellow-spy Kim Philby was actively involved. On the other political wing, Austrian Nazis in large numbers had been imprisoned and deported. A key event had been an attempted coup d'état by the Nazis in which the Prime Minister, Dr Engelbert Dolfuss, had been assassinated.[18]

Radio had been crucial to the Austrian Nazis' plans. We have seen the impact of the German broadcasts to Austria. When the rising began their first move had been to seize the radio station in Vienna and broadcast a programme which would have been a signal to their comrades all over Austria to rise. However, the plan failed for an unforeseen technical reason: although the radio station's studios were in Vienna, the transmitters were outside the city. Those in control there immediately switched off the transmitters when they realised what had happened, and the rest of Austria then heard music instead of their normal programmes, broadcast from transmitters at provincial stations such as Linz. Dolfuss had been at the second centre of attack, the Chancellery, and there the Nazis had succeeded. Dolfuss was killed in the very room where he had given his broadcasts over the previous years.[19]

The coup attempt had been accompanied by sympathetic broadcasts from Germany which ceased as soon as it was clear that it had been a failure. Schuschnigg took Dolfuss' place in what was a totalitarian regime which was anti-Nazi and anti-Communist. Things became stable for a while. Then, in early 1938, the existence of a further clandestine Austrian Nazi plot was discovered in Vienna. Known as the Teinfaltstrasse Plot, it was discovered during a raid by the police on an office block in that street which also housed a 'Committee of Seven' whose purpose was to act as a liaison group between the Nazis and Schuschnigg. Extensive contingency plans had been discovered for the planned Putsch, and these Schuschnigg had

[18] Dolfuss was assassinated on 25 July 1934.
[19] There is an illustration in Saerchinger, op.cit., of Dolfuss standing in this room, before a microphone, about to broadcast.

taken with him to Germany on a visit to Hitler. This visit has often been described; far from being able to make an effective protest, he found himself beaten down by one of Hitler's by now legendary tirades. He returned to Austria with a new cabinet wished upon him by Hitler and a National Socialist, Seyss-Inquart, in the key post of Minister for the Interior and Public Safety.

On 23 February Seyss-Inquart made his first broadcast to the Austrian people from Vienna radio using, also for the first time, his customary address, 'My German fellow-countrymen'. In the speech he pointed to a rapid development of affairs by authorizing the return of legal use of Nazi insignia, notably the swastika. The following day Schuschnigg made a speech in the Austrian Parliament which proclaimed with fierce intensity his intention to maintain Austrian independence. Then, a few days later, he made the fateful decision to have a plebiscite in Austria to give the Austrian people a chance of making clear their wish for independence.[20]

For the plebiscite to have any great chance of success it was obvious to all that Schuschnigg would have to come to terms with the left in a common front against the Austrian Nazis. This underlying fact made Hitler's response inevitable. It has frequently been pointed out that the plebiscite was a blunder, a slap in the face for Hitler which he could not possibly accept, but this underlying reason has not always been explained. Hitler rapidly issued an ultimatum to Schuschnigg insisting that the referendum must be cancelled. Schuschnigg as rapidly rejected it; it was of course an intolerable intrusion into a friendly country's internal affairs. But the true facts of the situation became clear when the radio programmes that were to take place before the plebiscite were announced. For the first time since the suppression of the workers' parties after the 1934 battles, the socialists were to be allowed to come to the microphone and appeal to the workers to support Schuschnigg. Two broadcasts were announced for the evening of 11 March, one by Minister Rott, a leader of the Christian Social Trade Unions who had been brought into the cabinet by Schuschnigg to bring about a rapprochement between the

[20] In this and the following paragraphs I have made use of the account of events given in Eugene Lennhoff, *The Last Five Hours of Austria, with an Introduction by Paul Frischauer* (1938). There are many accounts, including two books by Schuschnigg. However, Lennhoff, besides being editor at the time of the anti-Nazi daily newspaper *Telegraf*, had also been foreign political correspondent of the Austrian Broadcasting Company. His narrative makes frequent reference to the radio and the part it played in day-to-day happenings, and is accurate on such matters wherever I have been able to cross-check with other sources. The book as a whole is open to criticism. Paul Frischauer, who seems to have made its publication possible, also worked for Grand's section 'D' of MI6 at the time; see below, p.118.

Government and the estranged socialists of all kinds. The other was to be by the young workers' leader, Sailer, previously an editor of a Social Democratic newspaper.[21]

Once the plebiscite had been announced a stream of broadcasts from Germany had attacked it and spread false reports of a red uprising. Among those quoted at the time were: 'Czechoslovakia is supplying the red mob in Vienna with artillery to support an immediate Bolshevist uprising'; 'Germany is saying that serious labour disturbances have broken out in Austria and that blood is flowing in streams. Schuschnigg is no longer in control of the situation'; 'Dr Schuschnigg and the Burgomaster of Vienna have formed a Popular Front with the Communists in order to set Marxist hordes at the throats of the people.'[22]

When the news broke that the Socialist leaders were actually to be allowed to broadcast, it must have seemed sure confirmation of all this propaganda. Today merely making the microphone available for recognized trade union leaders would not seem grounds for great alarm; in Vienna of 1938 in an increasingly totalitarian Europe to offer the microphone to people who had been on the other side in a ferocious civil war less than five years before genuinely seemed likely to plunge the country once more into chaos. Berlin Radio heard within minutes of the proposed broadcasts and immediately attacked the proposal. Whatever time-table Hitler and the Nazis had planned for their coup was now speeded up. That the coup had already been planned is certain, for messages to the Austrian people by Seyss-Inquart had already been prepared with Nazi songs and military anthems, on disc ready for broadcasting over the Austrian radio system when the hour came.[23] Within hours Hitler's ultimatum was renewed, but this time it was not withdrawn. With the continuing struggle in Spain, and the undeniable fact that Czechoslovakia had

[21] I am indebted to Professor Peter Pulzer for the observation that Lennhoff is the only source that mentions two broadcasts, by both Rott and Sailer. All others mention only that Sailer was to have broadcast. I have not been able to check the Austrian Broadcasting Company's day-to-day programme announcements.

[22] Lennhoff, op.cit., p.41.

[23] The references to pre-recording are given in Charles Rollo, *Radio Goes to War* (1943), p.40, but without giving a source. David Irving refers to 'a speech for Seyss-Inquart to broadcast next evening, 11 March' as being given by Hitler to Glaise-Horstenau to take to Austria (see David Irving, *The War Path: Hitler's Germany 1933-39* (1978, Papermac ed. 1983), p.83), also without quoting a source. Seyss-Inquart's speech was repeated continuously and must therefore have been on disc, but when exactly he recorded the script is not clear. The recordings referred to by Rollo seem to have been made earlier as part of general arrangements to ensure that there was no repetition of the debacle of 1934.

become involved in the sort of movement that the Berlin radio attributed to them, Hitler felt that immediate action was imperative to prevent a possible link up between Czechoslovakia and a socialist Austria.[24] What the result of an appeal to workers would have been can only now be guessed at. As always with the political changes in Germany itself, with the imposition of totalitarian rule the opposition leaders fled abroad or went underground, and the ordinary workers then became indistinguishable from the enthusiastic supporters of the regime. Information about the anti-Nazi underground was unknown at the time and only discoverable by prolonged academic research decades later.[25]

The socialist broadcasts never took place. Instead, after a slight delay when music was played, Schuschnigg came to the microphone and announced his resignation and the end of Austria. The pre-recorded speeches by Seyss-Inquart followed, interspersed with the Horst Wessel song, played over the Austrian air waves for the first time, with other martial airs.

The following day Hitler entered Linz, his home town. From there he made an historic broadcast. As Chamberlain was later to declare war with Germany over the radio before he spoke to Parliament, so Hitler's speech announced the Anschluss without any other statement. The contrast between the two broadcasts, Schuschnigg's impassioned plea for a free Austria[26] and Hitler's equally impassioned and spontaneous appeal to his fellow Germans to witness his achievement, could not be greater.

> Austrian men and Austrian women! This day has placed us in a tragic and decisive situation. I have to give my Austrian fellow-countrymen the details of the events of the day.
>
> The German Government today handed to President Miklas an ultimatum with a time limit attached, ordering him to nominate as Chancellor a person to be designated by the German Government and to appoint members of a Cabinet on the orders of the German Government; otherwise German troops would invade Austria.

[24] There had been extensive traffic in Czech arms at the time of the left rising in 1934. Schuschnigg remarked after the war: 'Czech weapons were not purchased direct from Vienna [sic–Prague?] but via the Communist International in Zurich ...'. See Kurt von Schuschnigg, *The Brutal Takeover* (1971), p.83. This traffic was also a factor in the Spanish Civil War. It appears in fact to have been organized by Max K. Adler. For an account see Chapter 8 'Gun-running for the Shutzbund' in his autobiography *A Socialist Remembers* (forthcoming).

[25] See for example Ian Kershaw, *Popular Opinion and Political Dissent in the Third Reich: Bavaria 1933-45* (1983).

[26] That is, free from German control; the system of government operated was totalitarian and definitely not 'free' in the accepted political sense of the word.

I declare before the world that the reports issued in Austria concerning disorders created by the workers and the shedding of streams of blood and all the allegations that the situation had got out of control of the Government were lies from A to Z.

President Miklas asks me to tell the people of Austria that we have yielded to force since we are not prepared in this terrible situation to shed blood and we decided to order the troops to offer no serious resistance ...

So I take my leave of the Austrian people in this hour with a German word of farewell uttered from the depths of my heart: 'God protect Austria'.[27]

The broadcast took place at 8 p.m., shortly after the time announced for the speeches by Roth and Sailer. The following day came Hitler's speech:

Fellow countrymen and countrywomen, thank you for your words of welcome. Above all, thank you who have come here to witness the fact that it is not just the desire of a few persons to create this great Reich of the German nation, but that it is the will of the German people themselves.

This evening, I would like to have some of our international know-it-alls see what is going on, and admit it afterwards. Years ago when I left this city I carried with me the same faith that fills me today.

You can imagine my emotions now that I have given reality to my faith after so many years. If Providence called me from this city to the leadership of the German Reich, then it must have given me an order. And it can only have been one order, namely, to incorporate my beloved home country into the German Reich. I have believed in it; I have lived for it; I have fought for it. And I believe I have now carried it out, and you are witnesses of this. You are all witnesses and guarantors of it ... See in the German soldiers who march from all districts of the Reich in these hours – see in them warriors who are willing and ready to make sacrifices for the unity of the whole great German nation, for its liberty, for the power of our Reich, for its greatness and glory, now and evermore. Germany, Siegheil![28]

As with the Saar, although not on so total a scale, the people were swept up after the event had actually happened into an immense enthusiasm. British officials, earlier sanguine about the Austrian

[27] As given in the English translation in Kurt von Schuschnigg, *Farewell Austria* (1938), p.238. There are slight variations between this and the normally used translations which appeared in *The Times* and elsewhere.

[28] As published in the press. The origin of the translation is unknown, but it was presumably Goebbels' Propaganda Ministry.

people's wish for independence, remarked that they had clearly misunderstood the situation. Numerous independent witnesses wrote then and later of the fervent enthusiasm to be seen on all sides. Only those who knew the inevitable aftermath were missing from the crowds, many already well on the way to the borders and a lifetime's exile, others, less fortunate, to go into hiding until their discovery and real persecution began. The plight of Polish Jews was particularly acute since the Polish government announced that all those who had been abroad for more than five years had thereby lost their Polish citizenship.

Unlike previous great changes in the political state of Europe in the days before World War I when diplomacy was a matter of secret action, what had happened was there on the surface, to be heard by everyone in the actual voices of the leaders themselves over countless radios all over the world. There was no time needed for understanding, analysis or debate. The actual administrative changes could take place within hours of a radio announcement. Conventional diplomacy became redundant and diplomats themselves could add nothing to what was to be heard on every street corner and over the loudspeakers of radios in every café.

5. Britain's First Radio War

The first hint that the British authorities had of a propaganda war between herself and Italy, her ally in World War I, came in the earliest days of international broadcasting. The actual broadcast that alerted them was an internal talk in Italian, but it chanced to be heard by one of the few amateur radio enthusiasts in the Foreign Office, Sir Arthur Willert.[1] He was 'listening in' to the Italian radio to get background information for the Five Power Naval Conference that was to be held in January 1930 and had got a considerable surprise. He wrote immediately to the British Embassy in Rome:

> For the last week or two we have been listening-in in the country to the Milan broadcast. Apparently they have a weekly talk there on events of the world and so on. Anyhow, the last two talks we have heard have been quite venomously anti-British and anti-American with regard to the conference. Last week there were sneers and innuendoes about having to go and sit at the same table with such predatory creatures as the British lion and the American eagle. Last night the Italian wireless 'fan' was told that Mr Sterling and Mrs Dollar, or the other way around, expected to have things their own way in London but they are going to be jolly well mistaken, or words to that effect. One wonders if this sort of thing goes on all over Italy and, if so, how much the authorities in Rome know about it ...[2]

A week later he received a very illuminating reply from the British Ambassador:

> My Dear Willert, McClure showed me your letter regarding the Milan broadcast. Something of the same sort had been brought to my attention by a friend in Switzerland, who had listened to a broadcast from Milan about a cinema film about 'Trafalgar'[3] and was struck by

---

[1] Sir Arthur Willert (1882-1973). Chief Correspondent of *The Times* in the USA 1910-20; joined the Foreign Office in 1921 where he became Head of the News Department and Press Officer; member of the UK delegation to the Five Power Naval Conference 1930; resigned from FO 1935.

[2] Public Record Office: FO 395/439; P1928/1928/150.

[3] Unidentified.

the bitter way in which the broadcaster attacked Nelson and England generally.

As I was seeing Grandi[4] this morning I took down your letter and read it to him. He was perfectly furious and said that this was the sort of thing that happened when he was doing all he possibly could to influence Italian opinion to fall in line with that of Britain and America. He took a note of the matter and promised to deal with it suitably. So I hope there will be no further broadcasts from Milan of the nature you indicate.[5]

Grandi's anger no doubt stemmed from the actual line which Mussolini had said should be followed at the conference being prematurely revealed. He had been made aware in the most abrupt way of the new international factor in politics represented by the radio. The British Ambassador, by contrast, failed to appreciate what was happening. No doubt, like the majority of British diplomats abroad, he had no radio, either at his home or in the Embassy,[6] and was consequently not able to perceive that the authorities at home who listened, like Willert, had from now on at least as good an understanding as the man on the spot.

The failure of the Naval Conference to bring Italy and France to some agreement was thus not entirely unexpected in Britain. At one point Italy had walked out of the conference, or rather her delegate had returned to Italy because of illness, and was not present at the final ceremony. The Italian-French naval question was left unresolved. In a press conference before the actual conference began Ramsay MacDonald had said:

> The British Government is in favour of the complete abolition of the submarine category and, failing abolition, it hopes that the number of these craft will be reduced to a minimum, though obviously the question of producing a satisfactory equilibrium between nation and nation will be a very important and difficult one.[7]

But by the time the Abyssinian crisis developed Italian naval strength was a matter of pride and her submarines, far from being restricted, were prowling the Mediterranean and actually sinking ships in time of peace, as has been mentioned. In his broadcast at the beginning of the conference MacDonald had gone further and pointed to the dangers already present to those alert to the changing climate of world opinion:

[4] The Italian Foreign Secretary.
[5] Public Record Office: FO 395/493; P1930/1928/150.
[6] See above, p.25n14.
[7] As reported in the contemporary press.

Every country today – wealthy and poverty-stricken alike – feels the burden of arms, dreads their competitive development, doubts the value of the security which they give and would like to escape from their influence and power. And yet, as has been shown again and again the difficulties in the way are manifold. All, however, come from one main source, a lack of confidence. The spirit of doubt whispers: 'There will be *some* state which will refuse to carry out its obligations to the community of peaceful states; the machinery of arbitration will break down *somewhere* and *somehow*; do what we may a situation will arise one day when a deadlock of *some* kind will have to be faced, and there will be but one remaining method, the old fashioned one of a fight.[8]

By 1934 the theatre of this possible breakdown had emerged as the state of Abyssinia in North Africa. Hope for the League as an efficient part of what MacDonald had called 'the machinery of arbitration' was still being defended. Even Churchill in a broadcast on the Causes of War[9] had said on 21 November 1934:

I look to the League of Nations as being an instrument which, properly sustained and guided may preserve the threatened peace of the world. I know it is fashionable in some quarters to mock at the League of Nations; but where is there any equal hope? The many countries great and small that are afraid of being absorbed or invaded by Germany should lay their fears and their facts before the League of Nations. The League of Nations if satisfied that these fears are genuine should call upon its members to volunteer special constables for the preservation of peace against a special danger ...[10]

As was natural to him, Churchill looked to Germany always as the threat, but the breakdown envisaged by MacDonald was caused, it seemed, by Italy. In March 1935 Abyssinia appealed to the League of Nations and, ironically, she appealed against Italy, the nation who had sponsored her when she joined the League ten years before. The background to the dispute is still not clear, but Britain was far from an innocent bystander. She had been attempting to negotiate an arrangement with the ruler of Abyssinia whereby Britain would be

[8] Ibid.

[9] This sounds as though Churchill did in fact have access to the BBC when he wanted, in contrast to his protestations to Burgess (see above, p.57), but actually the talk was one given in a series arranged many months in advance, Churchill's script being vetted and edited along with the others. The speakers were Norman Angell, Lord Beaverbrook, Sir Austen Chamberlain, G.D.H. Cole, Major Douglas (of the Social Credit movement), J.B.S. Haldane, Aldous Huxley, the Rev. W.R. Inge and Sir Josiah Stamp.

[10] The series was published in *The Listener*.

given the Ogaden desert in exchange for aid and recognition. However, these negotiations seem to have been carried out by the local representative[11] and may not have been fully understood in London. All communications locally were being monitored by the Italians who soon became aware of what was afoot in a country where they had themselves envisaged action. Unfortunately British public opinion was completely unaware of this background and had also been influenced by some very successful propaganda from the League of Nations Union concerning Abyssinia. When Italy acted the case appeared a straightforward one of an imperialist power bullying a smaller one; indeed the situation could be seen in that light. Diplomatically the position for Britain was one of considerable difficulty. Not only was she actively, but secretly, involved in a situation in which the British public expected action of the most idealistic kind on the highest principles, but she also had, in Palestine, a most severe local problem to deal with. It was here that the first radio war which Britain became involved in broke out.

Italy was fully aware also of Britain's problems in Palestine and she found a ready weapon to hand in the form of the radio station at Bari. As tension in the area mounted she developed the anti-British tone of her broadcasts, already noticed by Willert. But she added a whole new range of broadcasts in Arabic aimed first at the Palestinian Arabs and then the Arab people in general. If Willert thought the tone of the Milan broadcasts was 'quite venomously anti-British' the Bari broadcasts made these seem mild humour in a satiric vein.

In June 1935 Anthony Eden went to Rome in an attempt to deal with matters. Britain had shortly before signed the naval agreement with Germany, and Mussolini drew attention to this as an example of British hypocrisy, although on the subject of Abyssinia he clearly had other examples of British hypocrisy in his mind as well. There was fierce disagreement between the two men which had unfortunate consequences of an extremely serious kind during the remaining years of the decade. At the time Eden was only a Junior Minister, holding the post of Minister for League of Nations Affairs. While in this post, which involved much attendance at Geneva, Eden had become more

[11] The report in the relevant Foreign Office file is clear: 'Before the Wal-Wal incident occurred Sir S. Barton had for some months been carrying on a series of very secret informal conversations with the Emperor of Abyssinia concerning the possibility of concluding an Anglo-Abyssinian Agreement which, inter alia, would include certain territorial rectifications likely to facilitate the administration of British Territory adjacent to the then Abyssinian Empire. One of the rectifications envisaged was the cession of a large part of the Ogaden to British Somalia ...' See Public Record Office: FO 371/20201; J647/3957/1.

sympathetic to the left and, in Britain, the viewpoint represented by the League of Nations Union;[12] he had broadcast from Geneva a well-publicized speech welcoming the Soviet Union to the League of Nations.[13] He was not sympathetic to Fascism as a system or to the man universally identified with it and would seem to have been a very bad choice for negotiator. Over the next few months the Foreign Secretary Samuel Hoare dealt with matters in a way which reflected his own sympathies which were very much with Italy.[14] When he in turn came to broadcast from Geneva it was in a very different spirit from Eden:

> You will want to know how Mr Eden and I have been getting on in Geneva during this difficult week. You will want in particular to know whether we think the chances of a settlement between Italy and Abyssinia are better or worse than they were a few days ago. I wish we could give you an answer that they are better. We cannot, but I think we can also say that they are not any worse ... I have felt over and over again the weight of the responsibility of representing a Government to which so many countries seem to be looking for guidance and advice. I have done my best to express to them what I believe to be the feelings of the great majority of my fellow countrymen. I have tried to put to them the typical British point of view, and in particular to express to them first of all our universal desire to live and let live in peace, and, secondly, our determination to keep our word that we have solemnly given in the Covenant of the League of Nations. How much I hope that in striving for these two objectives and in doing justice to Abyssinia, we shall still be able to remain friends with our Italian ally in the Great War. More than most people, I hate the idea of differences between Great Britain and Italy. I myself served for a year and a half in Italy during the war, and I still have the greatest admiration for Italy, the Italians, and the progress they have made in recent years. Let them

[12] For a critical view of the League of Nations Union, which also makes clear how politically contentious such independent-sounding bodies could actually be, see *The Origin and Development of the League of Nations Union* (n.d., *c.* 1931), published by the Boswell Printing and Publishing Company.

[13] A recording of Eden's speech of welcome has survived. National Sound Archives: NSA 12609.

[14] Sir Samuel Hoare, as he then was, had been an intelligence officer in Italy at the end of World War I. In his memoirs he candidly describes his role in obtaining funding for Mussolini from British Military Intelligence. No doubt Mussolini received funds from other sources as well, but this background explains Hoare's understanding of the situation and his ability to find a solution where others had difficulty. Lord Templewood, *Nine Troubled Years* (1954): '[Mussolini] was a powerful mob leader in Milan who had helped to bring Italy into the war and was then hesitating on which side of the barricades he would fight. A little timely help might keep him on our side. I at once telegraphed to Sir George Macdonagh, then Director of Military Intelligence in London, and asked him to authorise me to approach this unknown agitator. He agreed and gave me the means ...' p.154.

believe me when I say that I am as anxious as anyone in Europe to find a settlement that will do justice alike to Abyssinia's National rights, and to Italy's claim for compensation. Let the air carry tonight these words to Italy that, whatever bitter things may be said, are the words of a friend.[15]

Hoare's approach went a long way to counteracting Eden's influence. There followed shortly the ill-fated formal approach to Italy which became known as the Hoare-Laval pact, but events had meanwhile developed rapidly. In October Italy had actually invaded Abyssinia. With Britain playing a leading part, the League had imposed sanctions on Italy, going some way towards the sort of strong action which Churchill had suggested in his broadcast the League might embark upon, although he had not envisaged its use against Italy. There was also, in September and October, an intense propaganda war waged by Italy with the aim of getting her viewpoint put over on the radio in Britain to a public which had heard little of her side of the case. The question of Mosley's broadcasting in Britain has been dealt with in Chapter 1, but the most important direct attempt made by Mussolini to get his case heard involved General Garibaldi, grandson of the famous Garibaldi; it is worth examining in some detail.

In the middle of October General Garibaldi approached the BBC with a talk that he wished to give over the radio to the people of Britain. Unlike a previous request from Marconi, which Reith had turned down without any reference to the Foreign Office, Vansittart was told, after the decision had been taken, that Garibaldi's request had been made, but refused on the grounds that 'certain passages in what he proposed to say were obnoxious'. Vansittart sent the draft of Garibaldi's speech to Hoare on 23 October remarking that it had been brought to him by 'a friend who had been in direct touch with Signor Mussolini. The latter (Mussolini) was very anxious that facilities should be given to General Garibaldi and was prepared to offer equivalent facilities in Rome.'[16] He went on to give a brief account of the BBC's refusal and stated:

I do not think, however, that they would object in principle if you asked them to allow it. My own view is that if we wish to continue the detente with Signor Mussolini we should allow General Garibaldi to make

[15] Public Record Office: FO 371/19134; J4780/1/1.

[16] Nothing seems to have come of this proposal and I have seen no other reference to it. Mussolini arranged for English broadcasts to be set up using Ian Hope Dundas and others. On one occasion only he himself broadcast in English, for American audiences, after taking lessons for the purpose. The result was not a great success. See

these quite innocuous remarks over the wireless. We should expect some criticism of our action and be prepared to face it, but, from what I have heard, I have no doubt that Signor Mussolini is himself behind the General, whom, as a matter of fact, I had agreed to see for a few minutes tomorrow.

In a manuscript note he added:

If we turn this down, we shall certainly tend to put the clock back again in Rome, since Signor Mussolini has made the request in person through an intermediary.

Hoare took this advice in the first instance and replied:

I think that we had better allow this broadcast and wire to Sir E. Drummond[17] telling him that he can so inform [illegible]. We had better get as much credit as we can. The BBC however may well have to let someone else reply to General Garibaldi.[18]

In mentioning the BBC Hoare had raised the whole question of the relationship between the BBC and Government. The BBC were not of a mind to take kindly to remarks of the sort that the Secretary of State would 'allow' this broadcast. Reith had forbidden Garibaldi's broadcast and intervention by the Government would not be tolerated. In addition, of course, Reith's own views were anti-Italian on the Abyssinian question, besides being normally of the left. The civil servant entrusted with conveying Hoare's views to the BBC wrote a very apologetic memorandum.

I conveyed to Mr Graves of the BBC the Secretary of State's view that it would be politic at the present time to allow this broadcast in its revised form.
   Mr Graves, after consulting Sir John Reith, asked me to say that Sir John, while fully appreciating the considerations which were in the Secretary of State's mind, felt bound to suggest that such reasons of

---

Saerchinger, op.cit., p.65. The quotations that follow are from the files on the incident. Public Record Office: FO 371/19157; J7115/1/1.

[17] Sir Eric Drummond, subsequently Lord Perth; see below, p.164n91.

[18] A valid point, for the BBC were soon approached with an offer of a broadcast by Haile Selassie, arranged by an American broadcasting company. In view of their refusal of the microphone to Garibaldi they were obliged to decline the offer. This was shouted by the left as censorship by the BBC, or even the Government, which of course it was. There was no reply possible since the Garibaldi incident described here was secret; like so much connected with the Abyssinian crisis it has remained a secret to the present day.

1. Sir Reginald ('Rex') Leeper. As head of the Foreign Office News Department Leeper had a vital influence between the wars on Britain's broadcasting and propaganda. His interest in broadcasting and politics was far ahead of his time.

2. Sir Robert Vansittart, Permanent Head of the Foreign Office and later Chief Diplomatic Advisor to the Government. Vansittart was a fierce critic of the BBC and supported Leeper on every occasion. He is shown here broadcasting during the war.

3. Sir Horace Wilson, *eminence grise* of Neville Chamberlain. Wilson was responsible for coordinating arrangements for Chamberlain's secret broadcasts to Germany through the 'D' section of MI6.

4. Neville Chamberlain, Prime Minister. Chamberlain is shown here returning from his second visit to Munich in 1938. It was at this time that, in the greatest secrecy, he made the broadcast to Germany through Radio Luxembourg that began the radio war with Germany.

5. Major-General L.D. Grand, creator of the 'D' section of MI6 and founder of the Joint Broadcasting Committee. Grand appointed Guy Burgess to head the secret section of the JBC and coordinated all clandestine broadcasts to Germany, including those by Chamberlain and other leading figures.

6. The headquarters of the Joint Broadcasting Committee at Chester Square. Conveniently for him, Burgess also lived at Chester Square, a few minutes' walk away.

7. Guy Burgess. A candid snap-shot taken shortly after his defection. Burgess's mysterious activities for the Joint Broadcasting Committee formed a brief interlude in his career as a radio producer at the BBC. One of the best producers of his day, he worked at the BBC with his friend and colleague Sir George Barnes.

8. Guy Burgess. A portrait taken in Moscow shortly before his death.

9. Sir George Barnes. Seen here (far left) taking a group of Soviet officials on a tour of the BBC. Knighted for his services to broadcasting, Barnes began his career in the Talks Department where he was directly responsible for Guy Burgess's work.

10. James Strachey Barnes, half-brother of Sir George Barnes. He was a Fascist sympathiser and close friend of Mussolini from the earliest days, when he was supported by Britain, to his fall. He broadcast for Italy during the war.

11. Anthony Blunt, sometime Surveyor of the Queen's Pictures. Blunt played a leading role in Burgess's circle before the war, broadcasting for him at the BBC and providing him with a continuing link to the academic world at Cambridge and elsewhere.

12. Anthony Blunt's pre-war London residence in Palace Court, a central meeting place for Burgess and his circle.

13. Kim Philby at home in London after the war. Philby was a close political associate of Burgess, though not involved directly in his broadcasting ventures.

14. H. StJ. Philby (centre) at home in Riyadh, with the all-important radio close to hand. Philby broadcast for the BBC before the war, when he took an active part in right-wing politics, standing for the fiercely anti-semitic British People's Party, founded and run by the Duke of Bedford.

THE MENACE
of
DICTATORSHIP

15. An anti-Nazi cartoon
emphasising the part played by
radio in the propaganda war. This
was published by the Trades Union
Congress on 7 September 1933.

" Tell the world how well you're being treated "—" *The Nation* "

16. Lord Perth. As Secretary-General of
the League of Nations, Perth was
responsible for the setting up of the
League of Nations Radio Station 'Radio
Nations'. His experience of international
broadcasting made him a stern and
outspoken critic of the BBC.

17. Otto Strasser (right), leader of the Black Front and pioneer of many secret radio station techniques. He is shown here at the grave of Rudolf Formis, killed by the Gestapo while operating an underground station. The other man in the picture, Heinrich Grunow, was to suffer the same fate, executed by the Germans for running another Strasser station in France.

18. Konrad Henlein, shown here outside Churchill's London flat after a confidential meeting on 13 May 1938. Henlein was one of the first to have a warrant for his arrest for high treason issued against him solely for making a broadcast.

19. A cartoon published in the Nazi paper *Völkischer Beobachter* after the daily BBC broadcasts in German were announced in early 1939.

20. P.P. Eckersley. A brilliant radio engineer, Eckersley was obliged to leave the BBC for domestic reasons. He subsequently joined Oswald Mosley in his highly secret plans for a radio station. Eckersley's wife broadcast for Germany throughout the war, but Eckersley convinced the authorities of his loyalty and remained at liberty, though prevented from working for the war effort.

Registered as a Newspaper.

BLACKSHIRT

No. 57   MAY 25th—MAY 31st   "BRITAIN FIRST"   ONE PENNY

YOUR SPEECH MUST BE CAREFULLY PREPARED

Says—

William Joyce

APART from mastering the facts of policy, the student should make some attempt to acquire the language of controversy. For this purpose he should read:— "*Fascism in Relation to British History and Character*" and "*Letters of Lucifer.*"

We now have to consider the problems of form. According to Aristotle, no composition can be effective unless it has a beginning, a middle and an end. Otherwise, like the peace of the Lord, the speech would pass all understanding and seem likely to endure for ever. Before, however, the divisions can be considered, a few observations on the preparation of speeches may be acceptable. Generally a speech, if worthy of delivery, is worthy of some preparation. The few who can speak extempore with excellent effect constitute a small minority on which training would be wasted.

No matter how good an impromptu ● speech may be, the speaker will afterwards reflect that it could have been bettered by forethought. Indeed in the eighteenth century, "par excellence" the age of oratory, members of Parliament were at great pains to secure that the reports of their orations should surpass the originals. The great Dr. Johnson acted as a Parliamentary Reporter; and he was true to the spirt of the age when he exclaimed, "I always saw that the Whig dogs got the worst of it." As we, however, cannot rely upon such a stout champion as brave old Samuel, we must avoid the necessity for such kind assistance.

It is often asked if a prepared speech should be memorized. No definite answer can be given to the individual, since an affirmative would presuppose the possession of a good memory; and, as Nietzche says; "Many a man has failed to become a great thinker merely because his memory has been too good." The man who has difficulties with his memory should make no attempt to learn his whole speech by heart since his energies will be unhappily divided between attempts to impress the audience and attempts to remember what he must say next.

Such a conflict is fatal. The speaker who can memorize an entire speech may enliven it as an actor enlivens his lines; but he should always remember in preparation the total difference between the written and the spoken word. A composition may be splendid to the eye and intolerably monotonous to the ear. Thus it was that Edward Burke, a magnificent writer of speeches, emptied the House whenever he rose to speak.

However capably a speech has been learnt, the speaker would be unwise to resist the impulse to alter, add, or amend as he proceeds. Cadence, balance and emphasis are not alike upon peoples or platforms.

Once it is realised that there must be a dynamic interaction between speaker and audience, it follows that there must be some degree of mutual adaptation which will necessarily produce an effect upon the form of words. A speech is a living, resilient thing, not a stately corpse.

We all know, of course, how much pathos can be thrown into a recitation from one of Shakespeare's tragic passages; but the effect depends upon the genius of Shakespeare and the talent of an accomplished actor. A speaker who combines the two is not very commonly found.

Thus it is that complete memorization is not to be commended. If the main arguments are thoroughly known and their sequence clearly visualized, it is enough that the introduction, the conclusion, and certain special passages be committed to memory. These latter passages should never be long and they should always embody the principles

*"True art is nature to advantage dressed
What oft was thought but ne'er so well expressed."*

Perhaps one such passage for each section of policy should be enough.

Whilst it is not to be presumed that every speech must express and explain the whole policy, the present state of the public mind demands that the principles of Fascism should on all occasions be given the fullest expression possible. The audience which attends a public meeting will desire to know our attitude towards each important problem of the day and, not infrequently we shall be required to bestow a few words on trivialities which some people have magnified into obsessions. Hence, unless the subject is strictly delimited, the public will expect to hear the case for Fascism as a whole.

The speaker's next requirement is to know the time allowed. No fluency of introduction will compensate for awkward compression of the argument. Being informed as to the limits of time and scope, the speaker can arrange his arguments under various headings such as will be suggested in the next article.

The Leader speaks at Olympia June 7

Your part in Sales Drives

SUMMER heralds the best period of the year for outside sales. More people are about on the streets, the warmer weather allows pedestrians to linger on their walks, and Blackshirts can display our uniform to advantage without the necessity for being muffled up to the eyebrows.

Members will have read in the last issues of the "*Fascist Week*" and "*Blackshirt*" of the coming merger. The return to the old title, coupled with the reputation which the "*Fascist Week*" has established for itself, will have a great pyschological effect upon the public, and will prove to be one of the greatest selling factors we possess. The utmost use must be made of this new incentive to sales.

However good a publication may be, unless it is brought before the notice of the public it will fail in its object. The new "*Blackshirt*" must be on sale throughout the length and breadth of the country, so that there will be no town, village or hamlet where it is not possible to buy the official newspaper of the B.U.F.

To achieve this purpose, it is necessary to create a sales force of which every member of our Movement will be an agent.

In the past branches have done admirable work, and it is due to their loyal and unremitting effort that we have achieved so much in the marketing of our publications. But we are only starting. The response in the past has justified the belief that our organisation will, in a very short period, double the sales of our propaganda paper. It is a colossal task, but one which can be easily achieved by our members, whose slogan is "Service and Sacrifice."

One or two useful hints might prove of value to branch organisers. Branch sales drives should be held at least thrice weekly. On these drives sellers should keep well together and not be scattered all over the town. The ideal would be to proceed down one side of a street with about four paces in between sellers. The result will have a good effect upon the passer-by, and will often have the effect of making the passer, buy.

The latter sees one Blackshirt selling papers; he wonders what it is all about. Then he sees another, and thinks he will buy a paper, but while he is making up his mind the Blackshirt has passed. If only two Blackshirts were together selling, that potential sale would be lost, but with perhaps a dozen coming on behind, the intending buyer has no excuse. He can make up his mind, seek out his small change, and make his purchase before the column has passed.

A great deal depends, of course, upon the effect created upon the public by the Blackshirts. If the members are slovenly turned out or unkempt in appearance, an unfavourable impression will be made, and people will pass in disgust, but if the team is smart and well-groomed, even our opponents will be compelled to admire.

If these suggestions are followed, selling will become more interesting and you will look forward to the next drive with zest.

21. An issue of *The Blackshirt*, the British Union's first newspaper. William Joyce issues academic instructions on how to compose a speech above a photograph of Mosley at the microphone. In fact Mosley only succeeded in broadcasting after the war.

22. *above left* William Joyce fighting for Fascism at Chiswick shortly before he left the British Union to found his own party. He is seen wearing the characteristic British Union black fencing-jacket uniform with its lightning-flash emblem.

23. *above right* William Joyce in British Army custody at the end of the war, after his career as a script-writer for such programmes as Workers Challenge and the New British Broadcasting Station. The scar prominent here was obtained when, as an undergraduate, he was defending a meeting against Communist intruders.

24. *left* A propaganda cartoon of Lord Haw-Haw, popularly identified with William Joyce – an identity he assumed towards the end of the war after the myth had become well established. The contrast between Joyce and the caricature is obvious.

25. Maxwell Knight, MI5 officer. Knight knew members of Joyce's family and was almost certainly the MI5 officer who alerted Joyce to his impending arrest under 18B in August 1939. He appears to have known Joyce from his earliest days with the British Fascists.

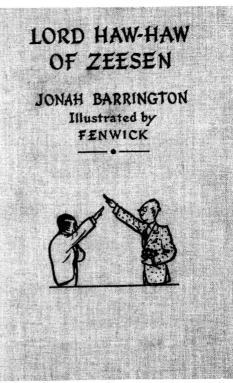

26. The cover of the biography of Lord Haw-Haw of Zeesen by Jonah Barrington, who invented the character which was taken up by the British counter-propaganda authorities. The idea was based on the upper-class accent of the Nazi English-language newscaster, which was certainly not the accent of William Joyce.

27. The Duke of Windsor, then Prince of Wales (bottom left), whose world-wide appeal for peace broadcast in May 1939 was banned in Britain, shown here in a regimental photograph with Norman Baillie-Stewart (top right) who began broadcasting for Germany in April 1939 and whose voice inspired 'Haw-Haw'.

28. Norman Baillie-Stewart in Dublin after the war, a photograph issued on the occasion of his engagement.

29. Sefton Delmer, one of the most accomplished exponents of black propaganda during the war, shown here listening to German broadcasts at Woburn Abbey where he worked with Rex Leeper and R.H.S. Crossman.

30. John Hilton, broadcaster on unemployment before the war and a most successful wartime broadcaster. A Cambridge Professor who started life as a mill apprentice in Bolton, Hilton was a close friend of Guy Burgess and Sir George Barnes. Burgess produced many of his talks at the BBC.

31. Harold Nicolson, politician and diarist. At the time of Munich his talks, guided by Guy Burgess, were the only topical political talks being broadcast by the BBC. Nicolson was also a central figure in the pre-war social world in which Burgess and Blunt flourished.

high policy could unfortunately not be openly adduced by the BBC who, he felt sure, would be the target of a great deal of criticism from the general public as well as from the press. The BBC had throughout this dispute been purely objective and had not allowed either side to air its views. General Garibaldi's would be the first ex parte appeal, for so, in spite of its innocuous character, it would be interpreted by the mass of listeners. The effect might be very good at the Italian end, but it was the British end which was the primary concern of the BBC. They would be willing to do it if they were allowed to say that General Garibaldi had been introduced to them by the Foreign Office.

I said that of course this, as they must know, would be impossible.

Sir John asked that this aspect should be put before the Secretary of State, with whom he would be glad to speak if the Secretary of State desired.[19]

Matters were complicated by the fact that there was an election to be held in November and another civil servant minuted:

I am a little worried about this from the Parliamentary or rather the electoral point of view. The Secretary of State's speech the other day I thought went exactly far enough without going too far; by which I mean that the Opposition, who were only too anxious to denounce a weakening by H.M. Government, if not indeed an Imperialist bargain with Italy, were quite unable to do so. But I am sure they are still looking for the chance. I feel sure too that if Garibaldi broadcasts even these platitudes the fact will be seized on on election platforms. In any case, would not the BBC insist on a counter-blast from Abyssinia? I do not know who would do it, but it seems to me that the spokesman for Abyssinia could only retort to Garibaldi by blackguarding Italy, so we should be no 'forrader' in the end. I must say that from the Parliamentary point of view I should very much like to see the thing dropped.[20]

Vansittart saw that there was an obvious difficulty here and added his written comment to Hoare:

I do not wish to embarrass you from the internal point of view. I only feel obliged to draw attention to the effect of refusal on Mussolini, who has personally interested himself in this.[21]

Hoare, by this time, had appreciated that the power in questions of broadcasting rested with Reith whatever the nation's interest might require and he declined the fight saying:

[19] Public Record Office: FO 371/19157; J7115/1/1.
[20] Ibid.
[21] Ibid.

> We have discussed this and we agree not to intervene at all. Let the
> BBC turn it down on their own responsibility.[22]

There could be no clearer demonstration of the independent role of
the BBC at this time on which they prided themselves; it was not
independence as envisaged by the charter, for the Governors of the
BBC were never consulted or informed, it was merely a question of
Reith's fiat in an organization of which he was in sole control. Hoare's
comment that the BBC had better ban the broadcast 'on their own
responsibility' of course raised the question of what this responsibility
was, and to whom. The answer, clearly, was that it was a
responsibility seen by Reith in terms of a *Realpolitik* view, as defined
by him, of what the BBC's public would think of any broadcast, and
the responsibility was to him personally acting in deliberate isolation
from the views of his Governors.[23]

The broadcast did not take place; in case its real nature should be
misunderstood, we print it here.

> I am honoured to be able to talk to the noble and friendly people of
> Great Britain by wireless to-night.
>
> The opportunity of addressing you is permitted to me out of love and
> respect for my grandfather, Giuseppe Garibaldi, champion of all just
> causes. In 1864, he was received in this country with sincere
> enthusiasm and welcomed by all the nation.
>
> He was granted the Freedom of the City of London, a great honour
> for a foreigner. In replying to the address made when that honour was
> conferred upon him, he stated that he was prouder of being granted the
> Freedom of the City of London, cradle of modern civilization, than of
> any other honour received during the War.
>
> This has never been forgotten in my family, and we still feel
> spiritually linked to the people of Great Britain, not only by family ties
> through my Mother, who is English, but also by deep feelings and
> conviction.
>
> England and Italy have always been friends.

[22] Ibid. General Garibaldi, by a strange coincidence, ended World War II with
Capt. Sigismund Payne Best (see below, p.191f.) among the prisoners of war, political
prisoners and hostages who reached Niederdorf in the South Tyrol in April 1945. See
S. Payne Best, *The Venlo Incident* (1950), p.256.

[23] There is of course the possibility that Reith made an unrecorded telephone call to
one of his Governors, or the Chairman, but this at the time would have been unlikely.
Today the reverse is the case. Telephone calls, rarely recorded even on vital matters,
are universal, and memoranda and letters have almost ceased to exist: the future
historian's task will be a difficult one. It is to Reith's eternal credit that he insisted
from the first on the highest standards in this matter for the BBC with a registry to
match.

England afforded refuge to exiles of Italian Independence, from Foscolo to Mazzini.

England denounced to the World, by means of Gladstone's powerful pen, the misrule of the Bourbons in Naples.

England supported Garibaldi's Legions and Italy's unity by arms and diplomacy.

England sent volunteers to fight in the famous expedition of The Thousand, shoulder to shoulder, with Garibaldi's Legionaries in 1860.

These facts are engraven on the hearts of the Italian people and will never be forgotten.

Threatening war clouds have been gathering over our two countries. Is there an Englishman or Italian who would not use every human effort to avert such a calamity?

Among my listeners there are many who fought beside us in the Great War.

I fought with them and to-day if my voice is not clear, it is the result of wounds received in this comradeship.

I am confident that a satisfactory solution can be found, which Italy will not hesitate for a single moment to accept. I, Ezio Garibaldi, repeat to you what Mussolini affirmed a few days ago – 'The Italian soldier in Africa is awaiting, with impatience, the order to turn his arms into ploughshares.'

My countrymen, men and woman, are second to none in their love and respect of the chivalrous characteristics of the womenfolk of Great Britain. We look to them with confidence, to help in the solution of the existing problem.

Through me the Italians salute you with affectionate appreciation of the past, and assurance as to the future.

To-night, thanks to the courtesy of the British Broadcasting Corporation, I am able to address you Italians,[24] who are listening, I give you Giuseppe Garibaldi's motto: 'Humanity, peace and civilization.'[25]

Deprived of any way of getting his opinions to the British public within Britain, Mussolini decided to try English-language broadcasts from Italy, and soon found English expatriates who were happy to come to the microphone and voice their opinions of the weaknesses and failings of British policy. Foremost among these was Col. Cyril Rocke, a fiery and eccentric individualist who had written articles for the Italian press and travelled the world to put Italy's case.[26] No actual recording's of Rocke's controversial broadcasts have been

[24] There were, of course, numbers of Italians living in Britain; Garibaldi had requested that he be allowed to repeat this part of his speech in Italian.

[25] Public Record Office: Fo 371/19157; J7115/1/1.

[26] The papers from which the following account is drawn are in the Public Record Office: FO 371/19227; J8413/8283/1.

traced, but it is clear from papers in the Public Record Office that they corresponded exactly, as far as the text went, with addresses he regularly gave to the British expatriate community, a circle which included Ezra Pound and British sympathizers with Italian Fascism such as Ian Hope Dundas and James Strachey Barnes.[27]

One of the most striking points made by Rocke was on the question of slavery in Abyssinia. Despite the existence of a League of Nations report which had drawn attention to the flourishing state of slavery in North Africa and the fact that Abyssinia was the centre of this trade in people, the question was largely ignored by the left-wing League of Nations Union in Britain and also by the press, which was seemingly uninformed on the question. All attempts to get the ruler of Abyssinia to put a stop to the traffic were in vain; the practices by which the people of the country obtained their living and had done so from time immemorial were vigorously defended as being essential to the country's economy. The young Haile Selassie, later fêted by the British, could do nothing to alter the practices of centuries, from which, indeed, part of his personal income derived. Rocke reached the topic in his broadcasts through the question of vivisection.

Many of the far-right in Britain were also ardent Anti-Vivisectionists[28] and Rocke's audiences naturally thought, when he raised the subject, that they were to hear again the horrors of the ritual killing of animals as practised by Jew and Arab alike. Instead he revealed that the Emperor of Ethiopia, the Lion of Judah, every year sent thousands of his subjects into slavery, and that the first step on their journey was their castration by the dealers to whom they had been sold. No medical attention was provided in these time-hallowed rituals, which were indeed vivisection; many died as a result and were mercifully saved from a life of degradation and misery, although their death was not a painless one. It can well be imagined what effect these

[27] The connection between Ezra Pound and Mussolini's British sympathizers is illustrated by the appearance of Pound's 'Does the Government of England Control the BBC?' in the British Union paper *Action*, no.150, 7 January 1939. There is an account of Pound at this time in E. Fuller Torrey, *The Roots of Treason* (1984), p.157f.

[28] The connection might seem obscure but was actually quite specific. Sir Oswald Mosley used the London and Provincial Anti-Vivisection Society, run by a supporter, Mrs Dudley-Elam, as a cover organisation. The rival party to British Union, the Imperial Fascist League, was run by a veterinary surgeon who was also a fanatical Anti-Vivisectionist and used this platform to obtain followers and funds. It has been suggested that the driving force behind such movements was a sublimated horror at the slaughter of World War I. Whatever the reason, those who became involved carried their campaigns against cruelty to animals and vivisection to great lengths. An echo in the present day can be seen in reports that the Duchess of Windsor desired that her fortune go to medical research, but on the condition that no project involving vivisection be supported.

broadcasts had on audiences in Britain who heard them. No doubt they explained the special attention paid to Rocke's activities by the security services. He was even made the subject of a report by Claude Dansey, founder of the 'Z' organization,[29] as characteristic of Dansey as its subject:

> Lt.Col. Cyril Rocke called at this office this morning ... I laughingly referred to his having taken to writing letters to the press and suggested that it was a sign of old age. This appeared to make him lose his temper and he informed me that he was up to his neck in it, fighting against sanctions with all his power, that he had been to Washington in connection with this and had distributed ten thousand copies of the letter which was published in the *Messagero*.
>
> I asked him why he should oppose sanctions and he replied, with great temper, that he thought Italy had been damnably treated, that he knew Abyssinia better than any living man and he thought Italy was right in everything she had done. I replied that I also knew something of Abyssinia and, without having any particular love for the people, I thought the Italians might have done things in a very different manner and without so many falsehoods.
>
> He became still more excited and said that the British had broken their word on every possible occasion and told many more lies than the Italians had. He then rushed out of the room and was overheard to mutter 'Swine' as he went.[30]

Ian Hope Dundas, Sir Oswald Mosley's Chief of Staff, was, as we have seen, the man who opened the negotiations with the BBC attempting to get the British Union of Fascists included in the BBC's roster of political parties that were allowed to the microphone. His broadcasts from Italy were numerous at this time but, again, no recording of them appears to have survived. Unlike the broadcasts by Rocke, the texts themselves have also gone. There was comment in the British press and he can be seen as the first of the radio 'traitors' of the kind epitomized later by William Joyce, apart, of course, from the fact that Britain and Italy were not at war.

A man of greater intelligence, and a more devoted supporter of Fascism, was James Strachey Barnes. During the Abyssinian crisis he was the Reuter correspondent with the Italian Expeditionary Forces and, although he does not appear to have broadcast himself, much of

---

[29] For a life of Dansey, see Anthony Read and David Fisher, *Colonel Z: The Life and Times of a Master of Spies* (1984).

[30] Public Record Office: FO 371/19227; J8413/8283/1. When Rocke died in 1968, aged 92, Lord Alexander of Tunis wrote of him: '... I remember so clearly seeing him, during the attack [at the battle of the Somme] leading our men forward against terrible hostile fire. Only two Officers and 82 men came out of that action unscathed. Cyril Rocke was a gallant man and a good soldier.'

what he wrote formed the basis of the Italian news broadcasts.[31] Among Barnes's fellow reporters with the Italian forces was General J.F.C. Fuller,[32] one of Mosley's senior officers but present as special envoy of Lord Rothermere. Fuller's knowledge of military matters may account for some of the most interesting observations made by Barnes at the time. For example he wrote on aerial warfare:

> The most striking achievement of the Italian Air Force was the manner in which the whole Army Corps on the Northern Front were supplied entirely from the air for days on end. Even live cattle were parachuted down. This had long been regarded as a theoretical impossibility, but the Abyssinian war had demonstrated its practicability. The lesson will need to be adopted immediately by European staff plans.[33]

On the question of who was to blame for the war in Abyssinia Barnes was outspoken, influenced by the fact that many of his closest Italian friends were killed in the war:

> All the economic difficulties, all the suffering, all the cruelty, all the grave losses which have been suffered on both sides of gallant and valuable lives must therefore be put down entirely to British policy: to Mr Eden, to Sir Samuel Hoare, to Mr Baldwin, to the rich men of the City of London who hoped to grow richer through a League mandate over Ethiopia ...[34]

He reserved his most savage attacks for Anthony Eden, which are worth recording if only because the differences between Eden and Italy were to have such a serious effect.

> Sir Samuel Hoare referred to him [Eden] earlier as an *ideologue*. He added: 'As Napoleon used to say, "Les ideologues sont plus dangereux que les chiens enragés." '

[31] The Italians were particularly conscious of the significance of radio in Abyssinia and would not allow any broadcasts to be made outside their control. This gave rise to an extraordinary incident in which the British Consul was refused permission to transmit on his own set and his office was entered by the Italian forces, who put the transmitters out of action. The result was that the British Government had no way of knowing what was going on throughout the war, except through messages sent by surface mail. There is a full account of the incident in the Public Record Office: FO 371/20201; J6198/3957/1.

[32] General Fuller was an active supporter of Mosley at this time, but also a freelance agent; he followed up his visit to Abyssinia by visits to the Spanish Civil War fronts, sending his detailed observations to the War Office. His reports may be read in the Public Record Office: WO 106/1578 and WO 106/1579.

[33] James Strachey Barnes, *Half a Life Left* (1937), p.168.

[34] Ibid., p.157.

This is the real Mr Eden, a very clever young man with a 'way with him'. He would have made a first-class commercial traveller. Unfortunately diplomacy is not commerce and his original excursions all over Europe in the guise of an 'honest but penniless' broker only brought on him a certain amount of ridicule. His appearance on the news-reels – in Russia with Stalin, in Warsaw, in Berlin – was invariably greeted all over Europe with titters of laughter. But these facts were ignored in England, or were put down to got up demonstrations.[35]

It is clear enough from the words and action of these men alone that Mussolini must have felt that there was considerable sympathy in Britain for his point of view. The propaganda broadcasts from Bari in Arabic, mentioned earlier, also received considerable support from expatriate Britons who knew the situation of the Arabs. Prominent among these was the Arabist H.StJ. Philby,[36] at the time as famous as his son Kim Philby[37] was later to become. Philby wrote strongly worded articles which the Egyptian press were only to happy to print, in the hope that their message would reach a wider audience. Writing in the *Egyptian Mail*, Philby drew attention to British bombing of open unprotected native villages in a way which makes chilling reading today:

That aerial bombing is freely used by the Aden administration is not denied by the Government. It is actually defended by those responsible as a rapid and humane method of keeping peace in the outposts of Empire. We are told that the inhabitants of the villages selected for aerial destruction are always warned with plenty of time to get away. Our enemies in the next great war will doubtless note that the destruction of London by bombardment after due notice to its inhabitants to quit will not be challenged on moral or aesthetic grounds.[38]

This article was forwarded to London by Sir Miles Lampson[39] with a letter to Sir Lancelot Oliphant observing

[35] Ibid., p.303.

[36] There is a recording of a talk given by Philby on 'Mecca and the Arabs' in the National Sound Archives: NSA LP 2342 3.f.1. The recording was made on 30 November 1937.

[37] There can be few Englishmen who have achieved such fame in their own lifetime as Harold Adrian Russell Philby – a fame, moreover, which reflects in such a unique way the political contradictions in the history of the world in the twentieth century.

[38] *Egyptian Mail*, 18 January 1938.

[39] Sir Miles Lampson, Baron Killearn (1880-1964), responsible for coordinating negotiations leading to the Locarno Treaty. Ambassador to Peking 1926-33; subsequently the first Ambassador to Egypt.

... our task is not made any easier by the fact than an Englishman – the well known Philby – is publishing stuff for which he might well, judging by its nature, have been paid as an Italian propaganda agent though actually I think that it is his blind pro-Arabism that has warped his vision (in this belief I am more charitable than my staff!)[40]

And the Italian station at Bari did not stop at Arabic broadcasting; struck by the success of their attack on Britain and her interests in the Middle East she embarked on broadcasts in Hindustani aimed at India. These broadcasts had an inestimable value for the Indian underground movements supporting the Congress Party and all opposition to British rule in India. Britain did not immediately take action against the Italian Hindustani station,[41] but on the question of Arabic broadcasts she was driven to act as events became more serious with the outbreak of the Arab revolt in 1937. Although the Abyssinian question had ended, with Italy occupying all the disputed territories and Haile Selassie in exile in Britain, the trouble in Palestine continued. So did the Italian broadcasts from Bari. Indeed they got worse, especially after Britain introduced her 'tough measures' to deal with Arab terrorism. The answer, obviously, was a radio station run by Britain to counteract the Bari broadcasts. Eden felt very strongly on this issue. He made the cessation of Bari propaganda an essential condition of making peace with Italy after Abyssinia and, indeed, finally resigned on this question. But he also went ahead strongly on the setting up of the British Arabic Radio Station which came to be known throughout the Mediterranean as 'Radio Eden'.

It was thought at first that the BBC would provide these broadcasts, and Reith has often been quoted as seeing the need for foreign broadcasts. But what exactly Reith meant by this is not clear. Certainly a rival BBC foreign policy to that of the Government would have been inevitable.[42] The time that passed between the Foreign Office perceiving the absolute need for the broadcasts and their actually coming about was yet further illustration, if any were needed, of the almost impossible relations between the BBC and the Government. Leeper attended one of the first joint BBC Foreign Office meetings and reported back in despair:

[40] Public Record Office: FO 371/21834; E749/50/65.
[41] The station finally established by the BBC to answer these broadcasts later became well-known through the chance selection of George Orwell to work there. For an account of the station and Orwell's programmes, see W.J. West (ed.), *Orwell: The War Broadcasts* (1985) and *Orwell: The War Commentaries* (1986).
[42] Allusion to the possibility of such a policy was made by John Coatman: see above, p.41.

The attitude of the BBC is not as helpful as it should be ... I was left to do all the insisting that this thing *must* be done. Mr Johnstone of the news department is to attend a Sub-Committee on Tuesday 29 June. The BBC have submitted a memo for that meeting. It consists very largely of technical difficulties which are their business and not ours. The last paragraph also contains that very foolish argument which is so dear to the BBC that the moral purity of their programmes should not be impaired by propaganda, ie. news in foreign languages.

One would think from the BBC's attitude that there was no international crisis at all, that the halcyon days of the post-war period had come to stay for ever, that no other country was threatening our interests seriously.[43]

He went on to recommend great sternness by the Foreign Office at the meeting. Vansittart agreed, adding:

... the thing has *got* to be done and done quickly, on grounds of high policy. Too much time has passed already and the matter must now be treated as an emergency.

Such attitudes got nowhere with the BBC, no matter how serious the question or how urgent the need. It was impossible to bring them to an understanding of the actual situation in any terms other than those understood by a bureaucracy: that here was one organization trying to impose its will on another, and it was not going to get away with it! It was a further six months before the first foreign-language broadcasts actually went out from the BBC. In the meanwhile the Foreign Office had established most successfully a news team for Middle East affairs and gone a long way towards making alternative arrangements which involved a number of possibilities, including broadcasting from Cyprus.[44] In retrospect it is clear that they could have carried out the work themselves, and finally this was done, as we shall see, when the alternative broadcasting system called the Joint Broadcasting Committee, for which Burgess worked, was created. But in those days there was a very great mystique attached to broadcasting; with this went vastly inflated ideas of the cost of any proposal that was going to produce any worthwhile result and this caused alarm at the Treasury. It is tempting to think that, without Eden's strong emotional involvement in the project, it might never have got off the ground.

[43] Public Record Office: FO 395/547; P2682/20/150.
[44] There were rumours at the time that a station was set up on Cyprus by MI6. For a later history of secret broadcasting from Cyprus at the time of Suez, see Julian Hall, *Radio Power* (1978) p.121.

Eden at length made formal proposals to the Cabinet for the establishment of medium-wave broadcasts to the Middle East in Arabic including in his report the gist of what Leeper and Vansittart had recommended to him:

> The time has now come when some more positive steps should be taken than that of asking the Italians to desist. Without attempting to imitate the tone or the methods of Bari, it is essential for His Majesty's Government to ensure the full and forcible presentation of the British view of events in a region of such vital importance.[45]

This ensured that things proceeded and, as good earnest, a committee called the Arabic Broadcasting Committee, or ABC, was set up. It held its first meeting on 15 September 1937 under Sir Kingsley Wood; the BBC was not invited to attend. After considerable discussion of all the possibilities – medium versus short wave; Cyprus, Palestine or India as possible locations for the transmitter – it was realized that the best answer would be a short-wave transmitter in Britain. The Empire Service refused to consider putting out broadcasts in any other language than English on the grounds that it would damage its reputation and was supported in its view by the Dominions Office. This meant the BBC creating an entirely new service, for setting up a Government station in Britain was thought impossible. After extensive discussions the Committee recommended that programmes in Arabic, Spanish and Portuguese be put out by the BBC in collaboration with the Foreign Office. The BBC had already agreed to put out programmes in Spanish and Portuguese, of 'straight news' for South America, to counteract the extensive propaganda being directed there by the German system at Zeesen. They now agreed to do the Arabic broadcasts as well, provided they maintained their independence of Government control. On a gentlemen's agreement between the BBC and Foreign Office that both would consult with the other on matters of international political significance the programme was launched on 3 January 1938.[46]

The inaugural broadcast and news service in Arabic put out by the

[45] Quoted in Taylor, op.cit., p.194; memorandum by Eden 13 July 1937. Public Record Office: CAB 24/270. CP185(37).

[46] Reith noted in his Diary for 5 November 1937: 'Our not being made to have a written agreement with respect to the Foreign Office on foreign language broadcasts was a great tribute to us – me especially. Eden had wanted something definite but the Cabinet minute referred only to a gentleman's agreement between Vansittart and myself.' Cited in Mansell, op.cit., p.53. Reith's very reference to a possible written agreement betrays the reality of the situation, for what would the nature of such an agreement have been?

BBC bore out all the worries of the Foreign Office and was a disaster, causing major diplomatic repercussions immediately, although attempts were made to suggest that it was a 'storm in a tea cup'. For, in the very first broadcast aimed at the Arabs, the BBC had chosen for its central news item the fact that an Arab terrorist in Palestine had been executed for being found in possession of a revolver. In Saudi Arabia the Court had been gathered together to listen to the first broadcast put on largely for their benefit. The ceremonies at the opening of the channel[47] created a favourable impression; the news that followed was greeted with a stunned silence. No greater insult could be imagined. In the attempts made afterwards to find out what happened it was suggested that it could not be avoided because the news had already been announced on the Empire Service shortly before. This was, of course, no answer and, looking at the matter today, it is difficult not to feel that the item was included deliberately by a BBC member of staff anxious to prove their independence while totally oblivious of the effects his actions would have on the world outside, a world well known to the Foreign Office, staffed by experienced diplomats, and with an immense archive of documented cases to draw on, but totally unknown to the BBC who had little to guide them but the bureaucrat's *amour propre*.

The inquest that followed this event in the Foreign Office news department, with its echoes in the BBC, were very important, for, although they dealt only with the radio war between Italy and Britain, they gave crucial experience on questions of propaganda which were to become more and more important as war itself came nearer and finally broke out. The events at Munich gave matters an added impetus, but it was the arguments and discussions that took place at this time, the beginning of 1938, that first raised the crucial questions.

The file on the incident contains a detailed account by someone well versed in the realities of the Middle East.[48] He had an unclouded view of what in the Bari broadcasts was propaganda, and what merely clear statement of unpleasant facts. It is worth printing in full to show the cold air of reality which existed in the Foreign Office at the time and which could have been drawn upon had a solution been looked for closely:

[47] These included addresses by such dignitaries as the son of the King of the Yemen, the Emir Seif-el-Islam Hussein, and the Ambassadors of those countries who would be covered by the service.

[48] G.W. Rendel, who was in regular communication with the man on the spot, Sir Reginald Bullard. In the file mentioned, Rendel also pointed out that they had both foreseen the troubles and submitted a memorandum in November 1937 '... when it was first proposed to use "strong measures" in Palestine' – to no avail.

I have ventured to point out in the past, perhaps too often, that Italian propaganda against us would have been innocuous had it not been for the actual facts which it reports, and that it is the *facts* which have damaged us far more than the ridiculous effusions of the Italian Press and the inventions of Bari broadcasts which have done us little harm. We are now in a dilemma, because, if we suppress these facts in our own broadcasts it will be clear that we are not giving straight news on the main question of interest in the middle East – i.e. events in Palestine – while on the other hand, if we give full news from Palestine we shall be daily injuring our own reputation and prestige.

The problem is a very serious one, and I think the solution lies far deeper than in any alteration of method or in any superficial palliatives that we might be able to apply ... I think it can now be said that the situation has steadily deteriorated since the strong measures were introduced. There is every indication that it will continue to deteriorate until something like a virtual state of war exists throughout the country. This probability has an important bearing on the question of how Palestine news should be dealt with in the Arabic broadcasts now being sent out by the BBC.[49]

The problem, finally, is one that is still with us, although Britain has ceased to have any direct responsibility since the creation of the State of Israel. Leeper made determined efforts to come to a solution to the problem, knowing that the matter was one which was affecting the whole stability of Europe, driving Italy more and more to permanent alliance with Germany, and bringing the prospect of a European war closer.

Commenting on the remarks mentioned above he first felt it necessary to explain how he had been misled by the BBC into thinking that some control over the broadcasts would exist to ensure that outright insults to friendly foreign powers would not go out over the air.

I have spoken to Mr Calvert[50] about this. He is uncertain what to do as regards Palestine news. For the moment I have merely urged him to refrain from broadcasting news which must be highly unwelcome to the Arabs. 'Straight News' (a BBC expression) must not be interpreted as including news which can do us harm with the people whom we are addressing. That seems to me sheer nonsense. I gave my own interpretation at the Kingsley Wood Committee in the presence of Sir John Reith and Mr Graves, and I understood that they had accepted it,

[49] Public Record Office: FO 395/557; P69/2/150.
[50] A.S. Calvert was an official of the Levant Consular Service who had been transferred to the Foreign Office News Department. He prepared his material in collaboration with the Palestine Press Officer in Jerusalem, a Mr Tweedy.

viz. that any news broadcast should be correct, that there should be no attacks on other countries, but that there should be selection and omission of news as our interests might require. It was because the BBC had made such a song and dance about their moral purity (implying that the F.O. were immoral and impure) that we laid down these conditions at the Kingsley Wood Committee before agreeing that the BBC should be entrusted with the Arabic broadcasts.[51]

It has been suggested by one commentator that Leeper was unaware that the formal excuse given for the BBC's including the news of the Arabs' execution in their first bulletin was that it had been in the Empire news service earlier in the day. The author, having actually quoted from the passage above,[52] did not, it seems, bother to read on to Leeper's very next paragraph:

> Mr Calvert has made the point that it is difficult for him to omit a news item such as the execution of an Arab which is included in the Empire News Bulletin. But is the BBC bound to broadcast to the Empire the execution of every Arab in Palestine? It seems to me unnecessary, though I suspect that it gives their conscience a warm glow.[53]

This selective quotation is interesting, for the writer was for nine years Managing Director of the External Services of the BBC, although after the war, and it stands out as a clear example of an institutional attitude being carried through to a following generation even in the face of documents released into the public domain which establish the actual facts. The same author had earlier briefly quoted from a memorandum by J.B.Clark:[54]

> The omission of unwelcome facts of news and the consequent suppression of truth runs counter to the Corporation's policy laid down by appropriate authority. If external bodies wish the Corporation to

[51] Public Record Office: FO 395/557; P69/2/150.

[52] Gerard Mansell in *Let Truth be Told* (1982), p.53. Mansell quoted briefly: 'Straight news must not be interpreted as including news which can do us harm with the people we are addressing', deleting, without mentioning it, the phrase 'a BBC expression'. He added: 'What he [Leeper] did not say, perhaps because he was not aware of it, was that news of execution had already been broadcast in the Empire Service without causing a ripple.'

[53] Public Record Office: FO 395/557; P69/2/150.

[54] Sir John Beresford Clark (1902-1968), described to the present author by Mulk Raj Anand who knew him during the war years, as the classic BBC bureaucrat. He played a considerable role in overseas broadcasting, having started out with the Empire Service under whose auspices he toured the world in 1937. He was one of the few who realized there was something not quite right about the Joint Broadcasting

modify an established policy, under which I have been directed to guide our news services, suitable representations should be made in an appropriate manner.[55]

And on this he commented:

It was a classic statement of the BBC's stand which still holds good to this day. It is to J.B. Clark's eternal credit that at this crucial stage, when even Reith seemed inclined to steer clear of confrontation with Whitehall and to deal with problems as they arose, he spoke out clearly and unequivocally. That he should have done so was heavy with consequences for the future.[56]

A classic statement it may have been, but it was also completely untrue and, within a few months, the BBC foreign language services were under almost total direct control of the Foreign Office.[57] Before putting forward his proposal Leeper dealt with the question of the content of the Palestine news broadcasts, establishing what was actually wrong with the BBC's approach:

It does seem to me that the treatment of the Palestine situation in these broadcasts is very difficult, and it is hardly fair to leave this to Mr Calvert alone. He will need some more authoritative guidance. In putting forward any suggestion myself I do so merely on the basis of how news should be treated as a general principle. Clearly Palestine cannot be ignored, and clearly official policy in Palestine must be upheld. But if it is to be upheld it must be explained. The inclusion of news items without any explanation of the reason why such a thing had been done by the authorities as part of policy seems to me wrong and merely harmful to our interests. Whatever we broadcast about Palestine must be done boldly and not apologetically and must be properly explained. In fact the news items must be written up in such a way that even if at times they may be unpalatable to the Arabs they are at least intelligible. The broadcasts must be constructive and not merely isolated news items, concentrating on what is important as regards policy and not omitting what may be news but what is not essential news.[58]

Committee (see below, p.114f.), although he was more worried by its successes in overt broadcasting rivalling the BBC than its secret side, if he knew of its existence.

[55] Mansell, op.cit., p.52.
[56] Ibid.
[57] See below.
[58] Public Record Office: FO 395/557; P69/2/150.

In fact what was to be avoided was the sort of sensational reporting that had been noticed by Vansittart before, and also the highly secret interventions of Reith or others at a high level which would suppress or include material according to their own private views – views, moreover, which had usually only been formed from the press agencies and popular press generally. No one in the BBC can have known of the exceptionally strong response by the Saudi Arabian court to the broadcast news item, and yet they spoke as if all matters in any way connected with the question of Arabic broadcasting and its effects were within their grasp and that their opinion must automatically be the correct one.

Leeper saw that being able to tell what was news and what essential news, as he distinguished them, would not be a skill given to a single individual unless he had wide experience and knowledge of diplomatic matters. As he put it:

> This requires not only knowledge of the subject but some journalistic skill. Mr Calvert by himself has not got the latter quality and for that reason Mr Barker[59] (hitherto Diplomatic Correspondent of *The Times*) has on my recommendation been appointed by the BBC the chief Editor of all foreign language broadcasts. He can be relied upon to steer his course through any awkward situation. ...I believe that if we explained the situation to Mr Barker he would be able to give sensible advice as regards the editing of the broadcasts. Until the problem is tackled in some such way I am afraid that Mr Calvert will be completely at sea. The matter seems to me to be of some urgency. Perhaps Sir Laurence Oliphant would prefer to discuss it first with those concerned in the FO.[60]

This arrangement was put into effect and the results were an improvement. The Foreign Office news desk was immediately able to give up-to-date information about world affairs which the BBC had no knowledge of or access to otherwise. Indeed, seen in the terms of those who wish to claim that the BBC has forever been entirely free and clear from Government 'interference', the surviving evidence is very damaging indeed. Information and comment was usually provided over the telephone. Occasionally, by the nature of things, people were not available to speak to directly and on these occasions information in a letter was sent over by special messenger. Enough of these letters survive in the BBC's archives to establish the nature of the connection between the BBC and the Foreign Office on the question of foreign language broadcasts.

[59] Arthur E. Barker, son of Professor Ernest Barker. This account of his appointment differs from that given in Mansell, op. cit., p.96.
[60] Public Record Office: FO 395/557; P69/2/150.

A letter written to Barker on 23 May 1938 might seem on the face of it to be a normal press briefing, were it not for the circumstance in which it was written:

Dear Barker,

Herewith the text of the speech which Lord Plymouth hopes to make in the Lords tonight. The passages we are particularly keen you should refer to in the broadcast to South America are marked. We are *not* keen that the part referring to the differences of attitude between the United States and ourselves should be mentioned. I am arranging that the Empire News should be informed by telephone whether Lord Plymouth in fact makes the speech or not.[61]

A further, much fuller, letter on South American affairs written to Barker on 27 August makes the matter clear beyond any reasonable doubt:

Dear Barker,

With reference to our telephone conversation yesterday regarding Brazil's National Day, I think that you will be able to make use of the following.

Brazilian relations with this country during the past year can only be described as disreputable, and it is as usual difficult to find anything to say which, while being somewhere near the truth, will not be offensive.

It will, however, be safe for the BBC to state that the major event of the year was the assumption by President Vargas of the full executive power pending the holding of a plebiscite to decide the form of the constitution. An allusion might also be made to the fact that Senhor Oswaldo Aranha, who is now Minister for Foreign Affairs, is a man of proved ability who cannot fail to see that Brazil's foreign affairs are conducted with skill, intelligence and tact. Senhor Aranha was previously Brazilian Ambassador to Washington, and we should be glad if you would pay him a suitable compliment. The other major event of the year was, of course, the Brazilian default, to which unfortunately we can make no allusion. For padding I can only suggest that the BBC might refer to the fact that the Anglo-Brazilian Commission which had been delimiting the Brazil-British Guiana boundary has at last completed its work, which was extended over some ten years owing to the great difficulties of the *terrain*. An allusion might be made to the close cooperation maintained by the two commissions, each working on its own side of the frontier.

With regard to cultural relations it would, I think, be prudent to say very little as the Government has recently passed a decree against foreign organizations on Brazilian soil and although we understand

[61] BBC Written Archives Centre: R28/73/1.

that our cultural societies will not be affected I think it better not to refer to them. On the other hand, we learn that a very good impression has been created by the decision of the British Council to bring two distinguished young Brazilian scholars to this country for two years; one student will go to Oxford and the other to Cambridge.

Lord Willingdon will arrive at Santos on the 17 September and proceed to Sao Paolo where he will stay three days. From there he will fly to Rio de Janeiro sailing for England on 27 September. During July and August HMS Exeter and HMS Ajax have visited a number of Brazilian ports including Rio de Janeiro, Para, and Pernumbuco.[62]

This is, indeed, a triumph of concise diplomatic briefing which is of value even now for understanding the relationships between Britain and Brazil at the time. Nothing remotely resembling this could have been provided by the BBC themselves; it seems particularly churlish, after the passage of so much time, that those writing of the BBC's affairs decline even to acknowledge the existence of these briefings, perpetuating the fiction of their absolute independence of Government.

The experience of fighting Britain's first radio war can thus be seen to have left lasting marks on the way radio propaganda was conducted in Britain, both at the time and in the world war that was to follow. The Italian broadcasts to India represented one of the earliest public hearings of the Indian Independence Cause; the Arabic broadcasts, both British and Italian, form an important element in the background of a situation which is still with us today. In Britain Eden's political fortunes became tied with this war which had been given, at least on one side, his own name, that of 'Radio Eden' against Italy's Bari.

The ending of the Abyssinian war did not end the tension between Britain and Italy that had built up, as we have seen. There is clear evidence that Chamberlain attempted to bring about some alleviation of the situation, perhaps influenced by the knowledge that Britain had not been entirely blameless in the affair, but certainly very conscious of the danger of Britain's World War I ally falling permanently into the new Nazi Germany's camp.[63] There were direct complications to a simple recognition of the Italian conquest of Abyssinia; the Spanish Civil War had broken out in 1936 and Italy had made no secret of her involvement in the conflict and of the presence of Italian troops fighting for the Nationalists. More seriously, for Britain as a maritime nation, Italian submarines had begun their attacking and sinking of ships that were taking arms to the Republican forces, as we have seen.

[62] Ibid.
[63] Winston Churchill shared these worries. See below, pp.242-3.

These were mostly Russian ships, but British ships and crews had also suffered. Eden had given the radio war another twist when, at the successful conclusion of the Nyon Conference that put a stop to these submarine attacks, he had broadcast from Geneva over the League of Nations radio station an attack on Mussolini, calling him a pirate.[64] However true this description might have been, making the comment on the League of Nations radio was the height of folly, for the over-riding question of *Realpolitik* was how to bring Italy back into some sort of friendly or at least neutral relations with Britain. Chamberlain's efforts to undo the harm done by Abyssinia have been seen as the classic example of appeasement, almost the equal of the 'betrayal' at Munich. In fact his policy towards Italy was one far more likely to have succeeded than Eden's which seems to have been based on private considerations at least as much as on those of policy. When Eden resigned he did so over the question of Italy and the conflict between himself and Chamberlain over whether the time was ripe for negotiations to begin.[65] The mark left by the propaganda war is seen in Eden's address to the House of Commmons explaining his resignation:

> It will be known to the House that certain exchanges of view have been taking place between the Italian Government and HM Government in respect of the opening of conversations between the two Governments. The immediate issue is whether such conversations should be opened now. It is my conviction that the attitude of the Italian Government to international problems in general, and to this country in particular, is not yet such as to justify this course. Propaganda against this country by the Italian Government is rife throughout the world. I am pledged not to open conversations with Italy until this hostile propaganda ceases ...[66]

Later he referred to the Anglo-Italian Agreement of January 1937 saying:

---

[64] There is a recording of Eden's broadcast in the National Sound Archives: NSA LP1535.b.1.

[65] The question of Roosevelt's proposals for a conference or other steps was raised at the time and has been seen by many subsequently as one of the great missed opportunities of avoiding war. However, Hitler's response to his proposals the following year suggests that Chamberlain's view of the value of the proposed talks was probably the correct one. The age of the Superpowers was yet to come, and Hitler certainly did not see America in an equivalent role.

[66] Hansard, Vol. 332 cols 45-6.

That same agreement contained a clause – a specific clause – dealing with the cessation of propaganda, yet propaganda was scarcely dimmed for an instant.[67]

The propaganda war was the first reason given for his disagreement with Italy, then the ramifications of the Spanish Civil War, and the failure of Italy to agree to a scheme proposed by Britain for the withdrawal of Italian troops. Chamberlain made it quite clear that he was anxious lest the situation deteriorate into a war between Britain and Italy:

> All this time suspicion was growing in Rome that we did not want conversations and that we were engaged in a Machiavellian design to lull the Italians into inactivity while we completed our rearmament with the intention presently of taking revenge for the Italian conquest of Abyssinia. The result of this suspicion was a series of activities on the Italian side: the movement of troops, the stirring up of propaganda, and other matters ... [continuing later] I was convinced that a rebuff to the Italian expression of their desire that conversation should start at once would be taken by them as a confirmation of those suspicions which I have described, and I thought if that were the effect the result would be disastrous. It would be followed by an intensification of Anti-British feeling in Italy, rising to a point at which ultimately war between us might become inevitable.[68]

But in referring to the propaganda war neither he nor Eden touched on the actual propaganda problem, which was not Spain and the question of when Italy would remove her troops, but Palestine. For the propaganda war which Britain was waging through 'Radio Eden' was one which could not in the end be won. Increased Arab belligerence caused great difficulty for the British, but still more for the embryo Jewish homeland which had become an even greater focus of Jewish hope now that there had been a dramatic rise in anti-semitism throughout Europe.[69] Eden's policy could only result in an exacerbation of this war, a war never avowed in public at the time, and this must have been as clear to him as it was to Chamberlain. Eden's resignation, at which Grandi the Italian Foreign Minister had a ring-side seat, was unquestionably a victory for Italian diplomacy, but it also marked a positive achievement for Chamberlain who was able to begin what we would call today a damage control exercise calculated to calm down fears of imminent conflict in the

[67] Ibid., Vol. 332 col. 46.
[68] Ibid., Vol. 332 cols 57-60.
[69] For the question of anti-semitism and the plight of the refugees, see below, p.155f.

Mediterranean and perhaps in Europe as a whole. It is interesting to notice that the line followed by Burgess and E.H. Carr in the BBC's Mediterranean series was close to Eden's, and that Burgess edited his text to appease the Foreign Office who were trying to follow Chamberlain's policy.

There has recently been a strong attack on Eden and his hatred of Italy by Richard Lamb,[70] showing how this went on to affect matters in World War II. Some explanation of Eden's feelings on these matters can perhaps be found in the fact that he read Arabic at University. He would thus have been able to understand the Bari broadcasts which were extremely malicious and hostile. In addition he was taught at Oxford by a noted arabist, D.S. Margoliouth, who, unusually, was also profoundly sympathetic to the Jewish people in their suffering, and it is possible that Eden was concerned by affairs in the area in some profound way. Whatever the reason, he formed views which created this first radio war and greatly affected the line-up when a general war in Europe finally broke out.

The Foreign Office struggles to get Italy looked at in a more positive way failed. The legacy of the radio war that began in 1935 was a 'phoney war' that ended, in 1940, with war in earnest.

[70] Richard Lamb, *The Ghosts of Peace 1935-1945* (1987) passim.

6. The Secret Air Waves

The terms 'clandestine', 'pirate' and 'secret' used of radio transmitters have caused considerable confusion. The term clandestine is normally used for stations that are supposed to be in, say, Britain, when in fact they are in another country. 'Pirate' broadcasting would be used of broadcasts known to be in Britain, claiming that they were in Britain, but being operated illegally. Both would of course be 'secret' but this term could also properly be used of, say, broadcasts by the British Government made quite legally, but not avowed as being by them. All these kinds of broadcasts proliferated between the wars but especially in the thirties when short-wave broadcasting's potential was realized. To simplify matters all these broadcasts will be called secret broadcasts, a characteristic which they all shared. It has been said that the first secret radio broadcasts were those put out by Otto Strasser's[1] broadcasting station hidden in Czechoslovakia which many thought to be in South Germany, but this is known now not to be the case.

The earliest secret broadcasts of any consequence were some put out by small Communist stations in Europe, but the first that was detected on a large scale and alerted the British Government was a Congress Party radio station in India, discovered in 1932.[2] The system

[1] Otto Strasser (1897-1974). With his brother, Gregor Strasser, later murdered in the notorious 'night of the long knives' (see above, p.29), Strasser played a considerable part in the early history of the Nazi Party. However, he broke with Hitler before he came to power, running an outlawed leftward-looking version of the party, which came to be known as the Black Front. Although little or nothing has been said on the matter, he was closely involved with Britain after the outbreak of war (see below, p.193f.). The British public knew of him as an alternative German leader through the work of a somewhat naive admirer of his, Douglas Reed: see for example Reed's book *Nemesis? The Story of Otto Strasser* (1940). As will be seen, he was much involved in secret broadcasting.

[2] This station, run by the son of a former President of Congress, was discovered on 6 October 1932. Five men were found in the station, and a contemporary press report described the working of the system: 'These five men used to transmit their anti-British propaganda from the central wireless station, now raided, to a series of transmitting sub-stations. The sub-station transmitting sets were portable and kept ready to be shifted in case of a raid by the authorities.' Indians also broadcast from

had been set up at great expense and consisted of a main radio station outside Delhi which in turn broadcast to outlying stations signals that were re-broadcast over most of India. The main Delhi station was soon located and the arrest of those running the other stations soon followed. From this moment on the British Government were fully aware of the possibilities of this new form of warfare. The Indian opposition's attempts to get on the air did not stop there. Indian exiles formed a number of groups in America, particularly on the west coast, and took an active part in the first broadcasts from San Francisco to India after the setting up of the radio telephone links. A number of Indians on the 'Black List'[3] were known to be in America and receiving support from American sympathizers who viewed Britain's behaviour in India with disfavour; official British attempts to have this matter dealt with seem to have fallen on stony ground. It was decided that no practical moves to bring about the extradition of those responsible for the broadcasts were possible.[4]

In Europe the first in the field of secret broadcasting were the Communist Party. There were many reports of small Communist stations being in operation during the thirties; during a strike in Amsterdam it was found that instructions and talks for the strikers were being put out by an unofficial transmitter. Secret Communist transmitters were found in Vienna; others were spoken of in Paris.[5] At the

---

America on a number of occasions. Gandhi, for example, broadcast on 13 September 1931, to the annoyance of the Security Services.

[3] Although the phrase 'black list' has now passed into common usage and might be thought unlikely to refer to a real list, at the time the Indian Government kept just such a register and called it by that name. It gave by number in order of priority the names of Indians being sought by the Security Services. Thus there is a file in the Foreign Office index A2613/173/45: 'Deportation of Indians on Black List from USA: Dulip Singh No.27 on the Black List.' It was their knowledge of such matters that gave the Indian security officers, much despised by the younger generation of MI5 and MI6 officers who were recruited on the outbreak of war, their worries about Communism. The majority of Indians operating in exile in America were Communist Party supporters.

[4] For the eventual British answer to Indian broadcasts from Axis stations, see above, p.94.

[5] For example, on 7 December 1931 it was reported: 'A secret short-wave broadcasting station has been discovered in Vienna. It proved to be connected with an international Communist espionage centre equipped with the most up-to-date apparatus, so as to be able to remain in contact with its agents independently of the postal and telegraphic services. So far two men and three women have been arrested. A station had also been established at Vienna Neustadt.' Sometimes the stations had quite specific purposes. In July 1934 supposedly spontaneous riots broke out in Amsterdam after a lowering of unemployment benefit. However, a press report remarked: 'Efforts to find a clandestine wireless post with which the Communists are

centre of many of these networks of small stations was a German, Willi Münzenburg,[6] a Communist who worked for the Third International and acted as an oracle for many young Communists and fellow-travellers who were determined enough to make their way to the heart of what was happening in revolutionary Europe. It is illuminating that two of the original British experts in secret broadcasting, R.H.S. Crossman and Guy Burgess, moved in Münzenberg's circle. Others such as Sefton Delmer[7] knew a great deal about him and the work that he had been doing. Unfortunately the literature in English on Münzenberg's activities is not as extensive as that dealing with the man normally regarded as the 'father' of secret broadcasting, mentioned above, Otto Strasser. Münzenberg's career ended after the German invasion of France, but for a considerable time before that he had rejected his earlier loyalties and made major contributions to a non-Communist 'Freedom station' financed by the French Government.

Strasser's broadcasts began in 1934. The idea seems to have been suggested to him by a brilliant radio engineer, Rudolf Formis.[8] He had been a vigorous opponent of Hitler and had once found himself, as engineer at the radio station at Stuttgart, relaying a speech of Hitler's; without hesitation he had cut off the Fuhrer and claimed a technical fault. He made the mistake of trying to do the same thing again and was found out and arrested. Luckily he escaped and joined Otto Strasser and his illegal organization known as the 'Black Front', setting up the

---

broadcasting reports of the progress of the rioting have so far failed.' (Both reports are reprinted in Keesing's Archives.)

[6] Willi Münzenburg (1887-1940). There is a biographical sketch of Münzenberg in Anthony Cave Brown and Charles B. MacDonald, *On a Field of Red: The Communist International and the Coming of World War II* (1981), p.464f. See also above, p.27.

[7] Sefton Delmer, author of *Black Boomerang* (1962), perhaps the most quoted book on secret broadcasting, giving the first genuine insight into the activities of the Government Secret Radio Station at Woburn Abbey where he, R.H.S. Crossman and others developed innumerable 'German' and other secret stations. It has been suggested recently that, despite working for the *Daily Express*, he was an active Communist sympathizer, if not actually an agent (see for example Anthony Glees, *Secrets of the Service: British Intelligence and Communist Subversion 1939-51* (1987), p.117f. It seems to the present writer that Delmer's view, especially in later years, was the exact centre-of-the-road Moscow line.

[8] Rudolf Formis was an engineer who was politically conscious; he can be compared with Mosley's radio engineer P.P. Eckersley. Among Formis's achievements was his advanced use of pre-recorded Strasser speeches and similar material, giving the impression of a very large station with studios attached, when in fact he was operating in secret from a room in a riverside hotel. This method was perfected by the Joint Broadcasting Committee, whose German programmes were produced by Guy Burgess. See below, p.118.

station in Czechoslovakia. It succeeded brilliantly and for more than a year a stream of propaganda poured from the transmitter and soon built up a following in Germany. There were other German-language broadcasts from abroad, the Strasbourg broadcasts mentioned before, and Russian broadcasts, at first legitimately transmitted for the Germans living in the Volga Republic, descendants of those who had gone there in Catherine the Great's time, but Strasser's were in a different category as they represented a genuine opposition within Germany.[9]

The Gestapo decided to act. Within a short time they discovered the location of the transmitter. To make sure, agents were sent and obtained some photographs of Formis. When his identity was confirmed they returned, intending to kidnap him and take him across the Czech-German border; their plans went awry and Formis was killed then and there, one of the first to die solely for broadcasting.[10]

There were other secret stations operating within Czechoslovakia, one of particular interest because it was mobile. Many such stations claimed that they were mobile and transmitting from all parts of Germany with the Gestapo only a step behind; *Die Deutsche Freiheitswelle* apparently actually was such a station, run from a large Buick car which was finally caught by chance when someone tripped over the aerial wire leading from the car to an aerial while it was broadcasting, and took the car's number. The whole purpose of these broadcasts was to get the political message of German opposition parties into Germany when all other means were banned. The pretence that the station was actually in Germany helped from a propaganda point of view, but was of little real value since no actual contact could be made with the audience without revealing the whereabouts of the exiles.[11] But there were other more powerful groups of people who wished to get their opinions over to the German people at times of crisis, namely the sovereign powers who were at odds with Germany.

Britain discovered the use of secret broadcasting at the time of Munich. The first attempts by the BBC to broadcast to Germany had

[9] Or, at least, so Strasser and a large number of people in the British Foreign Office and Security Services thought: see below, p.189.

[10] Others were to follow: for example, Heinrich Grunow, pictured standing alongside Strasser by Formis's grave (see plate 17) was also to be killed running a station for Strasser at Le Cannet in France.

[11] This problem was shared by all secret organizations. The advantage of having even a handful of agents in the country you were trying to reach was demonstrated in Britain during the war when posters advertizing the New British Broadcasting Station, actually in Germany, appeared all over London and the home counties, causing the authorities acute apprehension. See below, p.220.

resulted in ludicrous failure. A rapid answer had to be found; with war imminent it was thought essential that Chamberlain's opinion should be got directly to the German people. The answer provided by the Secret Intelligence Service was to have his broadcast sent out in German over the commercial station known as Radio Luxembourg.[12] This broadcast on the medium wave and had a large following for its light music programmes in Germany. The result was a brilliant success and a change in Hitler's attitude was noticed which may well have been due to the German people hearing the British Government's actual position for the first time. The great results achieved by seemingly simple and inexpensive means were immediately attractive and Chamberlain used the method repeatedly later. Other speakers followed him and the first large-scale secret broadcasting by the British Government began. It must be made quite clear that these broadcasts had nothing to do with the BBC, who were formally unaware of their existence. The BBC official who produced their own German-language programmes remained unaware of them until the present day.[13]

There were two problems that this secret, illegal, broadcasting had to surmount. First there was the technical problem of getting the broadcasts to the station at Luxembourg. The early Chamberlain broadcasts were recorded on disc in London and the discs then taken over to Luxembourg by plane. This did not always work and another method, that of sending the recordings over land-lines to Paris where they were then sent on to Luxembourg by transmission or creation of discs which were then sent to Luxembourg, rapidly superseded it. The agency which dealt with this difficult and highly secret matter in Paris was the Travel and Industrial Development Association of Great Britain & Ireland, known as the Travel Association.[14] This had begun arranging broadcasts on its own account in 1935, at a time when the BBC were unable or unwilling to broadcast abroad other than in the Empire Service. Their activities in broadcasting seem to have remained unknown to the present day. In March 1939 the British

[12] Radio Luxembourg and the other commercial stations were far more successful than standard accounts of broadcasting in Britain would suggest. At weekends they regularly polled 70 per cent of the mass audience, and many famous media names such as Roy Plomley and Hughie Green appeared on them. An idea of the range of their programmes can be obtained from the magazine *Radio Pictorial* which rivalled the opposition *Radio Times*.

[13] Private information: interview with Leonard Miall. But see below, p.128.

[14] For an early account of their broadcasting activities, which were extensive, see a letter from the General Manager, L.A. de L. Meredith, to Lord Eustace Percy at the British Council, 17 July 1936, in the Public Record Office: BW2/29.

Embassy in Paris sent the Foreign Secretary, Lord Halifax,[15] a full report by H. Noble-Hall, the Director of the Paris Office of the Travel Association, which is worth quoting at length.

> As regards political broadcasting, almost all of Mr Chamberlain's speeches since September 1938 have been recorded and broadcast in English, French and German. More recently, the various appeals made by British statesmen for national service have been broadcast by Radio Luxembourg in French and German. This is true of speeches by Mr Neville Chamberlain, Sir John Anderson, Sir Frank Bowater and Mr Anthony Eden.
>
> Radio Luxembourg also transmitted a French translation of the essential passages of the speech delivered by Lord Baldwin at the University of Leeds.
>
> Radio Luxembourg's station 'La Voix du Monde' has been entirely at our service for the last six months for broadcasts by prominent Englishmen passing through Paris; and during the past twelve months, I have had the use of Radio Luxembourg whenever I wanted. I have spoken myself on several occasions, and they broadcast on a world-wide link-up two speeches by Lord Lloyd and Lord De la Warr.[16]

The report then went on to report what it candidly referred to, by contrast, as 'straight reporting'.

The second problem was that of the illegality of what the British Government were doing. This was not merely a technical or moral worry. As Vansittart remarked at the time:

> There was unfortunately no possibility of arguing that these exceptional arrangements were appropriate enough at the time of Munich but ought now to be dropped. There was no doubt that we were in the presence of a continuing crisis and it was our duty to use every means that came to our hand to convey the truth to the people of Germany.
>
> There was no going back to the days of May 1936 Conference with its ban on 'the systematic diffusions of programmes or communications which are specifically intended for listeners in another country'. As a matter of fact the May 1936 resolution had been disobeyed by a good many other countries. We were latecomers in this field.[17]

[15] Lord Halifax (1881-1959) had succeeded Anthony Eden as Foreign Secretary in 1938. He had earlier been Viceroy of India 1926-31; like others associated with Chamberlain and 'appeasement', he has been much maligned. He wrote *Fulness of Days* (1957).
[16] Public Record Office: FO 395/626; P781/6/150. Memorandum itself dated 28 February 1939.
[17] Public Record Office. CAB 27/641.

It was assumed, in other words, that all countries were now engaged in secret broadcasting[18] and that there was no need to worry about such matters as long as complete secrecy was maintained. The difficulty lay in the fact that the BBC had long been fighting to get Luxembourg, a 'pirate' station, off the air. They were losing well over half of their audience at the week-ends and felt the pressure acutely. Their objections took the practical form of complaint whenever any international body met, and, unfortunately for the Government, just such a meeting to determine allocation of wavelengths was shortly to take place at Montreux.

The problem was raised at a meeting of the Cabinet Committee on Overseas Broadcasting which asked two of the visitors to the Committee, Major L.D. Grand[19] and F.W. Phillips,[20] to find an answer to the problem. They met on 14 February and drew up a document which met all contingencies.

(a)   The Government should not disown the policy approved in Command Paper 5205 in regard to the broadcasting of advertizement programmes in English from Continental stations.

(b)   In reply to any Question in the House on the subject Ministers should say that the Government has made representations on several occasions to the two Governments concerned but without success; and that it does not consider that, for the present at any rate, any good purpose would be served by making further representations.

(c)   If the Government is approached by commercial interests or by foreign Governments in regard to any scheme for the establishment of additional advertizing stations in Continental countries it should adopt a neutral attitude. It should draw attention to any answer given in the House on the lines of (b)

[18] Surprisingly Germany does not seem to have become involved in secret broadcasting before the war. Her 'white' broadcasting from Zeesen was, of course, on a massive scale.

[19] Major [subsequently Major-General] Laurence Douglas Grand (1898-1975). When Grand submitted his entry for *Who's Who* towards the end of his life the sole occupation he listed was 'Director of Fortifications and Works, War Office 1949-52'. There are further references to him here. See below.

[20] Frederick William Phillips (1879-1956). He entered the Post Office in 1895 and rose to become Director of Telecommunications 1935-40. He acquired great experience of international conferences in the inter-war years when the structure of international broadcasting was built up, acting as head of the British delegations for the conferences at Brussels (1928), Prague (1929), Madrid (1932), Lucerne (1933) and Cairo (1938). In evolving the paper given here, he would have contributed the substance, Grand the *Realpolitik*.

and should state that it does not wish either to support or to oppose any project of the kind.

(d)   The British delegates to the Wavelength Conference which is to be held at Montreux early in March should be instructed as follows:

1. To refrain from raising the advertizing question, and, if consulted by other delegations, to discourage them from raising it.
2. If, however, the question is raised by others, to avoid taking any prominent part in the discussion.
3. To try to avoid a vote being taken on the subject, but if this cannot be avoided to abstain from voting.
4. To refrain from making an attack on Luxembourg in regard to their pirated wavelength.[21]

This document was accepted; its truly Machiavellian recommendations involving Government representatives telling a large number of the most blatant lies all bear the stamp of Grand's mind. In forwarding the document to Leeper he even signed himself 'D', alluding to the organization which he in fact represented. His knowledge of Luxembourg and illegal broadcasting was not merely theoretical or administrative, as his capacity when present at the committee, 'Communications Department Foreign Office', might imply. He had already himself made extensive use of Luxembourg for a much more objectionable and scurrilous kind of programme produced for him by his own private secret broadcasting station set up immediately after the Munich crisis which was usually referred to by its initials, the JBC.

The Joint Broadcasting Committee represents quite the most daring excursion by the British into secret illegal broadcasting, going at least as far as Otto Strasser and Münzenburg. There have even been doubts expressed that it was a genuine Government department, with suggestions that it was an entirely clandestine affair run by the Communist Party in Moscow and grafted onto another quite genuine committee with a similar name that had existed briefly a few years before but which had become moribund.[22] Stories of this kind were bound to spread when the secret side of the JBC became known to those who made use of its more avowable 'straight' activities which were later absorbed into the BBC's Transcription Service. But there are questions still unanswered today which leave even such an

[21] Public Record Office: FO 395/646; P616/80/150.

[22] This was the Joint Committee on Broadcasting, which held its first meeting in July 1936. Reference to it may be found in the Public Record Office: BW2/29 It held its meetings at the British Council, Chesham Place,

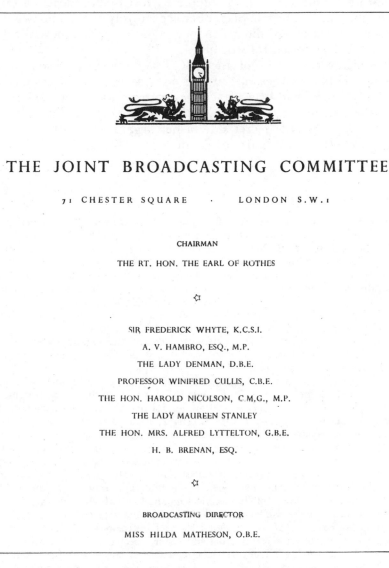

THE JOINT BROADCASTING COMMITTEE

71 CHESTER SQUARE   ·   LONDON S.W.1

CHAIRMAN

THE RT. HON. THE EARL OF ROTHES

✧

SIR FREDERICK WHYTE, K.C.S.I.

A. V. HAMBRO, ESQ., M.P.

THE LADY DENMAN, D.B.E.

PROFESSOR WINIFRED CULLIS, C.B.E.

THE HON. HAROLD NICOLSON, C.M.G., M.P.

THE LADY MAUREEN STANLEY

THE HON. MRS. ALFRED LYTTELTON, G.B.E.

H. B. BRENAN, ESQ.

✧

BROADCASTING DIRECTOR

MISS HILDA MATHESON, O.B.E.

The front cover of the only formal report produced by the Joint Broadcasting Committee. The committee shown here were selected by Miss Hilda Matheson at General Grand's suggestion and were described by her as 'biddable'. They never met as a committee, and it seems likely that only her friend Harold Nicolson knew what it actually did.

extraordinary suggestion as a complete Moscow broadcasting set-up working within the British Secret Service entirely open. The two main questions were: where did its money come from and how did Guy Burgess become so centrally involved?[23]

The clearest account of the JBC's activities was given by its Director, Hilda Matheson,[24] at the beginning of the war; Grand's Section 'D' Brief had been concerned with propaganda in Germany up to the outbreak of war and Matheson was clearly not sure what was to happen to the secret side of her organization, or indeed the entire group when war had broken out.

[23] When the BBC took over the JBC a report was drawn up which referred to funding from the Secret Intelligence Service (see below, p.199). However, this only began when war broke out. What is not clear is where the funds for its secret work before the war came from. Since this was set up by Grand, section 'D' of MI6 may have provided the funds. However, when the Foreign Office begun funding it on their vote at the start of the war, they appear to have known nothing of this. Actual funds were provided in gold sovereigns, which was, apparently, unusual. There is always the possibility that Grand was funding the operation from private funds, either his own or from elsewhere. The secretary of the Committee, Miss Hodgson, had been Grand's assistant in an earlier secret exercise in central Europe; her handling of this side of things ensured that they remained secret to all but Grand, who used the name Major Douglas when visiting the JBC.

On the second question it is, again, only possible to speculate with information available, in the hope that more will come to light as a result. Since Burgess was working as a courier for Horace Wilson (and Chamberlain, according to Tom Driberg: see *Guy Burgess: A Portrait with Background* (1956), p.40; see below, p.128) and since the arrangements for the transmission of Chamberlain's and the others' talks over Luxembourg were also made by Wilson with Grand, it seems likely that the introduction was made by those in the Security Services dealing with Wilson. Burgess was well known as a brilliant radio producer, and the value of secret stations, or the secret use of existing ones, had been made fully apparent. In addition Hilda Matheson was a close friend of Harold Nicolson and knew all about Burgess's skill as a producer, although she had left the Talks Department before he joined.

[24] Hilda Matheson (1888-1940), Broadcasting Director of the Joint Broadcasting Committee. From being secretary to Lady Astor, she went to the BBC as Talks Director 1927-32, leaving in controversial circumstances: a row with Lord Reith, and suggestions that she was having to leave because she was introducing left-wing speakers to the BBC. She then wrote a book for the Home University Library, *Broadcasting* (1933), which is still of considerable interest. In a chapter on Public Opinion she remarked (p.96): '... all broadcasting is ultimately a persuasive art, and Russia in her need has perceived more fully than most other countries the extent to which wireless may affect the smallest cog in the machine ... Often the actual expression is entrusted to a worker addressing fellow workers of his own area ... There are signs that other nations also are beginning to realise the way in which broadcasting can help to make the modern state work.'

I was asked by Major Grand in November 1938 if I would consider the possibilities of 'external broadcasting' (i.e. broadcasting from stations outside Great Britain, primarily to Germany but also to any other countries which proved available). I undertook to inaugurate such an experiment from the middle of February for a trial period of six months.

After an absence abroad of some three months, I returned to find a beginning had aleady been made with the commercial station of Luxembourg. This soon proved unprofitable and was dropped. I then advised the formation of a 'Good-will' Committee to sponsor broadcasts arranged through the broadcasting authorities of friendly countries, while the possibilities of other means of getting programmes into Germany were explored. The J.B.C. was the result.

Our activities in neutral and friendly countries were reported to the Foreign Office (Mr Leeper) and our preparations for recorded programmes in Germany were arranged with Major Grand.

It was made clear to me from the beginning that our functions in wartime would be:

(a) To prepare programmes for use in enemy countries on the instructions of Sir Campbell Stuart's department of the Ministry of Information.

(b) To prepare programmes for use in neutral countries, but aimed primarily at a German public, also on the instructions of Sir Campbell Stuart.

(c) To prepare programmes for use in neutral and friendly countries to the specification of Mr Macadam's department of the Ministry of Information.

It was agreed that a broadcasting unit was required with a personnel capable of covering these different activities, and I was authorised to assemble such a unit under the auspices of the J.B.C.

The plans for broadcasts to Germany were distinct from those openly carried out by the J.B.C.

A specially designed mobile recording outfit was made for the unit, and a large supply of German-made musical records was selected and bought.[25]

What Hilda Matheson did not make clear here was that broadcasts for Germany had already taken place on an extensive scale using the equipment prepared at the JBC's premises in Chester Square. This included not only portable recorders but an original form of portable transmitter which included a record player. While the JBC sent out programmes and discs to neutral countries they only *prepared* the German ones. Both before and after the war began these were actually

[25] Public Record Office: T 162/858/E39140/4.

delivered by the Security Services, most probably others in Grand's organization.

The secret section of the JBC produced records, at first only in German, which could be played on this equipment in Germany itself, or from neighbouring countries. The result hoped for was a *'Freiheitsender'* which would appear to be, not a mobile small transmitter, but a full-scale secret broadcasting station in Germany. The records contained not merely propaganda but variety programmes with the latest German hit songs.[26] The programmes were produced by Guy Burgess assisted initially by an Austrian refugee, Paul Frischauer, and his wife.[27] The precise extent of their activities remains a closely guarded secret. It is clear from a minute by Leeper to the Strategical Appreciation Sub-Committee of the Committee of the Imperial Defence that Government broadcasting units existed in Germany doing secret work. Talking about the ways that a message from the Prime Minister could be got into Germany he wrote that a pre-recorded message should be

> got ready for smuggling into Germany and then broadcast inside Germany. This is, I understand, technically possible. There are mobile units inside Germany today and contact with them can be established or a new mobile unit can be created.[28]

He had earlier referred to the possibility of a transmitter sending the message from a ship in the North Sea, clearly a reference to the *Freiheitsender* that was known to be operating there.[29] It is difficult to

[26] It was these that were referred to by Hilda Matheson at the end of her memorandum (above, p.117). When the JBC was absorbed into the BBC's London transcription service they passed to the BBC, where they were used for a number of purposes (private information: interview with Leonard Miall).

[27] Paul Frischauer (1898–1977). Frischauer had come to England some years before and formed part of an anti-Hitler group in London. How he became involved, and sufficiently trusted, to take part in the production of the highly secret JBC material is not known. In fact he was the cause of one of the JBC's few security breakdowns. His wife was Yugoslavian, and it was discovered by chance that she was in contact with that country's espionage service and sending details of the JBC's activities through their diplomatic bag. Faced with this disclosure, Grand arranged for them to be removed from the country and sent to South America. They duly departed and subsequently dealt with the JBC's affairs in South America. There is a file in the Foreign Office index referring to a request by Frischauer to use the British diplomatic bag to get his information back to the UK! See Public Record Office: A 4333/4333/51, 'Work of Mr Paul Frischauer: proposed transmission of reports by Foreign Office bag from Brazil, 1940'.

[28] Public Record Office: FO 395/647B; P1402/105/150.

[29] This ship became famous when it was raided by the German authorities. At least one commercial company attempted to get a ship flying the Panama flag to start

see what Leeper could possibly be referring to by 'mobile units inside Germany today' if they were not those established by Grand through the JBC.

Luxembourg was not the only commercial channel available, but it was decided to avoid using others after some difficult experiences at Liechtenstein and Strasbourg, the former involving Burgess. As a Foreign Office memo remarked:

> It would not do, however, to encourage the establishment of fresh advertizing stations in foreign countries. If pacts were made with the various groups which were eager to engage in such activities, the fact that the British Government's views had altered would soon become known. There would indeed be every chance of the Luxembourg Government's taking alarm, as a result of threats from Herr Hitler or otherwise, and refusing to permit its station to be used in the manner desired by the Foreign Office.
>
> There was no use in pursuing the suggestion of making use of the stations at Strasbourg[30] and Liechtenstein. Strasbourg was a French Government station and Liechtenstein was under the control of the Swiss Government who manage all the postal telegraphic and telephonic services of Liechtenstein.[31]

These worries were by no means theoretical. After an earlier attempt had been made to use the radio station at Neuchatel a cable had been received from the British Minister at Berne:

---

broadcasting, but this possibility only became a reality many years later with Radio Caroline. Ellic Howe, in *The Black Game* (1982), records the account of Werner Röder that the Deutsche Freiheitspartei ran a broadcasting station on board a fishing vessel 'in the English channel'. Prominent in this party was Dr Carl Spiecker (1888-1953) who later worked with Sefton Delmer at Woburn. If this is correct, Leeper may have been referring directly to this station, for Spiecker (also known as Mr Turner) was one of those Germans supported by Vansittart and his circle and well known to Leeper, Claude Dansey and the Foreign Office. However, the idea that the Foreign Office was supporting a dissident German party before the war, even backing a transmitter on the high seas, is so serious that direct evidence must be required to establish it as a fact – evidence which, in the absence of a Freedom of Information Act in the United Kingdom, is never likely to appear. Howe gives 1938 as the date for the station – actually it was 1939; the temptation, of course, is to see the JBC as providing material for the station, but this would be to place great weight on Leeper's remarks. If Frischauer were part of Dr Spiecker's circle this would provide some circumstantial evidence. For information about exile German groups, see Anthony Glees, *Exile Politics during the Second World War* (1982).
[30] Using Strasbourg would have been, to say the least, counter-productive. See above, p.33.
[31] Public Record Office: CAB 27/641.

Federal Councillor in charge of Posts and Telegraphs, who is ordinarily friendly to us, tells me that he is opposed to the project for a radio station at Neuchatel. He is struck by the fact that we are so anxious to establish radio stations so close to Germany and does not understand why we cannot circulate advertisements to England from our own stations. He expressed the view that Germans may soon object to Luxembourg station.[32]

The Cabinet committee had received a report that referred specifically to some of the groups who would be likely to approach the Government saying

...use could very likely be made of offers by any reputable British concerns, who, as in the case of Mr R. Boothby's group[33] ... wish to interest themselves in broadcasting from foreign stations and have offered to co-operate with HMG as regards the matter broadcast in foreign languages and who ask only that HMG should cease actively to oppose sponsored broadcasts in English from foreign stations.[34]

Boothby's group was typical of those who urgently wanted to get involved in commercial broadcasting, but it is still not clear today exactly which group he represented. In the case of Liechtenstein the first approach to the Government had been made by a group, of which Boothby later became a Director, called David Allens.[35] There is no evidence of Boothby's involvement at this time, as the person who made the approaches was P.P. Eckersley.[36]

As we shall see later, this group did not in fact have an autonomous existence, for it had been created with great secrecy by Sir Oswald

---

[32] Quoted by F.W. Phillips, ibid.

[33] There is no reference in Boothby's volumes of autobiography to his interest in broadcasting at this time.

[34] Public Record Office: FO 395/646.

[35] The firm published privately *David Allens: The History of a Family Firm* (1957). Although the book is ascribed on its title page to W.E.D. Allen, it was actually largely written by Allen's old friend Kim Philby shortly before his last return to the Middle East en route to Moscow. For W.E.D. Allen, see below, p.122n41.

[36] Peter P. Eckersley (1892-1963). The BBC's first Chief Engineer, he was a victim of the Corporation's strict moral code at the time and was obliged to resign after being cited in a divorce case. He went to work for Sir Oswald Mosley after a period working on private experimental ventures. He had shown an early enthusiasm for radio when at Bedales which translated itself into brilliant ability. His second wife, Frances Dorothy Eckersley, was a member of the literary Stephen family; she broadcast for Germany during World War II (see below). Eckersley wrote an informative book, *The Power Behind the Microphone* (1941). His brother, Roger Eckersley, also worked for the BBC as Director of Programmes, Assistant Controller and Chief Censor, and was author of *The BBC and All That* (1946).

Mosley. Eckersley was a full-time employee of one of Mosley's companies, 'Air-time'[37] although this was not revealed when he approached the International Broadcasting Union for permission to attend meetings on the strength of the promise of a licence that he had obtained from the Liechtenstein authorities. The secretary of the Authority was in close contact with the BBC and wrote advising them of what was happening. What followed is not clear, but, when a licence was finally granted, it was to another company entirely, led by a young Cambridge engineer, Peter Hope. Hope was actually working for Richard Gambier-Parry,[38] in charge of MI6's wireless communications. In company with Harold Robin, an engineer, he began creating the station, with a secret section. The confusion which the Liechtenstein authorities must have felt, expressed in the complaints of the Swiss authorities, must have been compounded when Grand's man, Burgess, also appeared on the scene. There are accounts of a row between the two organizations: it was considered foolish of the MI6 men to order their equipment from Germany, but clearly this was more than sensible for a station which was intended to be known as a German station.[39] The special equipment provided by Burgess's JBC would have been an open announcement of the existence of illegal activity associated with Britain, had the station been detected and raided by the authorities or by a Gestapo raid, as happened at Formis's station. If Burgess was directly under Russian control this would have been the clearest indication that he was acting as an agent provocateur, attempting to foster rows between Britain and Germany.

The initial approach that had lead to this classic crossing of wires had been made by Mosley's organization. As mentioned above Mosley was effectively banned from the British air waves. We shall now examine his secret project for broadcasting to Britain. Mosley

[37] There is an account of this company in Nicholas Mosley, *Beyond the Pale* (1983), pp. 134-7. There is also reference to it in Mosley's interrogation at the time of his 18B appeal.

[38] Sir Richard Gambier-Parry (1894-1965). From 1926 to 1931 he worked for the BBC in the Public Relations Department under Gladstone Murray (see above, p.15). He became Director of Communications to the Foreign Office in 1947, having being 'attached' to them since 1938 in the capacity mentioned here.

[39] See, for example, the brief account in Tom Driberg, *Guy Burgess* (1956), p.55: 'At one time it was intended to set up an "underground" wireless station in Liechtenstein, and Guy was sent there to see about it. He found that a foolish fellow-agent had, unfortunately, ordered the machinery and equipment from Germany. He therefore advised against the project and it was abandoned.' Driberg places this event in his chapter on the war years, 'Cloak, Dagger, Microphone'. There is, however, no doubt whatsoever that it took place before the war.

was in exactly the same position as Otto Strasser and other political exiles in Europe, but on the other side. At his interrogation Mosley steadfastly denied that he had any other intention in setting up his station than the perfectly laudable one, shared by all other commercial operators, of making money.[40] He had first heard of the radio advertizing business from W.E.D. Allen who had been a member of the original New Party which preceded the British Union.[41] Many advertizing firms were closely involved with commercial broadcasting from the continent, and David Allens intended to get involved in this. They had started to build a station in the Republic of Andorra when civil war broke out in Spain and halted development for three and a half years. Meanwhile they had hired time on Radio Toulouse, beginning their programmes with a talk on Anglo-French friendship written by Winston Churchill.[42] This was barely adequate, as the official history of the firm describes, without reference to Mosley:

> It was an enterprise which appealed to Geoffrey Allen's flair for rapid and spacious action. Peter Eckersley, formerly Chief Engineer of the BBC, a scientist of brilliant gifts and adventurous spirit, was engaged as technical adviser; and the company, for a time, ran its own six-passenger plane. Never reluctant to travel, the Allen brothers scoured Europe from Finland and Latvia to Greece and Portugal. Islands were not ignored. The authorities in Ireland and Iceland were canvassed, and visits were even paid to Sark and Lundy.[43]

Allens rejected Sark, but Eckersley could see the advantages of an island when it came to signal transmission: the rapid loss of signal strength which occurred over land was absent over water and a

[40] Had Mosley been successful in getting his station on the air he would have made a fortune. It is quite impossible to believe that he would not have channelled this money towards his political ends, just as Stafford Cripps, for example, donated the very large sums he earned at the Bar to the political organizations he fostered. What is suggested below is that Mosley's intentions went far beyond mere patronage and that he would appear with political messages on the channels, just as Cripps appeared in *Tribune* and on the platform of groups he funded.

[41] William Edward David Allen (1901-1973), scholar and businessman, author of *The Turks in Europe* (1922), *History of the Georgian People* (1932), *The Ukraine: A History* (1940), *The Russian Campaigns of 1941-5* (2 vols 1944, 1946), *Caucasian Battlefields* (1953), *Problems of Turkish Power in the Sixteenth Century* (1963) and, for the Hakluyt Society, *Russian Embassies to the Georgian Kings* (1970). With his wife Nathalia he gathered together an important collection of Russian ikons now at the National Gallery Dublin, exhibited as a collection at his request. For his involvement with Mosley, see Nicholas Mosley, op.cit., and below, p.230f.

[42] I have not been able to identify this talk.

[43] W.E.D. Allen [and Kim Philby], *David Allens: The History of a Family Firm* (1957), p.277.

transmitter on Sark would have given strong coverage over the whole of southern England. He discussed this with Mosley, whom he was by then working for full time, who immediately saw the possibilities. Mosley also succeeded in obtaining an introduction to the son of the Dame of Sark, L.C. Beaumont.[44] It became clear that, from a legal point of view, there would be no possibility of interference from the British Government or the BBC, and Mosley set up a company with a contract to broadcast from Sark signed by Beaumont as its principal asset.

Mosley's over-riding idea was to get similar sites on the other sides of Britain so that his programme would be able to give as good a nation-wide coverage as the BBC from their transmitters on the mainland. He made preliminary approaches for a transmitter site in Ireland, but then turned his attention to the North Sea. A site such as Heligoland, once a British possession, now belonging to Germany, seemed an ideal prospect. Others had seen the potential of such a location but the German Government had proved impervious to all attempts by commercial companies to become involved in commercial international broadcasting. Indeed the whole concept of that kind of commercial activity was alien to the National Socialist creed, besides being made extremely difficult to arrange financially by the international boycott against Germany.

Mosley decided to make the attempt, basing his hopes at least partly on his known sympathy with the Fascist cause in Italy. He had himself met Hitler on one occasion, but there seems to have been no active connection between the British Union and the German National Socialists in Britain for him to use. There was, however, a domestic connection, as Mosley's sister-in-law, Unity Mitford,[45] was a devoted admirer of Hitler who was frequently in his company. Lady Mosley often accompanied her sister on these visits, and a preliminary approach yielded encouraging results. Nothing was heard for some time, but then, in 1938, specific arrrangements were made. It was agreed that Germany would provide a site for the transmitter at Nordeich and that German engineers would build it. In exchange Mosley's company would pay royalties and liquidate the construction costs over a ten-year period. All payments were to be made in sterling,

---

[44] Lionel C. Beaumont; the introduction had been made by a mutual friend, Dudley M. Evans (see below, p.216n2). In his interrogation by the 18B committee Evans stated that Beaumont had terminated his agreement with Mosley shortly after the outbreak of war. Although Mosley did not refer to this at any stage and there is no reference to it elsewhere, Evans's statements are clear and precise. See Public Record Office: HO 45/25727.

[45] For Unity Mitford, see David Pryce-Jones, *Unity Mitford: A Quest* (1976).

a particular attraction to the German treasury because of the boycott. The agreement was duly signed and construction of the station started.

As with so many other public works projects, for this was in effect what this was, there were delays. The station was still not finished at the outbreak of war, although it later went on to broadcast to Britain and elsewhere as a normal German station. The fact that this secret station never broadcast did not prevent its existence being used against Mosley and his movement, as we shall see later.

This was not, it seems, Mosley's only attempt at getting round the ban on use of the radio. There was a further more sophisticated attempt of which nothing has been known until now. Nothing was said about it directly at Mosley's interrogation although he was asked a question, seemingly at random, about one of the principal participants in the scheme, Oliver Hoare,[46] brother of Samuel Hoare, Foreign Secretary at the time of the Hoare-Laval pact.[47]

Radio had great advantages over nearly all other means of communication on a mass scale, but it did have one serious disadvantage. In the case of total war it was possible for programmes to be jammed or, if a country was actually invaded, for vital transmitters to be destroyed. The German government made some arrangements for countering this, using telephone lines to create an emergency wire rediffusion service. Mosley's engineer Eckersley evolved a similar system for use in Britain. It was based on the electricity mains supply, a signal being imposed on the mains electricity coming into a dwelling which was then received on a special set. There was no tuning facility, as with an ordinary radio. Instead four channels could be selected by a switch; in addition a signal could be sent even when the set was switched off that would operate an alarm to let people in a household know that a message of importance was about to be transmitted so that they could then turn the set on and be sure of hearing it. This set had many advantages over radio, and all the problems that could be envisaged through war conditions were dealt with.

Eckersley approached the Government in partnership with Oliver

[46] Oliver Vaughan Gurney Hoare (1882-1957). A sportsman in early life, who played rackets for Harrow in 1900 and tennis for Oxford in 1904, he later went into business.

[47] The Hoare-Laval pact was an early example of diplomacy clashing with the new strengths of the media. A leak before the discussions started caused such an outcry among a public unaware of the true background to the situation and unenlightened by the press and radio, that the pact had to be dropped. This can now be seen as unfortunate, a step on the road to World War II that might well have been avoided.

Hoare, who had also previously worked for David Allens. The plan was put forward and given favourable consideration at first. It was then dropped by the Government entirely. There is no sign in the papers in the Public Record Office that deal with the project that it was referred to the BBC.[48] It must be assumed, if only because Hoare's name was raised in the Mosley interrogation, that the identity of Eckersley's and Hoare's backer had become known to the authorities. Had the project succeeded, Mosley could at any time have gained access to a transmitter chain that would have given him immediate entry to every home in the kingdom with a mains electricity supply, a facility which would have been extremely useful to him in May 1940.

Oliver Hoare, like Boothby, also approached Lord Perth about a new radio system that would unite the benefits of all commercial channels and be able to reach the entire population of the United Kingdom. No action was taken, and the matter was not mentioned specifically at Mosley's interrogation when Hoare's name occurred, but it is difficult to see what other system than Mosley's would answer the description he gave of its advantages. There is direct evidence that Eckersley was in continuous communication with Mosley, and he received a capital sum from him when his contract was terminated at the outbreak of war. The case with Oliver Hoare is not so clearcut. Other purely commercial concerns made exactly similar approaches to the Government, some of an overtly 'political' nature.

In July 1939, for example, Lord Perth wrote to R.A. Butler:[49]

A question arose at the meeting at the Home Office over which Sir Samuel Hoare presided this morning as to the possible utilization of certain radio stations which were of a commercial character particularly at St. Juan les Pins and at Ljubljana. These were under the control of a Mr Plugge,[50] who was ready to place them at the Government's disposal for any purpose which might be desired. Meanwhile Mr Plugge is going ahead on his own and building up what he called a good-will asset for these stations by musical and variety

---

[48] Public Record Office: FO 395/666; P2936/P3351/2930/150.

[49] Richard Austen Butler (1902-1982). At this time Under-Secretary at the Foreign Office. For the first biography of him to have been written with access to his personal and political papers, see Anthony Howard, *RAB: The Life of R.A. Butler* (1987).

[50] Captain L.F. Plugge MP, the founding father of commercial broadcasting in Britain through his International Broadcasting Company. The aptness of his name for such a venture has caused him to be treated with some humour. In fact he was a brilliant pioneer in the field, and his numerous questions in Parliament on all aspects of radio give considerable insight into the development of radio, as well as reflecting his own thoroughness and initiative.

entertainments. He is doing this of his own accord and no Government commitments have been taken towards him.[51]

Lord Perth did not mention whether Hoare's brother's interest in a rival concern was disclosed when the matter was discussed! It is clear though that Plugge was engaged on an exactly similar business and, as a direct rival of Allens, some of whose employees had previously worked for him, he would seem to have known exactly what was afoot. It was precisely the charge against Mosley that, while building up 'a good will asset for these stations by musical and variety entertainments' he would make them available for other purposes but not, as Plugge suggested, the Government's.[52]

In later life Sir Oswald Mosley identified as a spy within the British Union W.E.D. Allen himself. Certainly there was a mystery about the subsequent role of Allen in the war. Despite the fact that it was his bank account through which Mussolini's assistance to the British Union was channelled, and the fact that he seems to have kept this from the Security Services, he was not detained under 18B(1a).[53] There were other candidates, including, as we shall see, William Joyce, Mosley's propaganda chief, and his second-in-command, Neil Francis-Hawkins, but whoever was responsible, it is clear that the authorities knew about Mosley's contract with Hitler and the fact that the German Government were building an entire radio station for him. This alone would have provided moral justification, in their eyes, for the wilder antics of Grand, Burgess and the others though they could not have known of Burgess's ulterior purposes.

The effect of the British secret broadcasts was considerable. There was immediate response expressed through the British authorities in Berlin, which was conveyed to the Cabinet. There was also a response in the German press and, more directly, in pointed references by the German leaders to British propaganda. Writing on 16 June 1939 an official of the British Embassy in Berlin drew attention to direct attacks on members of the Foreign Office news department:

> In my letter of June 15th, I gave you a summary of an article in the 'Nachtausgabe' directed against Sir R. Vansittart. This had been followed up by a personal attack in the 'Völkischer Beobachter'

[51] Public Record Office: FO 395/631; P3176/6/150.

[52] The word 'charge' is used figuratively here – there was never a charge against Mosley of any kind, or against any of the people detained under the Emergency Powers Regulation 18B(1a).

[53] Reference was made to this in Mosley's interrogation. It may of course have been that the Security Services were aware of Allen's key role in getting money from Mussolini to the British Union, but if so they did not inform the Committee

[People's Observer] on Leeper. The ambassador does not wish to report these personal attacks officially, but considers that you should know they are going on.

Referring to the Prime Minister's statement in the House on June 15th regarding the establishment of what is called a Propaganda Department[54] in the Foreign Office, the London correspondent of the Völkischer Beobachter writes that the active and leading part to be played in the new department by men like Leeper throws significant light on the character of the new office. Leeper, an Australian by birth, is described as belonging to the section of Whitehall which has always demanded a policy directed against Germany.[55]

There were also frequent attacks against the British propaganda put out on Radio Luxembourg, both in speeches by the German leaders and in the press. The Foreign Office News Department on occasion referred such complaints to the BBC for denial, knowing full well, what the BBC did not, that their source was elsewhere.[56]

The programmes put out over Luxembourg by Grand's Section 'D', the JBC, were extremely secret, but the transmissions of Chamberlain's speeches were sometimes actually recorded on BBC premises. A close examination of the BBC's archives has produced evidence that, when the BBC studios were used, the engineers carried out the work in strict secrecy and frequently without the knowledge of the senior staff responsible. There was a breakdown in the arrangements for transmission of a German translation of Chamberlain's speech of 17 March 1939 which conveys the realities of the situation. The junior engineer in the BBC wrote a worried internal memo to his superior:

An attempt at secrecy – probably very necessary for political reasons – led to an unnecessary flap last Friday night, the 17th.

Apparently DDG, C(P), and Mr J.B. Clark made an arrangement with the Prime Minister or one of his secretaries that his speech in full

---

examining Mosley. Allen is not mentioned in any of the popular works on MI6. However, he is mentioned as head of station in Ankara in James Fox, *White Mischief* (1982), p.197. See biographical note above, p.122n41.

[54] This was the department that succeeded the Vansittart Committee. It was presided over by Lord Perth and became the Ministry of Information, in essence, when war broke out. It was considered particularly important that the existence of an embryo Ministry of Information should not become known, as this would be taken as a sign that war was imminent. Some Ministry of Information note paper was actually prepared and used in July, but immediately suppressed; I have seen one sheet of it used at this time, bearing the signature 'Michael Balfour'.

[55] Public Record Office: FO 395/647D; P2533/105/150. 16 June 1939.

[56] See below, p.159.

should be translated into German, recorded on discs and then flown over to Luxembourg for transmission at 07.00 the following day. This was kept so secret that neither the control room, R.P.Ex nor Maida Vale had any knowledge of it. A certain Major Skitt (?) who apparently spoke with the authority of the Prime Minister started ringing up the Control Room after the Prime Minister's speech on Friday evening, wanting them to make line arrangements for the playing of the records to Luxembourg the following morning as, due to one thing and another, they were not going to be ready to be flown over as originally intended. The Control Room knew nothing about this ... Thus you will see that junior engineers were at the eleventh hour rushing about so far as they could see to do things for a sponsored station [i.e. Luxembourg] without a word from any of their seniors that it was all in order ... I fully appreciate the need for secrecy on occasions such as this but would submit that those who decide to keep it hush-hush should, before they make their decision bear in mind the complications which result ...[57]

It has not been possible to identify Major Skitt. However, it is clear from other BBC memoranda that Sir Horace Wilson[58] either gave Skitt his authority or dealt with the BBC and Luxembourg himself. Burgess's statement to Tom Driberg, that he acted directly for Chamberlain as an intermediary, suggests that he might have been involved, as he was doing the 'secret' work for the JBC and Grand throughout this period. The spectacle of Burgess acting secretly for Sir Horace Wilson is not edifying. However it is clear that Leeper and the Foreign Office were not fully aware of the procedure followed. The Director of Outside Broadcasts, writing to the BBC's controller of programmes, reported a meeting at the Foreign Office on 21 December 1938

At a meeting at the Foreign Office on Monday afternoon Leeper spoke to me about the importance attached by the Government to the P.M.'s statement in the House that afternoon on Foreign Affairs. In response to a question I told Leeper that in the past arrangements for Luxembourg had originated in conversations between Downing Street (Sir Horace Wilson) and Major Skitt.[59]

[57] BBC Written Archives Centre: E1/1051, 20 March 1939.

[58] Sir Horace John Wilson (1882-1972). Entered the Civil Service 1900; Permanent Secretary, Ministry of Labour 1921-30; Chief Industrial Advisor to the Government 1930-39. Wilson has become known as Chamberlain's *eminence grise* throughout this period. His fall from power when Churchill became Prime Minister in 1940 was spectacular. 'Major Skitt' was possibly an alias of Grand's.

[59] BBC Written Archives Centre: E1/1051.

Vansittart had made it quite plain that Chamberlain both knew and approved of these steps:

> The Prime Minister has taken a great interest in it and had directed that every effort should be made to get the British view into Germany by wireless ...[60]

Vansittart's active involvement in this sphere suggests again that his alleged falling from favour and removal from his post of Permanent Head of the Foreign Office and 'promotion' to the newly created post of Chief Diplomatic Adviser to the Government needs to be re-examined. At meetings of the secret Cabinet Committee on Overseas Broadcasting Vansittart is specifically described as representing the Secretary of State for Foreign Affairs. The permanent Head of the Foreign Office, Sir Alexander Cadogan, was not present at these meetings. On other secret matters dealing with preparations for war it was Vansittart who dealt with Sir Campbell Stuart, not Cadogan, and Vansittart appears to have dealt directly with Chamberlain or Sir Horace Wilson. This extraordinary situation was in itself a reflection of the political nature of the confrontation between Germany and Britain, and the very possibility of political confrontation was due not to the old-fashioned printed propaganda but to the new world of foreign-language radio broadcasting. It was this secret war conducted by Britain no less than Germany, Italy and Russia that provided a seed bed for the World War itself.

Chamberlain's close involvement shows clearly that his policy of appeasement was only one side of his character and that he was quite capable of taking a tougher line. And there was more to his actions than mere contingency planning, for all issues between Britain and Germany could became a basis for a radio war out of which a real conflict could emerge, regardless of any formal cause.

[60] Public Record Office: CAB 27/641.

7. War Declared by Radio

The events leading up to Britain's declaration of war on Germany on 3 September 1939 must be among the most closely examined and frequently described sequences of events in English history. Yet, when looked at from the point of view of radio broadcasting, there are surprising and important omissions. The long run of broadcasts of speeches by Chamberlain, Eden and others in German from Radio Luxembourg were secret by their very nature, and were successfully concealed from the British public and later commentators. But other important matters have simply been ignored. A conspicuous example is the broadcast by the Duke of Windsor from Verdun in May 1939, when war seemed a matter of days away, appealing for world peace. It was heard by over 400,000,000 people all over the world, each intensely interested to hear the first words spoken in public by the Duke since his abdication speech, which had obtained a similar world audience. In Britain the broadcast was banned and has almost never been referred to since.[1] Another case was the proposal, as a means of dealing with radio and other propaganda questions, of an Anglo-German Cultural Agreement,[2] put forward by the German Government in January 1939 and rejected out of hand by the Foreign Office to the great annoyance of the officials in the British Embassy in Berlin, who were fully aware of the difficulties with Hitler caused by such questions, out of all proportion to their actual value. These and other events deserve further description and a place in the chronology of events leading up to the declaration of war which makes their importance quite plain.

The seemingly inevitable path to war began with the crisis in Czechoslovakia the previous year. After the Anschluss, the union of Austria with Germany in a new Greater Germany, commentators immediately turned to Czechoslovakia as the next most likely trouble spot.

The problem of the German minority in the new State of

[1] There is a recording of the speech in the National Sound Archives: NSA LP20246.b.1.
[2] See below, p.147.

Czechoslovakia had been realized at the time of Versailles. The minority was far from insignificant – more than 3,000,000 people – and they were concentrated in large areas close to the German border rather than spread out through the country as a whole. Masaryk, the founding father of Czechoslovakia,[3] had thought that the new state would be more stable without them, and Lloyd George had pointed to the inevitability of conflict within the new state as soon as Germany developed after the war.[4]

The educated British public were first made aware that the situation was very much a living one when the leader of the Sudeten German Party, Konrad Henlein,[5] had visited Britain on a speaking tour in 1935. Col. Christie[6] had introduced Henlein to Vansittart, who in turn had arranged for him to give a talk to the Royal Institute of International Affairs. The discussion which followed the talk was frank, and one impassioned outburst by a Jewish spectator first brought to the audience's attention the fact that Henlein's party was Nazi in sympathy and anti-semitic.[7]

In the next few years the problem developed continuously with discussions between Henlein and Benes taking place frequently over the question of Sudeten grievances. Violent outbreaks were common, resulting in deaths on both sides. Trivial matters were exaggerated out of all proportion; the world learnt, for example, that the Sudeten Germans traditionally wore white stockings and that the Czechs had a mind to put a stop to such things! White stockings were henceforth banned from any Sudeten leg; Hitler actually mentioned this serious

---

[3] H.A.L. Fisher remarked that Czechoslovakia was the first state in the world to be created by propaganda (quoted in R.H. Bruce Lockhart, *Comes the Reckoning* (1947), p.130) and this propaganda was carried on by Masaryk, largely in America. His son Jan Masaryk played an important role as Czechoslovakia's Ambassador in London and is frequently mentioned by Lockhart. See also David Irving, op.cit.

[4] See David Lloyd George, *The Truth About the Peace Treaties*, 2 vols (1938) for a full discussion of this question.

[5] Konrad Henlein (1898-1945). After service in World War I Henlein worked as a bank clerk with an amateur interest in gymnastics. In 1931 he was appointed leader of the German Gymnastic Union in Czechoslovakia – this represented an alternative to the Czech SOKOL organization which had figured largely in Czech nationalist circles before the creation of Czechoslovakia. Embarked on what was in fact a political career, Henlein founded the Sudeten German *Heimatfront* (Patriotic Front), as the German Nazi Party was banned. This became the Sudeten German Party. Henlein shared the fate of his patron and mentor Hitler in May 1945.

[6] For Col. Christie and his connection with Vansittart, see Christopher Andrew, *The Secret Service* (1986) and below, p.193.

[7] The talk, with the discussion, was published in *International Affairs*, vol.15, no.4, July-August 1936, pp.561-72. The outburst referred to was by Mr Israel Cohen.

matter in one of his speeches as an example of Czech oppression that could not be tolerated.[8]

As we have seen, radio was an important element in the development of events in Vienna, but commentators, particularly in America, had experienced difficulty in getting proper coverage of what was happening. The cause of this was that the transmitters in Austria were not powerful enough to send signals direct to America. Instead signals had to go by land-line to Berlin and there be retransmitted over the short-wave transmitters at Zeesen. It was obvious that, Germany being one of the protagonists in the struggles going on, there would be a severely imposed limit to the amount of objective reporting that could be sent through these channels. We have noticed already the troubles experienced by Vernon Bartlett and R.H.S. Crossman in their broadcasts, which were broadly speaking sympathetic to Germany.

Initially this was the situation in Prague also. Signals for America had to go by land-line to Berlin, where they were sent on via the Zeesen transmitters. However, the situation changed rapidly after new transmitters were built to overcome this, and in a way which itself considerably increased the tensions in the German minority areas of Czechoslovakia. One of the many complaints of the German minority was that, like the Germans in the Saar before the plebiscite, they had no radio programmes in their own language and had to listen to broadcasts from Germany itself which could not always be well received. This was a legitimate grievance and one symptomatic of the general cultural situation within the Czech state. But the problem of Sudeten Germans was remedied by the Czechs themselves. A German-language radio station was set up and put out over the new transmitters, which were now among the most powerful in Europe.

Instead of calming things down, this only brought them to a head, for the content of the programmes was very definitely anti-Nazi and often even anti-German. Or so they seemed to the Germans, for, worst of all, the signals were easily strong enough to be heard through great parts of Germany itself. There they became a far more insidious threat than the obviously biased programmes put out by the French from

---

[8] Hitler made this remark in his speech of 12 September 1938: 'When 3,500,000 [Sudeten Germans] who belong to a people of almost 80,000,000 are not allowed to sing any song the Czechs do not like because it does not please the Czechs, or are brutally struck for wearing white stockings because the Czechs do not like it ... when they are pursued like wild beasts for every expression of their national life ... I can only say to the representatives of the democracies that this is not a matter of indifference to us, and I say that as these tortured creatures cannot obtain rights and assistance by themselves they can obtain both from us.'

Strasbourg. A radio war developed which was the background to the crisis proper as it evolved through the summer and autumn of 1938. German broadcasts emphasized strongly the difficulties of the Sudeten minority under their leader Henlein, and tales of atrocities against them acted as a barometer of the day-to-day level of the propaganda war.

In May 1938 there had been a serious error of judgement by the Czechs. They had somehow been lead to believe that the Germans were about to invade or, in any event, that massive troop movements had recently been taking place on the frontier. They took the serious step of mobilizing their troops in the frontier areas. This ill-considered move was to have disastrous consequences which should have been plain to all. Mobilization is always extremely serious; the decisions to mobilize at the beginning of World War I could not be counter-manded once given, so the story went, and the result had been an unavoidable clash of great masses of men. Matters were not so serious in Czechoslovakia, which was not a world power, but, projected onto the world stage by the propaganda war, it almost seemed as though she was. Hitler was forced into the position of denying that he had mobilized or that there had been any troop movements – indeed there had been none – making it seem as though he had been forced to climb down by the Czechs. From this time war became an actual possibility.[9]

With knowledge of the importance of what they were doing, there was much discussion of what could have lead the Czechs to take such a serious step. A possible answer can be found in other false alarms and rumours which were spread at the time, and which were believed even by Britain: in 1939 first an imminent German invasion of Holland and then an invasion of Rumania were both thought to be likely on the basis of unfounded rumour. A rumour that Poland was about to be invaded was believed on no better evidence, as we shall see, than that of a *News Chronicle* journalist, Ian Colvin.[10] Another

[9] For an account of the change in Hitler's attitude brought about by this crisis, from the line 'It is not my intention to destroy Czechoslovakia in the immediate future by military action unless provoked ...' to the often quoted 'It is my unshakeable resolve that Czechoslovakia shall vanish from the Map of Europe', see David Irving, *The War Path: Hitler's Germany 1933-1939* (1983 ed.), p.100f.

[10] Ian Goodhope Colvin (1912-1975). It is a mystery how Colvin obtained the influence he undoubtedly had at this time. An answer might perhaps be found in the patronage he received from such figures as Lord Lloyd which frequently caused difficulty for the British authorities in Berlin, where Colvin was *persona non grata* with the German Government. See for example the telegram from Ogilvie-Forbes to Leeper on 5 January 1939: 'Colvin called on me today and said that he had been asked by Lord Lloyd to explore the possibilities of developing the work of the British Council in

story from the same source at the time of the Czech mobilization which is recorded in detail in the Foreign Office files shows how this sort of rumour developed.

The *News Chronicle* had carried a story about the alleged lessons the Wehrmacht were gaining from the campaign in Spain, citing a lecture given in Berlin by a German General. The German press immediately pointed out that the story originated in a German-language broadcast from Moscow which had named the alleged lecturer as General von Reichenau. A telegram from Sir George Ogilvie-Forbes in Berlin made the impact of the story in Germany unmistakable to the Foreign Office:

Telegram (en clair)[11] Berlin 13 July 1938. Enormous headlines cover the front pages of this morning's newspapers. 'In Moscow's service. The *News Chronicle* takes over the Soviet Campaign against Germany's Policy in Spain.' 'Incredible attack on Germany by English newspaper' etc. etc ... The *Völkischer Beobachter* states that a few days ago when agreement was reached in the Non-Intervention Committee[12] it prophesied that an effort would shortly be made to torpedo the effort by means of a press campaign ... Finally newspapers make the point that the *News Chronicle* is conducting a campaign not only against Germany but against Chamberlain.[13]

The interest here was that the story was spread through radio propaganda from Moscow, which Ian Colvin in Berlin must have confirmed; literally a rumour. But the full significance, and a pointer to a possible explanation of the Czech mobilization which precipitated the Munich crisis, was to be found in a further telegram sent by Sir

---

Germany and had been informed by him that he might possibly be employed in this connection. I warned Colvin of the delicacy of making enquiries and told him not to mention to any German the proposed development of the British Council's activities. He quite understood ...' (FO 395/633; P84/12/150). Colvin wrote two books, *Vansittart in Office* (1965) and *The Chamberlain Cabinet* (1971), which cover this period. They should be treated with caution. For a formal statement that Colvin was *persona non grata*, see FO 395/633; P858/12/150. Colvin was actually being considered for the Travel Association not, as he claimed, the British Council.

    [11] I.e. unciphered. Telegrams which were sent in code always began with the word 'decypher'.

    [12] The committee met in London under the auspices of the Foreign Office and was intended to deal with infringements of an agreement not to send arms to either side. It was widely regarded as a farce but had some useful function in a situation without immediate precedent.

    [13] Public Record Office: FO 371/21709; C7067/1261/18.

Nevile Henderson[14] a few days later:

> D.N.B[15] statement in question is printed under heavy headlines in all of the Sunday newspapers and alleges that the Czech troop movements are openly connected with the *News Chronicle*'s recent campaign as part of a general plot against the peace of Europe. Whether D.N.B's statements are partly or wholly fabricated it must be admitted that the *News Chronicle*'s campaign has greatly complicated the situation here. Moreover I understand that it was the failure of His Majesty's Government to announce and give credence to the German dementi of Reichenau story in Parliament which has caused the real disappointment here. Berlin. July 17 1938.[16]

Henderson understood well that, in a state ruled by propaganda, the reports in a paper such as the *News Chronicle*, probably not even seen by any British statesman in England, could seem of great importance and a source of potential incident. Czechoslovakia also saw matters in these terms and her mobilization might well have been caused, as the Germans suspected, by some such seemingly minor event in the propaganda war.

These events of May 1938 set Hitler off on a path which resembled that leading up to the Anschluss, but whereas with Austria there had only been an old plan to deal with the possibility of a Monarchy being re-established in Austria, Operation 'Otto',[17] with Czechoslovakia there was to be thorough planning for a full-scale invasion, with 'X-day', invasion, at the end of September. On 1 September Hitler issued his final commands to his army commanders and an invasion became inevitable unless diplomatic moves could provide an alternative solution. Czechoslovakia could not create an answer herself,

[14] Sir Nevile Meyrick Henderson (1882-1942). He began his career as Third Secretary at St. Petersburg, and was Envoy Extraordinary at Belgrade 1929-35, Ambassador to the Argentine 1935-37 and Ambassador in Berlin 1937-39. His *Failure of a Mission: Berlin 1937-1939* (1940) gives an invaluable picture of the time; unlike many commentators he was fully conscious of radio and the impact it was having. Talking of a reception being held by Goering on 11 March 1939, for example, he notices (p.24): 'The Schuschnigg and Seyss-Inquart radio messages were being anxiously discussed on all sides and it was quite obvious that every German present was wondering what was happening.' In the pre-radio age none present would have known that anything was happening at all. For his observations on broadcasts immediately before the invasion of Poland, a somewhat more important matter, see below, p.168.

[15] The DNB, the Deutsches Nachrichtenbüro, was the official German news agency.

[16] Public Record Office: FO 371/21709; C7067/1261/18.

[17] A reference to Otto, Archduke of Austria, claimant to the Austro-Hungarian throne. For his role in the war see Richard Lamb, op. cit., p.307f.

but she had allies and an audience in the rest of the world, most importantly in America where the idea of her existence as something more than a dream had first originated. And it was to America that Benes turned in a deeply felt broadcast on 10 September, which was put out over a nation-wide link-up with simultaneous translation.[18] He drew attention to the situation which he described as the most serious since the end of the World War. He pleaded for a solution to be found by calm negotiation, saying that Czechoslovakia had developed peacefully over the first twenty years of her existence and wished only to continue in the same way. The speech was heard with great clarity all over America, but, in case the average listener had not fully understood the seriousness of what he was hearing, the New York announcer made it clear with his final remark:

> The Press Radio Bureau brings word of another speech, [apart from Benes'] made at Nuremburg today, by Field Marshal Goering to the Nazi Labour Front ... The climax of the address which caused a sensation in the great assembly hall was the sentence: 'If fate should win and another world war come, Germany will conquer!'[19]

Goering was speaking at one of the numerous meetings at the Nuremburg Nazi Party rally which was then taking place. The climax of the week's events was to be a speech by Hitler on 12 September. It was widely thought that this speech was going to tell the world whether Hitler had decided on Peace or War. Again arrangements were made to broadcast the talk all over the world, the American networks providing simultaneous translation as the speech progressed. The announcer there on the early morning news programme told his listeners:

> This morning the entire civilized world is anxiously awaiting the speech of Adolf Hitler, whose single word may plunge all of Europe into another world war ...[20]

The speech when it came was the equal of any of his previous outbursts, inspired anew by the fact that he was addressing an audience which was for the first time drawn from the new Greater Germany, including his own native land, Austria. But it did not give the answer the world had been waiting for. There was no declaration

[18] Simultaneous translation was then still in its infancy. For about two years the BBC had been experimenting with simultaneous translation of Hitler's speeches for British audiences, but war began before they had perfected the technique.

[19] Quoted in H.V. Kaltenborn, *I Broadcast the Crisis* (1938), p.14.

[20] Ibid., p.19.

of war but, on the other hand, Germany was to turn an even sterner face on those who persecuted German minorities wherever they might be. The response among the Sudeten Germans was great with disturbances that looked so menacing that the Czechs made a further serious error and declared martial law of a most severe kind in those areas affected. Thanks to the existence of their German-language radio station the Government was able to make the declaration immediately to the entire population of the Sudeten lands. The savage penalties which included, apparently, a mandatory death penalty, execution within two hours of sentence without appeal, shocked ordinary citizens. Almost immediately the Sudeten German Party issued an ultimatum ending:

If within six hours of the delivery of these requests the Government has not accepted and published them, particularly by radio, the leadership of the Sudeten German Party refuses all responsibility for further disorders.[21]

The reason for the special reference to radio is not clear. Presumably the original broadcast declaration of martial law had been regarded as such as insult that only a withdrawal in the same way was held to be sufficient. The ultimatum was ignored, and Henlein followed it by a broadcast in which he demanded the cession of the Sudetenland to Germany and denounced the Czech Government as murderers responsible for the deaths of hundreds of innocent citizens. Whereupon the Czech Government announced, over the radio, that a warrant had been issued for the arrest of Henlein on a charge of high treason, perhaps the first occasion that a broadcast had lead directly to such a charge, and one which, under the martial law then in operation, carried the mandatory death penalty.[22]

It was at this point that Chamberlain decided to intervene directly in affairs. With the leader of one of the main factions under effective sentence of death, all negotiations involving Germany and Czechoslovakia were clearly at an end and war could only be a matter of days away. A special bulletin broadcast in America on 14 September, one of a stream of such bulletins and press reports coming from all over the world, said:

From the Sudeten German battle front [sic] comes the report that at least forty have been killed in the bloody fighting at Schwaderbach.

[21] As quoted in the British press; origin of translation unknown.
[22] The most obvious case of a person committing treason by broadcasting was that of William Joyce. See below, Chapters 8-10 and Appendix passim.

The Czech authorities had ordered their men not to fire back because they feared the shots might strike Germans across the border. After retiring from the police station the Czech militia finally opened fire and the fighting is still going on ...[23]

The British Cabinet had already been wrought up over the Czechoslovak situation in a fierce row with the BBC over a broadcast which Harold Nicolson had tried to put out over his weekly series, produced, as we have seen, by Burgess. Again Sir Horace Wilson was directly involved, as well as the Foreign Office, in attempting to get the BBC to see reason. Although Burgess produced the script and clearly acted as provocateur throughout, it fell to George Barnes to have to deal with the row caused by the attempt to broadcast it. He wrote a full account of what occured which is extremely valuable, incidentally, in showing the normal mechanism whereby the supposedly independent BBC was in fact monitored by Foreign Office consultation which was obligatory for political talks affecting foreign affairs.

12.00 noon: Received script from Nicolson. Rang up Foreign Office. Saw Mr Leaper [sic – Leeper] who read the script and said that so far as his personal opinion went, he thought it excellent, and could be broadcast as it was. In view, however, of Sir Horace Wilson's message to the BBC, and of the gravity of the situation, he would take it himself to Sir Alexander Cadogan. As the latter was then with the Secretary of State, the Foreign Office's decision could not be given until after three o'clock.

I went immediately to the Travellers' Club to tell Nicolson that we could not give him any information until after 3.00 pm. He agreed to remain at his chambers until he heard from me. He expressed his approval of the BBC's attitude in this matter and agreed that if the Foreign Office took objection to the script they would probably object to the script in toto and in that case he would be prepared to re-write it.

3.30 pm: Mr Leaper telephoned to say that the Foreign Office cannot take any responsibility for Mr Nicolson's script as submitted, and that in view of the gravity of the situation, and of the pace at which it is changing, the Foreign Office would prefer that no talk at all on that subject was broadcast tonight.

I asked if this was an instruction. He replied that the Foreign Office could not instruct the BBC on a matter like this, but that the recommendation was very strong.

Saw C(P) [Controller Programmes] who said cancel but that if Harold Nicolson would talk on some other subject that would be a better solution than an alternative programme, e.g. records. If he

[23] Kaltenborn, op.cit., p.29.

refused, we must cancel the talk, but the gravity of the situation must not be given as our reason for so doing.

Telephoned to Harold Nicolson and communicated Foreign Office's message and BBC wish that he would talk on another subject, giving as his reason the delicacy and the rapidly changing character of the situation. He suggested cancellation and asked for half-an-hour to think it over.

4.15 pm: Nicolson telephoned to say that he would give the talk and would not refer to the international situation. He told me in confidence that he had been in communication with the Foreign Office and had been told that his script had been seen by the Secretary of State in person.

He asked that no change should be made in the announcement.

Informed *The Listener* that script would not contain mention of international situation and agreed to post script to printers.

7.00 pm: Saw Mr Nicolson at King's Bench Walk. He showed me his new script. The first two pages were the same (A). The next two were an expansion of them and a careful working up to the phrase 'I am going to talk this evening about other things' (B). Then followed one-and-a-half pages describing the beating up at the altar of the Bishop of Rothenburg by Nazis (C). Then two paragraphs criticizing German diplomatic methods (D). The last half page of talk was about milk at 7d a quart, with the German babies of 1914 as the chief example (E).

I made some verbal changes in (B) which can be seen on the broadcast script. I asked that (D) should be deleted. Mr Nicolson agreed provided that he did not have to think of anything else to put in its place. I then said that in my opinion (C) should also be deleted because we had been asked by the Foreign Office not to mention the crisis, and it seemed to me that a story in which listeners' sympathy was enlisted against Nazi methods was not keeping to the letter of our promise. Mr Nicolson did not agree and said that he understood the Foreign Office meant that he was not to talk about the actual Czech crisis. He could see no reason for deleting (C) and as he had spent the whole afternoon re-writing he preferred to cancel the talk rather than alter it. I argued with him until 8 o'clock. In view of the importance which the Foreign Office would seem to have attached to this talk, it seemed to me that cancellation was as bad as allowing Mr Nicolson to go a little further than we wanted, since cancellation could only be interpreted by listeners as meaning that the international situation was very grave. Mr Nicolson was very angry and asked me to suggest alternative subjects if (C) was deleted. I suggested the Persian Railway and Lord Halifax's speech about the international accommodation for foreign students. He rejected both but eventually agreed to re-write his script if he had time, but still threatened to cancel if I objected to anything more, or if he could not find anything else to talk about.

I then returned to Broadcasting House and arranged with the

announcer and Mr Lidell, who was on duty, to be ready to fade out Mr Nicolson's talk if, in my opinion, he departed too far from his script. I also arranged for the talk to be recorded and copies to be made from this recording. I met Mr Nicolson at 9.30 and he produced a third script which was, in my opinion, innocuous. He apologised for the difficulties he had made and expressed himself as much more angry with the Foreign Office than with the BBC. As he did not wish me to remain I left him at 9.55 pm.

My impression on leaving Mr Nicolson was that he had been made angry

    (a)   by the waste of time in having to re-write twice;
    (b)   by the Foreign Office's veto on his talk after the nice things which they had said to him personally about his previous talks.

He felt that the Foreign Office were only able to take such a strong line because they could rely upon him not making public their veto. He said that he would have to think over very seriously about how to reply to the letters from listeners who were disappointed because he had not talked about the Czech crisis. I have spoken to Talks Ex. about an extra fee, and recommended that he should be offered an extra fee of twelve guineas. [The BBC actually offered six guineas].[24]

This astonishing battle of wills can clearly be seen in terms of a fight between anti-appeasement opinion, identified for the moment with Nicolson and the BBC, and the Government, intent on finding a solution and with the actual responsibility for doing so. Burgess remained in the background while the row was going on; if he was also acting as an unofficial messenger for Chamberlain at this time, as he claimed, his position was clearly delicate, although it did not stop him returning to the charge as soon as the trouble was over, as we have seen in Chapter 3.

We know now that Burgess was working for Russia, but it is still a large step to conclude that the line being put forward by Nicolson, standing by Czechoslovakia to the point of war, was exactly a Moscow line encouraged by her through Burgess. Clearly it would have been an advantage for Russia if war had begun then, for it would have been on the western front at a time when her own armies were weakened. Whether the line was Moscow's or Burgess's or simply Nicolson's own, the effective blocking of it by the Government's censorship of the BBC kept matters still within their control. It is ironic that when Chamberlain began fighting his secret radio war through Radio Luxembourg and the Joint Broadcasting Committee after Munich it was Burgess who did the work then also.

[24] BBC Written Archives Centre: Harold Nicolson contributor files.

Chamberlain's own final response to the crisis was to depart from the normal diplomatic procedures and instead go to Berlin and discuss the Czech crisis in person with Hitler. Today international politics have developed to the extent that the leaders of the two super-powers can talk to each other over the telephone in extreme emergency. In 1938 diplomacy was still not quite at home in the twentieth century; Chamberlain himself had never flown in an aeroplane before and his suggestion was widely seen as one showing actual physical courage. Indeed, as matters were to develop, with three journeys to Germany rather than one, any statesman in his seventieth year today, even with modern transport, would have found the going hard.

Conventional accounts of the events that followed soon to be known simply as 'Munich' are accurate and precise as far as they go. But they mostly fail to capture the atmosphere of the time and the important role played by broadcasting both in building up tension and in causing the universal feeling of euphoria when the discussions ended in peace not war. The strain on those taking part of having news broadcasts giving almost minute-by-minute accounts of events, and at the end of each leaving the question of peace or war undecided, must have been great and a potent force on all those taking part to come to some solution. One of the accounts of the radio reporting of the crisis put this point quite specifically:

> In September, war came closer than it has come since the Armistice. We were saved from war, I am convinced, by the mobilization of world opinion for peace. When the crisis came we had mastered a force of which we knew almost nothing in 1914. Through it and because of it the peoples of the world demanded and got an exact accounting of every important move by their leaders ... Radio became of itself one of the most significant events of the crisis. It was significant because it showed that in every great crisis in which it plays a part the ultimate issue of peace and war is to be decided by all mankind in the great forum of the air. The air has become the battleground; and in the war which is waged there night and day between arguments for war and arguments for peace, I think that the arguments for peace will finally prevail.[25]

Clearly this shows an American view, but something broadly similar was held by many people all over the world; politicians, Chamberlain and Hitler included, could not escape a well-nigh universal constituency of all who could listen to a radio. Although it is not

[25] Kaltenborn, op.cit., p.3.

mentioned in Kaltenborn's book or in any other account of the crisis, the most important broadcast was one given by Chamberlain which was widely heard in Germany and brought the factor of German public opinion into play, to the great annoyance of the German authorities.

The broadcast was that given by Chamberlain to British audiences on 27 September towards the end of the prolonged crisis. After the first meeting with Hitler Chamberlain had flown back to England and got the agreement of the British Cabinet to almost all of Hitler's demands; the French also concurred. He returned to Germany but, at his second meeting with Hitler at Bad Godesburg, he was taken aback to hear Hitler say that this agreement was now no longer sufficient. After further discussion he again returned to Britain and then gave a broadcast talk going over all that had occurred and conveying the British case with manifest sincerity. Both he and the Foreign Office saw that it was essential to get this talk with its candid message to the ears of the German people. But despite the known imminence of war no way had been thought of to do this. Later, as a result of the crisis, departments were set up to fill the gap in such vital arrangements as we have seen; on September 27 all that existed was the embryo Ministry of Information which proved useless. It was decided to oblige the BBC to broadcast a German translation of the speech to Germany direct. To ensure that the signal reaching Germany was as strong as possible, all transmitters, London and regional, were to carry the programme. The British public were astonished to hear, instead of their published programmes, a lengthy talk in German. Those who knew German were even more amazed, for the translation was obviously very hesitant and the talk itself broken up into brief sections that destroyed the force of the speech entirely. To make matters worse reception was still not good in Germany, and the talk clashed with a broadcast by Hitler.[26]

At the last minute someone, probably Grand, suggested that one of the commercial stations might be used, such as Radio Luxembourg. The suggestion was seized on, despite the illegality of what was being

---

[26] The question of reception of BBC broadcasts in Germany was to cause the BBC some difficulty, surprisingly. It had been suggested that the new German People's sets were so made as to prevent listening to overseas broadcasts. A set was brought to London and tested by the BBC engineers who found this to be untrue – the set merely had no short wave, otherwise it was the equal of any set on the market in Britain. To get the required information the BBC finally intended sending an engineer to Germany clandestinely who would be able to judge reception. It is small wonder that meanwhile Chamberlain had resorted to Luxembourg.

done and the fact that it breached the International Convention which Britain had signed barely a year before.

The result was a brilliant success; a competent translation of the speech was put out over the main Luxembourg German channel at eleven o'clock on the morning of 28 September, when a large proportion of the German listening public heard it. Its impact was all the greater because it was the first time they had heard the British case.

It is always difficult to assess the result of any broadcast, but there was an immediate protest from Berlin to the Luxembourg authorities, which was followed by further protests. Until this broadcast all information reaching the German public had been controlled entirely by Goebbels[27] and his Propaganda Ministry and the encroachment through Luxembourg was bitterly resented. The broadcast was made at the exact time that Hitler was deciding whether to invade, or instead reply favourably to an appeal by Chamberlain for a last visit, which had been echoed by a last-minute suggestion from Mussolini that any decision be postponed for twenty-four hours.

When Chamberlain rose to speak in the House of Commons he had still not received a reply from Hitler, but while he was actually speaking a message was handed to him arranging a meeting for the following day. Chamberlain announced this to a House which broke into hysterical cheering; had the proceedings of Parliament been broadcast in those days no doubt the whole country would have joined in. The achievement was a triumph for Chamberlain, and all the more so if it had resulted even in part from his decision to play the Dictator's propaganda game.

This triumph in the House, and the agreement which followed, were soon turned against him, and the very word 'Munich' became synonymous with betrayal. Every detail of his return, the waving of the piece of white paper at the aerodrome, seen clearly on the television pictures of the event,[28] his appearance at 10 Downing Street

[27] Joseph Goebbels (1897-1945). Goebbels had become Reichsminister for Public Enlightenment and Propaganda in 1933. This post gave him absolute control over all the media, and those who doubted the strength of this control soon saw the press become a Nazi monopoly and virtually all the staff of the German broadcasting system removed. Goebbels' diaries contain numerous references to radio and broadcasting. For his rapid development of overseas radio propaganda, see above, p.71.

[28] It has been suggested that Chamberlain was actually instructed to wave the paper so as to make it, and himself, clear on the television outside-broadcast pictures, then a very new thing. This might seem far-fetched were there not a specific reference to the visibility of the paper on the screen in the account of the broadcast, with illustration, in the BBC's year book.

leaning from the same window that Disraeli had on his return in 1878[29] and greeting the crowds with almost the same words, 'Peace with honour', have all been repeated again and again as the classic example of a diplomat fooled by a man younger and more clever than himself who, instead of leading his country to peace, was plunging it towards inevitable war.

Had the Munich negotiations failed, war would have resulted from a German invasion of Czechoslovakia, or possibly from a declaration of war by Britain, France and Russia. It would have been a different war from the one that broke out almost exactly a year later, for the Polish and Hungarian Governments had made it clear that they too had claims on parts of Czechoslovakian territory. On 23 September the Soviet government had informed Poland that an invasion of Czechoslovakia would result in the termination of their non-aggression treaty. However on 25 September Benes, the Prime Minister of Czechoslovakia,[30] came to a provisional agreement with Poland, who took over the contested lands at the same time as Germany absorbed the Sudetenland. War would have seen Poland and Germany as allies.[31]

Within days of the Munich agreement Chamberlain was to discover the likely course of future events, and it was through radio propaganda that the first clues were obtained. Reports began to come in that the German propaganda stations were now turning their attentions to Slovakia. A determined attempt was being made to persuade the Slovak people to turn away from the Czechs and set up their own state. In six months this campaign, building on a well-established Slovak movement, achieved success, but Chamberlain can hardly have thought it would come so soon. This information did not remain secret for long as a Parliamentary question from a Labour MP asked for confirmation of the broadcasts' existence. Chamberlain confirmed that they did and added:

[29] For an account of this, see Robert Blake, *Disraeli* (1966). *Peace with Honour* was also the title of a popular often reprinted pacifist book by A.A. Milne.

[30] Eduard Benes (1884-1948). For an account of his attitude at the Paris Peace Conference in 1919, at which he was Czechoslovak representative, see Lloyd George, op.cit. Benes went on to become President of his country from 1935 to 1938, having been Foreign Minister until then. There were mixed feelings about Benes at the time: Ian Colvin quotes Nevile Henderson as saying of him (*Vansittart in Office* (1965) p.239): 'Benes is a traitor, a traitor to his people', although this may be an instance of the need to treat his remarks with caution. What is less in doubt is the existence of transcripts of highly damaging telephone calls between Benes and Masaryk in London at this time. See David Irving, op.cit., pp.136-7.

[31] Improbable though this may seem, it is no more improbable than the Soviet-German Pact. In addition Poland and Germany had very similar views on what was called the Jewish Question; see below, p.155f.

His Majesty's Ambassador in Berlin has already represented to the German Government the desirability of restraint ... on German wireless.[32]

But he of course knew that he had himself become involved in the grey world of secret broadcasting and there was little point in Henderson making representations of that kind to Hitler because this very question was the one most consistent complaint voiced by Hitler and one to which Britain could not give an answer.

There were those in Britain who objected to the settlement and took no part in the subsequent celebrations. Duff Cooper[33] resigned from the Admiralty; Harold Nicolson made a speech, without referring to his banned broadcast, attacking Sir Horace Wilson as well as Chamberlain,[34] but the most resounding attack came from Winston Churchill, in a speech in the debate that followed Chamberlain's return. Churchill was still banned from the BBC, but he felt so strongly about what had happened that he agreed to an arrangement made by one of the commercial companies for a speech to be broadcast to America. The speech went ahead and caused a diplomatic incident, for direct broadcasts to America were few and America was acutely conscious of anything resembling political propaganda aimed at their shores. Randolph Hearst[35] wrote a spirited isolationist reply to Churchill which appeared all over America and caused the British Ambassador in Washington to write to the Foreign Office with a warning against the likely effects of future broadcasts of the same type. Lord Halifax, the Foreign Secretary, minuted the file:

I had a letter yesterday from Colonel Murray[36] who happened to be stopping with the President, and he said that the effect of Mr

[32] Hansard, Vol. 339 col. 164. The MP was Mr David Grenfell.

[33] Sir Alexander Cadogan remarked succinctly of Cooper's resignation: 'Duff Cooper resigned. Good riddance of bad rubbish' (Cadogan, op. cit., p.111). The actual motives for the resignation are obscure. The decision seems to have been taken spontaneously late in the evening at his club and put into operation the following morning. For an account of his life, see John Charmley, *Duff Cooper* (1986).

[34] This attacking of a civil servant was considered very bad form, as Nicolson seems to have felt at the time, for he told Sir Robert Bruce Lockhart that he never made the remarks attributed to him, having deleted them from a draft script which a secretary mistakenly passed to the press unedited. See R.H. Bruce Lockhart, *Comes the Reckoning* (1947), p.18.

[35] Hearst's reputation was at its height at this time and the speed and accuracy of his reply to Churchill commanded great respect. A measure of his influence can be seen in Vansittart's use of the word 'Hearstliness', presumably his own invention!

[36] I have been unable to identify Colonel Murray.

Churchill's broadcast in the USA had been very unfortunate![37]

In fact these consequences were exactly what Churchill might have hoped for and his views were made known to a much wider audience than if he had succeeded in getting to a microphone in Britain. Hitler made his next important speech after Munich in Saarbrucken, the scene of his first great triumph against the Versailles settlement. He gave faint praise to Chamberlain but then pointed to his weakness as the leader of a democracy to be replaced perhaps without warning by another Government under Duff Cooper, Eden or Churchill. These men, Hitler said, openly planned another war against Germany.

Chamberlain was no doubt shocked by this intemperate language so soon after Munich. His next important move was in some sense an answer to this new tone, a visit to Mussolini in Italy in company with Lord Halifax. The highlight of the visit was a formal banquet in Rome when Chamberlain, in replying to Mussolini's speech, proposed a toast to the King of Italy, adding after a slight pause 'and Emperor of Ethiopia', thereby formally acknowledging Italy's claims in a style to which Eden had always been opposed. When he returned he made a speech, broadcast world-wide, outlining again his policy in regard to Italy. The formal occasion of the speech was an address to a trade association in Birmingham. His speech covered all aspects of his efforts in foreign policy both before and after Munich and shows his very clear grasp of what he was doing and the extreme seriousness of the affairs he was dealing with. He was careful to mention in detail the significance of his agreements with Mussolini, pointing out:

> I go further and say that the preservation of the peace last September was only made possible by the events which had preceded it, by the exchange of letters between myself and Signor Mussolini in the summer of 1937 and by the conclusion of the Anglo-Italian agreement in February of last year. Without the improvement in the relations between this country and Italy I could never have obtained Signor Mussolini's cooperation last September, and without his cooperation I do not believe peace could have been saved.[38]

Chamberlain ended his broadcast on a note which gave a clear indication of the way his mind was working at the time:

---

[37] Public Record Office: FO 395/623; P3030/2645/150.

[38] The speech was given, and broadcast live, on 28 January. Text as quoted from National Press in Keesing's Archives, p.3422. National Sound Archives: NSA T28034/6/1.

Conscious of our strength, avoiding needless alarms equally with careless indifference, let us go forward to meet the future with the calm courage that enabled our ancestors to win through their troubles a century and a quarter ago.

The implied comparison of Hitler and Mussolini with Napoleon must have flattered those in Germany who heard the German-language version of his talk broadcast over Luxembourg.

In fact it was at this moment that the German Ministry for Foreign Affairs chose to propose an Anglo-German Cultural Agreement to cover a wide range of matters, including radio broadcasting. Sir George Ogilvie-Forbes[39] sent a telegram from Berlin on 27 January outlining the proposals and expressing his enthusiasm for it:

> I feel that a cultural agreement would be of inestimable benefit to us from the point of view of introducing propaganda into this country and that we should have far more to gain from it than Germany. I hope therefore that you will be able to inform me at an early date by telegram that you agree in principle. In that event we should ask the ministry of Foreign Affairs to submit definite proposals for your consideration.[40]

The telegram was received by Rex Leeper. He was immediately totally opposed to the idea. His actual reasons for outright rejection can only be speculated upon; it does not appear from the papers that he consulted Sir Alexander Cadogan,[41] or his Minister, Halifax. However, from his own knowledge of what was going on in broadcasting, it would have been obvious that any agreement would have proved very embarrassing; it would almost be as if Germany had

[39] Sir George Ogilvie-Forbes (1891-1954). University of Bonn; entered Foreign Office 1919 and served at Mexico City 1927-30, the Holy See 1927-30, Baghdad 1932-35, Madrid 1935-37, and then, at this time, as Counsellor at the British Embassy, Berlin 1937-39. Ogilvie-Forbes was good support for Nevile Henderson and, as is clear from these events, firmly determined to make whatever moves were possible to lower the chances of war, in the face of British recruitment appeals and similar talks being broadcast in German over Radio Luxembourg.

[40] Public Record Office: FO 395/633; P297/12/150.

[41] Sir Alexander George Montague Cadogan (1884-1968). Entered the Diplomatic Service 1908; Head of the League of Nations Section of the Foreign Office until 1934, when he went to Peking as Minister and later Ambassador in succession to Sir Miles Lampson (see above, p.93) 1934-36 (there is no record of his having met Agnes Smedley, Sonia Kuczynski or, indeed, Roger Hollis, all of whom were there). At this time he had risen to Permanent Under-Secretary at the Foreign Office (1938-46), during which period he kept brilliant and incisive diaries, published posthumously: David Dilks (ed.), *The Diaries of Sir Alexander Cadogan, O.M., 1938-1945* (1971). Later in life he became Chairman of the BBC Board of Governors.

after all come in to the League of Nations International Convention on Broadcasting. His reply to Ogilvie-Forbes came as a shock:

> We do not like the idea of a regular cultural agreement such as those concluded by Germany with other Governments, as the practice is quite alien to us. This is a totalitarian technique not suited to our methods, and in any event we do not possess the necessary funds and resources. We are anxious therefore not to put cultural matters on this footing.
>
> At the same time we agree with you that it would be unwise to snub the cultural department of the Ministry Foreign Affairs in the approach they have made to you, as this would give Ribbentrop an excuse for his anti-British venom. We should like you therefore to toy with the idea in a friendly spirit by saying that from time to time when anything useful for cultural relations can be done and done effectively we might discuss matters and see how we could assist the cause of better relations. You might hint for example at the usefulness of a few exchange visits of the Youth or the sending of exhibitions from time to time or an occasional lecturer, but you will understand that we are not anxious to spend large sums on an elaborate programme of exchanges which will in fact bring us a very small if any return.
>
> Since I wrote to you last November we have gone carefully into the possibilities of propaganda in Germany and we cannot see very much that the British Council can do on purely cultural lines which would produce any real results.
>
> In general therefore we must leave it to you to be friendly by not closing down abruptly the approach which has been made, but at the same time not committing us to a programme which we should regard as expensive and unremunerative.[42]

Ogilvie-Forbes' reply on 28 February is also worth quoting in full as it shows the last desperate attempt he made to get some sort of rapprochement between the British and German people established through the nowadays well-known medium of cultural exchange. His letter went unanswered and the last paper has an instruction by Warner, Leeper's deputy in the News Department, saying 'Enter soon 2/3 [i.e. 2 March]'. The registry file stamp is dated the same day.[43]

> I need hardly say that we are rather disappointed at your reply in regard to the approach of the German Ministry for Foreign Affairs to us for the conclusion of a cultural agreement, particularly as we find it

[42] Public Record Office: FO 395/633; P297/12/150.

[43] The Registry stamp indicates the date on which the file was deposited and entered in the FO index. Files frequently did not reach Registry for a considerable time after the last action had been taken on them. An instruction 'Enter soon' would suggest that the file was not wanted around.

extremely difficult in any case to know exactly on what lines to proceed in order to improve relations between our two countries and we presume that the Foreign Office desires us to do anything possible in this direction.[44] As regards the issue of a cultural agreement, we feel impelled to return to the charge. There is no reason at all, if you dislike totalitarian technique, to conclude a full-dress agreement such as those signed by Germany with other powers.[45] Why not tell us exactly what points you would be willing to contemplate and we could then arrange an exchange of notes on a limited scale and extend our activities later at our discretion. Surely it is hopeless to ask us 'to toy with the idea'? We find it difficult to agree with you that a cultural agreement would bring us very small benefit. On the contrary it is just the kind of propaganda which is going to be of the greatest advantage to us. We realize that you may not wish to spend large sums, and we do not press you to do so, although in your letter to the Ambassador of November last you stated that anything on cultural lines must be done on a serious scale and that you would have to get extra funds for the purpose. Within the last few days we have been approached by representatives of the Hitler Jugend with suggestions for some official arrangement between Germany and England for the interchange of students in schools and private families and for the placing on a proper basis of the existing system of summer camps for male and female students. Could not these ideas be considered and figure in a limited cultural agreement? If so a representative of the British Council might come over and discuss possibilities with the Ministry of Foreign Affairs.

I am sorry to be so importunate, but we feel here that a cultural agreement is one of the best ways of improving relations and getting our propaganda into the country. We trust therefore that in the light of the considerations set out in this letter you will be able to re-examine the whole matter.[46]

At the same time another independent approach was made to the BBC for an exchange of talks by the leaders of each country over each other's radio system: Chamberlain would be offered an opportunity to speak to the German people, and in exchange Hitler would speak to Britain over the BBC. The approach was welcomed by Ogilvie,[47] the

[44] An ironical reference implying, of course, that it did *not*: that is, that appeasement was no longer the policy. Whether that would have been the reaction if anyone other than Leeper and Warner had seen the file is an open question.

[45] The Japanese had been early in this field. See for example *Kokusai Bunka Shinkokai (The Society for International Cultural Relations) Prospectus and Scheme* (Tokyo, 1934). The scheme is very similar in outline to that proposed by the German Government.

[46] Public Record Office: FO 395/633; P297/12/150. There was no reply.

[47] Frederick W. Ogilvie (1893-1949). Ogilvie had spent his entire life, except for the war, in the academic world. When appointed he was Vice-Chancellor of Queen's University, Belfast, having been Professor of Political Economy at Edinburgh for

new Director-General of the BBC, and would also, unquestionably, have helped put an end to the clandestine radio war being waged over Radio Luxembourg. The Government intervened to stop the broadcasts and none ever took place. Finally Germany decided to reply in kind, and their English-language broadcasts, by Norman Baillie-Stewart, began in April, another twist in the propaganda spiral.[48]

The next break in the pattern of events that Chamberlain hoped to be able to meet with calm courage, as he had said in his broadcast, came over Czechoslovakia, once again.

Immediately after Munich, as we have seen, German radio propaganda had begun encouraging the Slovak population of Czechoslovakia, never very firmly set in the post-war state, that they should seek independence from the Czechs. After Munich even the spelling of the country's name had been altered to 'Czecho-Slovakia' in deference to Slovak feeling.[49] The German propaganda fell on fertile soil, and there was a great increase in Slovak national feeling. So much so that a possible coup had been reported to Prague that was to take place some time after 10 March. They had taken precipitate action, arresting Monsignor Tiso,[50] the Slovak Prime Minister, in an effort to forestall any possible revolt. However, one of the Slovak Ministers escaped and proceeded to Vienna where Seyss-Inquart immediately made the facilities of the radio station open to him.[51] He

some years before that. The reasons for his appointment as Director-General are still a mystery. Among those canvassed for the job in succession to Reith were figures as prominent as Vansittart; Ogilvie was entirely unknown.

[48] There was remarkable official complacency about this development. Leeper minuted Cadogan: 'The Germans are going to like our broadcasts less from today onwards. I don't think it matters in the least if they repay the compliment by broadcasting in English. Their propaganda here will have little effect.' To which Cadogan replied: 'Yes, I agree. I should not be afraid of German broadcast propaganda in this country ...' (FO 395/626; P445/6/150). Indeed this must rank as one of the most astonishing errors of judgement in the brief history of radio propaganda to that time. As we shall see, the effect of the German propaganda was devastating, particularly after the outbreak of the 'phoney war'. See below, p.173f.

[49] To avoid confusion the original spelling 'Czechoslovakia' is used here throughout.

[50] Monsignor Jozef Tiso (1887-1947), President of Slovakia, author of *The Ideology of the Slovak Populist Party* (1930). At the time Tiso was described as 'a modest, sound, healthy, quiet popular man', quoted in David Irving, op.cit., p.187. He was executed at the end of the war.

[51] This was Dr Ferdinand Ďurčanský, the Slovak Deputy Prime Minister. Irving mentions that it was an early-morning telephone call from Seyss-Inquart to Hitler's liason officer with Ribbentrop, Walter Hewel, that alerted Germany to the Czech occupation of Bratislava on 10 March. However, he does not mention the broadcasts by Ďurčanský, which were clearly absolutely vital, indicating to the Slovaks that they

gave a series of broadcasts which urged the Slovaks to show every resistance they could to the Government in Prague. Apologists for Hitler have later attempted to show that there was no actual German instigation of the coup which followed. They have failed, however, to mention, let alone account for, the broadcasts made from Vienna or those earlier broadcasts which had begun after Munich. On the other hand, there is no doubt that the Slovak cause was a genuine one. No one could invent the scene in the Slovak assembly when all rose and sang the Slovak National Anthem after declaring themselves independent, nor suggest that they were acting from any other than patriotic motives; none the less the *Realpolitik* of the situation must have been obvious to all of them. Monsignor Tiso's visit to Berlin only confirmed what all knew, that the State would exist by courtesy of a guarantee from Germany.

With the independence of Slovakia the state of Czechoslovakia ceased to exist. It would have been possible, in theory, for the powers that had arranged for that State's protection at Munich to have attempted some further adjustment, but the question was decided in a matter of hours by Hitler's action. The first intimation that the Czechs had of their fate was a broadcast at 4.30 in the morning to the military authorities in Czechoslovakia informing them that their country no longer existed and that German troops would be crossing the border in an hour and a half's time to occupy the Reich protectorate of Bohemia and Moravia.[52] At the same time a state of emergency was declared in the border areas which had the interesting condition that all radio sets in those areas had to be handed over to the authorities. Clearly, if any resistance was expected, it was thought that it would be co-ordinated or encouraged by broadcasts from Prague, or elsewhere, a backhanded tribute to all those who had been running secret radio stations there with the Prague Government's tacit agreement. Another unusual detail in those early hours of occupation was the insistence that the steel works at Witkowitz be captured intact as soon as possible. These works were some of the largest in Europe and were owned by a family of international bankers who had been in dispute with the German authorities over a number of matters. Two members of their family had been held after the Anschluss and an attempt had been made to involve the steel works at

---

had support. Irving remarks: 'We are insufficiently informed on the decisions that Hitler now took.' It is clear he must have given the go-ahead for Ďurčanský's broadcasts from Vienna. See Irving, op.cit., pp.186-7.

[52] Presumably those concerned must have been alerted in some way to expect such a broadcast, unless listening habits have changed markedly over the intervening years.

Witkowitz in a settlement. Shortly before the occupation of Bohemia and Moravia the works had begun dumping their steel in a conscious attempt to break the world steel cartel. Their actions had a world-wide effect, causing unemployment in Britain on a large scale in that industry, according to papers released in the Public Record Office.[53] It also drastically affected the German steel industry. The British Government were involved partly because large Admiralty orders were being manufactured at Witkowitz. However, the main reason was that attempts were made through General Spears, a Director of Witkowitz, to involve the Government in a buy-out of the firm by the Czech Government. The cartel dispute had finally been settled a few days before the occupation. Whether the situation had anything to do with the timetable for Hitler's action will probably never be known; the matter would have remained entirely obscure had it not been for the decision by Neville Laski[54] to place a statement of these matters on record.[55]

Ribbentrop[56] lost no time in coming to the microphone himself to tell the population of Bohemia and Moravia why he was there and what the future held for them. The use of radio meant that every citizen, literate or illiterate, knew from the first moment what had happened:

[53] The greater part of the papers relating to this matter may be found in the Public Record Office in FO 371/22902; C1003/C1695/C1984/C1985/C2095/C2280/C2300/C2424/C3076/C3957/etc./1003/12. However, those relating to the breaking of the steel cartel were filed, for some reason, in an unrelated sequence. In one of the few references to Witkowitz, Cadogan remarked: '[X]' came about German offers to buy Witkowitz works. This significant. If they are prepared to pay $ or £ for it, it doesn't look as if they are going to march in and take it. Talked to Strang about it; we must see Hankey as Admiralty have placed large orders ...' Diary entry 5 May 1938, op.cit. In fact walk in and take it is exactly what they did, using, as Irving remarks, a special force drawn from the elite SS regiment Leibstandarte Adolf Hitler to secure the works intact.

[54] Neville Jonas Laski (1890-1969) QC, President London Committee of Deputies of British Jews 1933-1940. He wrote at this time *Jewish Rights and Jewish Wrongs* (1939).

[55] The Witkowitz papers concerning the breaking of the steel cartel were sent to the Government by Laski acting in his capacity as President of the London Committee of Deputies of British Jews.

[56] Joachim von Ribbentrop (1893-1946), Hitler's Foreign Affairs advisor, who first came to prominence when he negotiated the Anglo-German Naval Treaty of 1935. From 1936 to 1938 Ribbentrop was Ambassador to London, and he returned to Germany to become Minister of Foreign Affairs until the end of the war. Of all the Nazi ministers he came to be the most despised – the fact that he had connections with the Champagne industry was irresistable to a certain kind of British snobbery. Accounts of him are frequently savage: see, for example, the entry for him in Robert Wistrich, *Who's Who in Nazi Germany* (1982). For his own account, see *The Ribbentrop Memoirs* (1954).

Bohemia and Moravia have for a thousand years belonged to the 'Lebensraum' of the German people. Force and unreason have arbitrarily torn them from their old historical setting and finally their incorporation in the artificial structure of Czechoslovakia created a breading ground of constant unrest. Year by year grew the danger that from this region there might emerge as already once in the past a most terrible threat to European peace ...[57]

He then went on to outline the new constitution. The timing of these events caused Chamberlain some embarrassment, besides the shock of the actual news itself. When he first spoke of the matter in the House of Commons on 15 March he had been criticized for being vague in his condemnation of Hitler's tearing up, as it seemed, of the Munich agreement. In fact, as he explained, he had not been able to gain any adequate knowledge of what had actually occurred. The following day he broadcast a speech, again relayed world wide, and later in German over Radio Luxembourg, that made his attitude clear.

The Government was at a disadvantage because the information that we had was only partial; much of it was unofficial. We had no time to digest it, much less to form a considered opinion upon it.[58]

He went on to assure his audience that people who thought he did not care about what had happened were mistaken, and that he intended to correct that mistake:

...no greater mistake could be made than to suppose that, because it believes war to be a senseless and cruel thing this nation has so lost its fibre that it will not take part to the utmost of its power in resisting such a challenge [to peace] if it were made. For that declaration I am convinced that I have not merely the support, the sympathy, the confidence of my fellow countrymen and country-women but I shall also have the approval of the whole of the British Empire and of all the other nations who value peace indeed, but value freedom more.[59]

Perhaps the most poignant comment on the occupation of Prague was a broadcast by Benes from Chicago on 19 March. He had left his country at the time of the Munich agreement and his message to the people of Czechoslovakia from half way round the world must have seemed like a last desperate wish rather than a prelude to events which were to develop continuously until the country was finally

[57] As published in the national press. Origin of translation unknown.
[58] Ibid.
[59] Ibid.

re-established in 1945, only later to fall once again under a foreign yoke:

> The independence of Czechoslovakia has not been crushed. Until my last breath I shall continue to fight for my people and their rights, and I am sure they will ultimately emerge as proud as they always have been of their history and their freedom. I know that in history brute force has always fallen after such a terrible and brutal misuse of power. Germany has declared that all this was done in the name of the peace of Europe. It is the peace of the cemetery.[60]

On March 29 the French Premier Daladier[61] added to the tension in Europe and the world, if anything further were needed, by a broadcast sent out from France in seven languages world-wide. There was alarm in every sentence he uttered and, for those who did not hear the broadcast in their own country live, it appeared in the world's press the following day:

> How can Europe be otherwise than in a state of alarm? There is not a single man today who does not know that war would be a catastrophe for every nation. None would be exempted from destruction. We do not want this. We want to help Europe save herself. In the name of my country I invite the confident support of all powers which think as we do, all those who, like ourselves are ready to persevere in the path of peace but would rise as one man in the face of attack ...[62]

Two days later Chamberlain announced in the House of Commons that Britain would give full support to Poland if she was attacked; the guarantee which followed this in a few days was to prove the crucial step that brought about World War II.

The world had first become conscious of a new phase in Polish worries about Germany in a broadcast, on the same day that Benes spoke from Chicago, by President Moscicki; the date also happened to be the birthday of Marshal Pilsudski[63] and the tone of the broadcast was one of confidence:

---

[60] As published in the national press. Origin of translation unknown.

[61] Edouard Daladier, at this time Prime Minister and Minister of National Defence.

[62] As published in the national press.

[63] Marshal Pilsudski had become well known and highly regarded in England partly through the publication of a dramatic account of the stopping of the Red Armies at Warsaw at the end of World War I: Viscount D'Abernon, *The Eighteenth Decisive Battle of the World, Warsaw 1920* (1931).

Poland was weak, now she is strong. The basis of her policy is freedom and independence, and we shall not surrender her destiny to alien protection.[64]

Fierce denunciation of Polish atrocities had by then begun on the German radio in the familiar build-up to some kind of confrontation that would bring benefit to Germany; the Polish press was fully aware of what these broadcasts meant:

Poles understand the tragic example of Czechoslovakia; therefore Poland is ready for war even against the strongest adversary. The Poles have no inferiority complex and will fight for victory whatever the odds, remembering the battles of history in which Poles have beaten numerically stronger German armies.[65]

On April 3 Chamberlain made the guarantee in formal terms and made it plain that France would also stand by Poland. The following day the Polish Foreign Minister, Colonel Beck,[66] arrived in Britain and began brief discussions with Chamberlain on a variety of matters, some connected with the Guarantee, others not.

One of the main questions, indeed the central question, which was exacerbating all matters in Europe was raised by Colonel Beck at the press conference at the end of his visit. This was the question of Jewish emigration from Poland, which he said he had raised with Chamberlain and, by prior arrangement, on behalf of the Government of Rumania, which was also feeling acutely the results of massive emigration caused by Germany's anti-semitic policies. The official British communiqué on the visit contained no reference to this matter, although a statement confirming Colonel Beck's remarks was issued from the Foreign Office later. However, before Beck left Poland, the *Times* special correspondent there had been given an exclusive briefing on the plan for settlement of the question which Beck brought to London for discussion.[67] It involved, as had plans suggested by

[64] As quoted in *Keesing's Archives*, p.3506. Origin of translation unknown.

[65] Ibid.

[66] Colonel Jozef Beck. Generations of British students have drawn their opinion of Beck at this time from A.J.P. Taylor's *The Origins of the Second World War* (1961 and still in print). For an alternative view, see Piotr S. Wandycz, 'Poland between East and West', in Gordon Martel (ed.), *'The Origins of the Second World War' Reconsidered* (1986).

[67] His reports formed the central feature of *The Times'* reporting of the proposed visit. On 4 April, for example, beneath a headline 'The Jews of Poland a Scheme of Dispersal', he wrote: 'Apart from questions of war and peace which have recently arisen the chief subject which Colonel Beck, Foreign Minister of Poland, hopes to discuss during his visit to London is emigration, especially that of Poland's Jews. It is

Germany,[68] an arrangement whereby Jews asked to leave Poland, or leaving voluntarily, would put their money into bank accounts in Poland before leaving which would be managed by banks either in Palestine or elsewhere. Poland had been among the earliest to attempt to find a practical solution to her difficulties in these matters, coming to an agreement with the French Government to explore the possibilities of emigration to Madagascar.[69] Poland had no doubt thought to raise the question with Chamberlain, partly because Britain was the mandatory power in Palestine, but also because Britain had announced on 19 February that she had accepted an American offer to send an expert mission to British Guiana to examine the possibility of Jewish emigrants from Europe being settled there. The position in Palestine itself was critical and virtually insoluble, as became clear with the opening of the Palestine conference in London on 7 February; the earlier refusal by the British Government to allow 10,000 Jewish children from Germany to go to Palestine, despite the offer of the Jewish Agency in Palestine to take them, had already shown how matters stood.

It was this factor alone which made Germany's expansion in Europe of acute and actual concern to every other country in the world. No one could then have foreseen what was to be the result of a European war for the Jewish community who were still there at the mercy of a totalitarian power whose central concern was their removal from Europe.[70] After the Czechoslovakia debacle a fund known as the

expected that he will not merely ask for space and facilities for the settlement of emigrants in the British Empire, but that he will present comprehensive suggestions and a plan of his own.' *The Times*, 4 April 1939, p.15.

[68] For discussion of these arrangements, which were actually carried out, between various banks in Palestine and the authorities in Germany, see Francis R. Nicosia, *The Third Reich and the Palestine Question* (1985).

[69] 'It was announced from Warsaw on 30 December [1937] that, after an understanding had been reached between the French and Polish Governments, Jews from Poland are shortly to be allowed to colonise in Madagascar ... A Polish-Jewish delegation visited Madagascar last summer and, according to the official statement, found it suitable for settlers of the peasant type. During the recent visit of M. Delbos to Warsaw, Colonel Beck stressed the desire of his Government for possibilities for the emigration of Polish Jews' *Gazeta Polska*, 1 January 1938.

[70] Bound up with the problem was the question of Germany being given some compensation for her colonies lost in World War I. To give only two examples: first, in a conversation with M. François-Poncet on 27 October 1938, Ogilvie-Forbes was informed that Germany would have to be offered something in lieu of her pre-war colonies and 'he mentioned Madagascar as a possible French contribution, instead of the Cameroons, which, restored to Germany would make too dangerous a salient in French Africa'. Had this come about, the 'Madagascar solution', which was at the base of the proposal, would have immediately become practicable. Secondly, Neville Chamberlain noted on a conversation with Oswald Pirow: 'Goering told him that he

Lord Mayor's Fund had been set up in London to give assistance to refugees who were in practical terms nearly all Jewish. It was known as the Lord Baldwin Fund, after the initial impetus given to it by Lord Baldwin, speaking from retirement. At a meeting in the Mansion House on 9 December 1938 with the Lord Mayor Sir Frank Bowater[71] in the Chair statements had been read from all over Europe, including one from the Pope, condemning the outrages being committed against the Jews. The most telling remarks were those uttered by Lord Rothschild:

> The slow murder of 600,000[72] people is an act that has rarely happened in history. It is an act you can prevent ... We have no primitive ideas of revenge against Germany for what it has done to our co-religionists ... we cherish Peace above all else, and there is not one Jew who would do anything to try to plunge this country into the bloodiest war the world could ever know.[73]

A practical step had been taken with the setting up of a camp for Jewish refugees at Richborough in Kent run by the Council for German Jewry. But the camp, which trained people, giving them practical skills they could use when they went on to Palestine, could only take 3,000 people.[74]

Had the British public not fully understood the connection between the totalitarian anti-semitic policies of Nazi Germany and the threat to world peace, the statements by Colonel Beck and the coverage of the question in *The Times* made it certain that they did.

The next major increase of tension was the result of the unannounced action by Italy against Albania. People who chanced to tune into Radio Tirana on 7 April would have heard an impassioned plea by King Zog for assistance as his country was being invaded by Italian forces. Two days later, over the same microphone, the new

---

would be prepared to surrender all claim to Tanganyika if that territory were used for the settlement of the Jews ...', 7 December 1938. Both papers may be found in the Public Record Office: FO 371/21791; C13497/13218/18 and C15270/13564/18.

[71] Sir Frank H. Bowater (1866-1947), Alderman of the City of London and Mayor of London 1938-39. Very considerable sums were raised for this organization. Among those on the Committee in Czechoslovakia was Wenzel Jaksch.

[72] This is the figure quoted. Over the following years it was raised as the situation developed, until finally, in 1942 in New York, the world was warned that 6,000,000 could die if something was not done.

[73] As published in the national press.

[74] For a brief description of this camp, see Norman Bentwich, *Wanderer in War* (1946), p.10. The book also contains an account of his meetings and discussions with Eichmann at the former Rothschild Palace in Vienna (p.13).

President of Albania, after the ousting of King Zog, M. Jaafar Ypi, was to be heard conveying a message of homage from the Albanian people to Mussolini. In the context of the rapid passage of events in the world at the time this does not seem to have caused uncontrollable alarm in Britain. Albania had had a curious history after World War I. It had been threatened with partition, and this had only been avoided through the persistent arguments of one of the experts in the British delegation, James Strachey Barnes. As we have seen, Barnes was now living in Italy and one of the foremost champions of Fascism. At one time he had been offered the kingship of Albania but had wisely declined, steering the crown instead towards his protégé, Zogu, who became King Zog I.[75]

Chamberlain reacted strongly at first, recalling Parliament on April 13, but after much discussion made it clear that he was going to do nothing. He remarked:

> No doubt some would say that we should now declare the Anglo-Italian agreement must be considered at an end. I do not take that view myself. Nobody with any sense of responsibility can in these days lightly do anything which would lead to an increase in international tension ...[76]

He then went on to point out that the Italians had agreed to withdraw all their volunteers from Spain, with their arms, armour and aeroplanes after the victory parade in Madrid, and were in fact doing so. This meant of course that the primary aim of the policy alluded to by Vansittart,[77] that Spain remain neutral and not become another Fascist State, was largely fulfilled. Critics from the left poured scorn on this achievement, especially the recognition of Franco's Government,[78] but it stood the test of time. Germany took another view; she saw the occupation of Albania as a brilliant gesture striking

[75] There was a widely circulated story that this title, 'King of Albania', was offered by Maundy Gregory to the head of a noble house who declined the offer on the grounds that it was not in his line. Always assumed apocryphal, it may well be that it had some actual basis in the events described here.

[76] Hansard, Vol. 346 col. 14.

[77] See above, p.39.

[78] See, for example, Attlee's remarks in the debate on his motion: 'That, in the opinion of this House, the decision of His Majesty's Government to grant unconditional recognition to Spanish insurgent forces dependent on foreign intervention constitutes a deliberate affront to the legitimate Government of a friendly Power, is a gross breach of international traditions, and marks a further stage of a policy which is steadily destroying in all democratic countries confidence in the good faith of Great Britain.' Hansard, vol.344, no.54, cols.1099-1218.

against what she referred to as encirclement but what in Britain was called the Anti-Aggression Front.[79]

In the greatly heightened tension caused by this act, and with a general conflagration expected daily in Europe, people turned again to Germany for further action. A little earlier, in March, there had been a war scare over a possible invasion of Holland by Germany; rumours had appeared on radio programmes which Germany attributed to Britain. Warner at the Foreign Office News Department had written to his opposite number in the BBC:

> Statements have appeared in the German Press to the effect that 'The British wireless has it on good authority that the Third Reich was mobilizing on 1 March, that it was going to annex Holland by force and what not.' The context implies that this sort of thing was in your German broadcasts. We have not been able to trace any such reference here, but, before replying to that effect to an enquiry which we have had we should be glad of your confirmation.[80]

With the Albanian invasion in progress these rumours were renewed. Holland put full emergency powers into operation and reservists were called up, borders were guarded and all main rivers and bridges were mined. The Dutch Premier, in a broadcast on 11 April, said that he had taken these steps 'to preserve Dutch neutrality against all possible eventualities' although he did not think that a direct attack on Holland was imminent.

Another well-documented false alarm was the case of Rumania. A German trade delegation was in Rumania, in fact on a routine trade mission; however, an attaché from the Rumanian Embassy in London went to the Foreign Office with information that this was merely a cover and that immediate German action against Rumania was to take place. The information proved to be completely false, but was followed by other warnings, spread by people of doubtful authority, that action of some sort was without any doubt imminent.[81] Finally,

[79] Not the strangest thing when reading contemporary accounts of affairs in the British press are the statements that Germany's fears of 'encirclement' were groundless, while the same papers were vigorously pressing for an extension of what was called the Anti-Aggression Front against the Axis powers to include Russia and any others who could be persuaded to join.

[80] BBC Written Archives Centre: R28/73/1, 16 March 1939. Possibly a JBC broadcast.

[81] The attaché was M. Virgil Tilea. There is an account of his 'scare' and its consequences in Cadogan's diaries, op.cit., p.159f. Irving describes his spreading of the rumour 'for purely commercial reasons' but without identifying his source. Presumably 'insider-dealing' had its attractions then as now, and wars, and rumours of wars, have traditionally caused exchanges to fluctuate more even than general elections.

the guarantee to Poland was extended to cover Rumania as well.

On 26 April, Chamberlain announced that he was introducing conscription. In doing so he scrapped a policy, first enunciated by Baldwin in 1936, that Britain would never introduce conscription in peace time and repeated by Chamberlain himself not four weeks before. The reason for Chamberlain's action, as he clearly stated when confronted by Attlee with this *volte face*, was that the guarantees given to Poland and Rumania together with the new conditions meant that mobilization could not wait on the formal declaration of war. The actions which actually made war now seemed to take place without warning and he had been obliged to go back on what he said. His declaration, in the terms in which he made it, seems almost to have amounted to a declaration of war. It was followed on 28 April by a speech given by Hitler to a specially convened session of the Reichstag. His speech began by referring to an extraordinary 'Peace Appeal' by President Roosevelt[82] which had been broadcast to the world on 14 April. As Hitler remarked:

> Before I actually received this document the rest of the world had already been informed of it by radio, and newspaper reports and numerous commentaries in the democratic world press had already generously enlightened us as to the fact that this telegram was a very skilful tactical document, destined to impose upon the states in which the people govern the responsibilities for the warlike measures adopted by the plutocratic countries.[83]

In fact, like the proposals which had been the formal cause of Eden's resignation the year before, they acted only as a lever to force a greater escalation of the cold war. Hitler dealt with Roosevelt's points with overpowering irony after responding to Chamberlain's introduction of conscription by scrapping the Anglo-German Naval Agreement, which had been the token of Britain and Germany's never going to war again in the famous 'scrap of paper' signed after Munich, and, on

[82] See reference to this talk above, p.104n65, à propos Roosevelt's suggested talks at the time of Eden's resignation.

[83] As reported in the national press. A translation on this occasion was distributed directly from the Anglo-German Information Service in London and shortly after published as a pamphlet, printed in Germany. The translation of previous Hitler speeches appearing in *The Times* and elsewhere had been edited, frequently quite severely; who was responsible for this is not clear. The authorities in Britain allowed the dissemination of these speeches when they were printed in Germany, but shortly after the Anglo-German Information Service began to have them printed in England and the Director, Dr Roessel, and members of his staff were then expelled from the country. No explanation of these complex affairs has ever been forthcoming.

the Polish front, by annulling the German-Polish Non-Aggression Pact. This, coupled with Chamberlain's speech on conscription, moved Europe to the very brink of war.

In this highly charged situation the world was startled by an announcement that the Duke of Windsor had decided to break the silence he had imposed on himself since his abdication, in May 1936, and broadcast to the world an appeal for world peace. Over 400,000,000 people heard the broadcast, but it has remained almost entirely unknown in Britain since it was banned by the BBC. The exact circumstances of the ban are obscure. The BBC at first referred the matter to Buckingham Palace but was directed by them to 10 Downing Street. It appears that, after consultation at the highest level, the BBC decided to agree to impose its ban. The BBC's archives contain no specific file on the incident and the matter was referred to in the Governor's minutes only in general terms. There was extensive coverage of the ban in the contemporary press, much of it, apparently, leaked from the Duke of Windsor's side, probably by the American broadcasting network which was naturally not happy about what was occurring. The King and Queen were at this time on board ship in the Atlantic, about to begin their tour of Canada and America,[84] and there were accounts of ship-to-shore telephone conversations between George VI and his brother in an attempt to get the talk cancelled completely. The truth of the matter will probably never be known, but the broadcast went ahead on a world-wide link-up. Before coming to the microphone the Duke went on a tour of the burial grounds at Verdun, looking at the graves of the hundreds of thousands of men who had been killed there. He made it plain that he was speaking on behalf of those dead whose graves he had visited that day:

I speak for no one but myself and without the previous knowledge of any Government. I speak simply as a soldier of the last war whose most earnest prayer it is that such cruel and destructive madness shall never again overtake mankind. I break my self-imposed silence now only because of the manifest danger that we may all be drawing nearer a repetition of the grim events which happened a quarter of a century ago.

You and I know that Peace is a matter far too vital for our happiness to be treated as a political question. We also know that in modern warfare victory will only lie with the powers of evil ...

Whatever political disagreements may have arisen in the past the supreme aim of averting war will, I feel confident, impel all those in

[84] Had war actually broken out at this time, as was feared, they would have been in Canada. This may be the source of the then current rumour that the Royal Family would leave Britain and go to Canada in the event of war. The rumour was repeated by German propagandists throughout the war.

power to renew their endeavours to bring about a peaceful settlement.

Among measures which I feel might well be adopted to this end is the discouragement of all that harmful propaganda which, from whatever source it comes, tends to poison the minds of the people of the world. I personally deplore, for example, the use of such terms as 'encirclement' and 'aggression'. It is in a larger spirit than that of personal or purely national interests that peace should be pursued. The Statesmen who set themselves to restore international security and confidence must act as good citizens of the world and not only as good Frenchmen, Italians, Germans, Americans or Britons.

In the name of all those who fell in the last War I urge all political leaders to be resolute in their discharge of this mission. The World has not yet recovered from the effects of the last carnage. The greatest success that any Government could achieve for its own national policy would be nothing in comparison with the triumph of having contributed to save humanity from the terrible threat which threatens it today.[85]

To assess the effect of this broadcast is extremely difficult. However, there was one extraordinary series of events which suggests that Chamberlain at the least was greatly influenced away from war at exactly this time. In the days before the Duke of Windsor's broadcast, war had been so close that the final steps to perfect the propaganda campaigns at the outbreak of war had been set in motion. This involved, as a central part of the campaign, the dropping of tens of millions of pamphlets over Germany, in the cities and over the front lines, stating clearly and briefly where the cause and responsibility for war lay. The drafting of the text of the document and the printing of the copies to be sent could only be arranged immediately before the outbreak of war – obviously, since the text could not be known until then and the printing and distribution was immensely costly and difficult to arrange. Responsibility for perfecting the text and arranging printing was shared between Sir Robert Vansittart and Sir Campbell Stuart at Electra House, and in fact this process had been started and the printing arranged when a sudden halt was called. On 8 May Campbell Stuart had written to Vansittart:

> I enclose herewith two copies of the amended leaflet in English and German which was agreed at our meeting today. I should like to know as soon as possible whether Lord Halifax and Sir Samuel Hoare approve them.[86]

[85] Text from the speech, National Sound Archives: NSA LP 20246.b.1.
[86] Public Record Office: FO 395/647c; P2288/105/150.

On 10 May Sir Horace Wilson, who had also received a copy of the proposed pamphlet, wrote to Vansittart:

> I think [Chamberlain] feels that there is difficulty drafting at the present time a leaflet which is intended to be used at times and in circumstances now *quite unforeseeable* [my italics] and perhaps the draft which has been prepared is as good as any for such a purpose. He shares, however, doubts which others have felt as to the utility of the leaflet which may prove to be quite unsuitable when the time comes. I think he feels, too, that if and when hostilities break out, let us say, with Germany, the minds of the people of Germany, like the minds of our people, will be too much occupied with the excitements attendant upon the event to pay much attention to leaflets ... I gather from the minutes of the meetings that the decision to print and hold a stock of this particular leaflet does not prejudge the question whether *at the time* distribution should in fact take place. The decision on this point will be taken by the Government of the day, in the light of the then circumstances.[87]

Both Vansittart and Leeper were astonished by this letter, and showed it in their reactions. Vansittart wrote to Halifax:

> It would seem in the light of this letter that unless there has been some misunderstanding we have all been rather wasting our time; but I cannot help thinking there must be some misunderstanding.[88]

But it appeared that there was no misunderstanding. Chamberlain had simply turned his back firmly on all the alarmists around him and had shaken himself free from the frame of mind where even the rumours of a 26-year-old *News Chronicle* reporter had brought him to thinking that war was imminent.[89] It is difficult to see what can have caused this change. Perhaps there was change in the air and the Duke of Windsor's appeal caught it, as did Chamberlain in his letter to Vansittart; but it is at least plausible that the broadcast, banned in England but heard with universal acclaim all over the world, did indeed change the climate of opinion and dispel the thought of war from Chamberlain's mind.

The discounting of Vansittart's alarmism, which Cadogan thought later had brought him to the verge of collapse,[90] was accompanied by

[87] Public Record Office: FO 395/647c; P2290/105/150.
[88] Ibid.
[89] I.e. Ian G. Colvin.
[90] Vansittart's sources had him expecting war almost daily for most of 1939. Cadogan in a typical entry in his diary wrote: '... Van rang up in high state of excitement ... I asked him to come around and gave him cold supper. I have never

yet another change in his fortunes. On 15 June Chamberlain announced that he was setting up a Foreign Publicity Department with Lord Perth at its head.[91] Its purposes were identical with the Vansittart Committee, and a memorandum to Vansittart's secretary from Leeper established that he would 'hand over the reins' to Perth, while keeping his old interest in Intelligence.[92] The change was not allowed to go unremarked by the public. On 19 June Arthur Henderson tabled a written question asking 'whether the new Information Department at the Foreign Office is to take over the work of the Vansittart Committee'.[93] The answer was in the affirmative.

Critics have suggested that this appointment by Chamberlain was a weak one, some going so far as to suggest that there was actual scandal attached to it. Philip M. Taylor remarks:

> The news of Perth's appointment created, in Oliver Harvey's[94] words, 'a real scandal'. Perth was certainly an unusual choice. Although he had enjoyed a long and distinguished diplomatic career, he could hardly have claimed to be well grounded in propaganda techniques. He had, of course, served as Secretary-General to the League of Nations before taking up the Rome embassy, during which time he undoubtedly experienced League publicity and Italian propaganda, but there is no indication that he took an active interest in either.[95]

Then, going on to quote Oliver Harvey's verdict on the appointment:

---

seen a man nearer nervous collapse. *His* source has told him H[itler] has chosen war ... Eventually calmed Van down a bit and packed him off about 11. This is the beginning of the "War and Nerves". And I have seen the first casualty!' Cadogan, op.cit., p.196.

[91] Lord Perth (1876-1951), formerly Sir Eric Drummond. Entered the Foreign Office in 1900; Précis Writer to the Foreign Secretary 1908, 1910-11; Private Secretary to the Foreign Secretary 1915-19; Secretary-General of the League of Nations 1919-33; British Ambassador to Italy 1933-39; Head of Foreign Publicity Department 1939; Ministry of Information 1939 and then Chief Advisor on Foreign Publicity to the Minister of Information 1939-40.

[92] Public Record Office: FO 395/647D; P2519/105/150.

[93] Ibid.

[94] Oliver Charles Harvey, Baron Harvey of Tatsborough (1893-1968). Entered Diplomatic Service 1919; became secretary to Anthony Eden and then Halifax; was in Paris at the beginning of the war and returned to become Eden's private secretary again after a brief spell on secondment to the Ministry of Information; succeeded Sir Orme Sargent as Deputy Under-Secretary (Political) 1946-48 and then became Ambassador in Paris, following Duff Cooper. His diaries were published after his death: J. Harvey (ed.), *The Diplomatic Diaries of Oliver Harvey, 1937-40* (1970).

[95] Philip M. Taylor, *The Projection of Britain* (1981), p.287.

It is a ramp of Sam Hoare and Horace Wilson, with the tacit and really unforgiveable acquiescence of H[alifax].[96]

Both Taylor's and Harvey's opinions are mistaken; if Perth's appointment could be criticized it was only on grounds of his age. Apart from that his experience at the League of Nations and later had given him a very great knowledge of propaganda and, in particular, broadcasting. In 1933 he had given the Broadcast National Lecture for the BBC on the subject of the League of Nations;[97] but his knowledge of broadcasting went much further than that of an accomplished essayist, for the League of Nations had set up, under his direction, its own radio station 'Radio Nations'. This had been the vehicle through which many of the statesmen of the League had gained a world audience. It had been through its microphones that Anthony Eden, for example, had broadcast to the world his welcome of Russia to the League and, later, his graphic description of Mussolini as a 'pirate'.[98] The station was also much used by the American commercial channels to send their broadcasts to America on the whole range of European affairs. After Perth had left, the League produced one of the first detailed studies of radio political propaganda, still unrivalled in its field.[99] No doubt, as he continued his interest in radio, he would have examined this closely. Certainly while at Rome he was acutely conscious of propaganda; Bari was one of the main thorns in the side of Anglo-Italian relations, and it is even conceivable that his appointment was related to his great knowledge of this form of propaganda. Even more useful for someone who would most probably lead a Ministry of Information in time of war, he had a deep suspicion of the BBC's abilities. As the one person in Britain, besides Reith, who had presided over the creation of a radio station, he was fully entitled to his opinion, which he did not hesitate to express. On 3 November 1938, for example, he wrote to Lord Halifax from Rome:

The BBC are really incorrigible! I was listening to the Empire News this evening and when mention was made of the reception in the Italian Press of the approval of the House of Commons to the bringing into force of the Anglo-Italian Agreement the announcer stated that the news had appeared on the back page of the Italian newspapers.

[96] Ibid., p.288.

[97] Also published by the Cambridge University Press for the BBC: Sir Eric Drummond, *The League of Nations: The Twelfth of the Broadcast National Broadcast Lectures* (1933). These lectures were the predecessors of the more lengthy 'Reith Lectures'.

[98] See above, p.104.

[99] Thomas Grandin, *The Political Use of Radio* (1939 *Geneva Studies*).

Although this is literally correct it is a very unfair presentation of the facts.

It is true that the front pages of the morning and evening papers were completely taken up by the Vienna arbitral award, but on the last page but one under the heading 'latest news' great prominence was given to the debate, the headlines were large and the discussion fully and fairly reported. This is by no means the first time that the BBC has given a tendentious twist to announcements about Italy and I think, if possible, something ought to be said to them about it. The case to which I refer seems to me to be peculiarly bad and misleading in its implications.

Incidentally the BBC report of the Prime Minister's speech in the House last night was, to say the least of it scrappy and inadequate and was read in a perfunctory tone of voice whereas the summary of Eden's speech, for example, was read with a sort of eager acquiescence.[100]

Chamberlain had himself suffered at the hands of the BBC,[101] no doubt an added reason for appointing someone who, although an outsider when compared with Leeper, for example, had a deep knowledge of propaganda and an unrivalled knowledge of international affairs.

When war finally broke out radio played a major part both in the sequence of events and in the coverage given it, which enabled the world to follow the approach of the cataclysm in programmes that were often only minutes apart. One American commentator, R.G. Swing, produced a book *How War Came* in which the approach of war was chronicled solely by his radio broadcasts.[102] The first part of the book, 'From Prague to Danzig', dealt with events as they evolved in that period, ending with a broadcast on 18 August 1939. The second

[100] Public Record Office: P3248/P3250/P3404/5/150.

[101] There had been a number of concerted attacks on Chamberlain by the BBC, usually in the form of selective reporting of speeches and debates. He was also acutely conscious that the BBC news often misunderstood or misinterpreted vital questions; see for example his worries about the BBC coverage of the guarantee to Poland which were sufficiently strong for him to want to telegraph Warsaw to correct any misapprehension. *Cagodan Diaries*, op.cit., p.178.

[102] Raymond G. Swing was one of the few pre-World War I reporters who became equally famous over the radio; his talks were broadcast in England as well as America. In the preface to his book *How War Came* (1939) he remarked (p.8): 'When I went to Berlin in 1913, international diplomacy was reserved for the elect. The general public knew nothing about it, intellectuals knew a little and that not too soundly, and the only true knowledge was reserved to those who had been admitted into the fellowship of diplomacy ... But today ... Hitler speaking at Danzig, talks to ... every German, every Englishman, Frenchman, Italian, everyone who can afford a radio set or can listen to a set of his neighbours. The change is far too great for its significance to have been sufficiently grasped or to be fully exploited.' As far as the modern history of the period is concerned, this remains largely true today.

part, of equal length, called simply 'The Fourteen Days', dealt with the events following the signing of the Soviet-German pact on an hour-by-hour basis. The contrast between this and the events leading up to World War I, when radio did not exist and news could only be established by those capable of reading between the lines of newspaper reports, is a measure of the impact of a single techno- logical invention on the culture of the twentieth century. Besides giving a detailed coverage of the unfolding of events, Swing's book was also itself part of the propaganda war being waged by the Germans. A single example makes this point graphically.

On the eve of the invasion of Poland an elaborate piece of play-acting had been put on to justify Germany's action. The stage chosen for this was the radio station at Gleiwitz, the same station that had been at the centre of the German-Polish radio war which had embittered relations between the two countries in 1930. The play acted out on this stage was a raid by Polish irregular forces, in uniform, on the radio station. They were to occupy the station briefly, make a short broadcast, and then be captured and killed by German forces. In fact the men were not Polish but German prisoners dressed in Polish uniforms, brought to the scene and actually executed. There have been numerous accounts of this unsavoury incident including one by the man who organized it.[103] But the question has never been asked: for whom exactly was this play-acting conducted? The answer was the German people on the home front, but beyond them the world's media, informed of the alleged outrage over the German radio and through the news services. And a detailed example can be seen in Swing's broadcast to America at 9.45 a.m. on 1 September:

> It should not be necessary to say, though it is worth keeping the record straight on the subject, that the twenty-one incidents of Polish border outrages which occurred during the night had nothing to do with starting the war. Hitler in his speech gave the impression that they had. Whether or not Polish soldiers exchanged shots with Nazis at one or more places during the night had nothing to do with starting the war. The strange attack on the Gleiwitz radio station on the German side of Upper Silesia had nothing to do with it. A band of Poles as you know, stormed the station, drove out its personnel and put out a broadcast calling on Poland to defend itself. Nazi police soon shot down many of the radio raiders.[104]

Less than twelve hours after the incident, full details of it were thus

[103] Louis Hagen (ed.), *The Schellenburg Memoirs* (1956).
[104] Raymond G. Swing, op.cit., p.228.

being broadcast over American radio as the truth, heard by millions of listeners and entering their memories as one of the central events that started World War II. From being a propaganda ploy of doubtful value it can be seen as a brilliant exercise which fulfilled every hope placed in it. The true events were later made known, but in countless other cases the story appearing in print all over the world has become as much fact as if it really happened as the propagandists said it had. And this relationship between radio propaganda and the printed word, already important, became vital during the war itself when virtually all the news appearing in the papers came from wireless reports.

In the hours before absolutely irrevocable military instructions were given Sir Nevile Henderson gives another brief insight into the role that the radio played in Nazi thinking. In the afternoon of the day before Poland was invaded Henderson went to see Field-Marshal Goering:

> He invited me to come and see him that afternoon, and I did so at 5 p.m. in the company of Sir G. Ogilvie-Forbes. Inasmuch as I had heard that the text of the proposals which Ribbentrop had refused to give me was to be broadcast on the radio that evening, my first remark was to point out to the Field-Marshal that this procedure would probably and finally wreck the last prospect of peace, and to beg him to do his utmost to prevent their publication. Goering's reply was that he could not intervene, and that the German Government felt obliged to broadcast their proposals to the world in order to prove their 'good faith'.
>
> Instead he talked for the best part of two hours of the iniquities of the Poles and of Hitler's and his own desire for friendship with England, and of the benefit to the world in general, and the advantage to England in particular, of such a friendship. It was a conversation which led nowhere ...[105]

Henderson saw that the broadcasts would mean that the 'sixteen points' would become public property, and that the Polish Government could not say that they knew nothing of them. The question of what exact knowledge they actually had of them is a matter merely for debate since without them being 'formally' presented they could not, in diplomatic terms, be said to be known. The radio blew away such old-world diplomatic niceties and added a direct insult as well. In fact the broadcast took place, and within minutes the Polish radio had published a resounding rejection. As

[105] Nevile Henderson, *Failure of a Mission, Berlin 1937-1939* (1940), p.275.

Henderson saw, no debate or diplomatic discussion was possible.

In Britain two days were to pass before a formal mechanism for declaration of war was decided upon and the decision to use it irrevocably taken. An ultimatum was issued on 3 September requiring Germany to withdraw from Poland and to reply within two hours, that is, since the ultimatum was delivered at nine o'clock, by eleven o'clock.

Shortly after the ultimatum had expired Chamberlain announced directly to the British people over the radio that they were at war. The broadcast from 10 Downing Street was recorded and has been replayed on countless occasions since. Later that day King George VI broadcast a message to the people of the Empire from Buckingham Palace.[106]

As Ramsay MacDonald had said in his broadcast after King George V's speech opening the Naval Conference in 1930:

> ...There will be *some* state which will refuse to carry out its obligations to the community of peaceful states; the machinery of arbitration will break down *somewhere* and *somehow*; do what we may a situation will arise one day when a deadlock of *some* kind will have to be faced, and there will be but one remaining method, the old fashioned one of a fight.[107]

Neville Chamberlain, listening to MacDonald's words, can scarcely have imagined that it would be he, a man of peace before anything, who would have to use that one remaining method.

[106] Both speeches are in the National Sound Archive: Chamberlain on NSA LP 2287/f/2 and King George VI on NSA LP 2287/f/4.
[107] As reported in contemporary press; see above, p.82.

PART THREE

8. Lord Haw-Haw
and the Anti-Lie Bureau

Chamberlain's broadcast announcement of the war was only one of a series of broadcasts by Ministers that supplemented the normal means of communication between government and governed. The arrangements for evacuation were co-ordinated in this way, and the numerous other wartime regulations were dinned into the public consciousness by constant repetition over the radio. As the war developed, this became in a real sense a substitute for the normal democratic processes.[1] The recruitment for the armed forces was also linked to broadcasting, as it had been before the war.

The German English language broadcasts which had been so scorned by Cadogan and Leeper when they were first threatened were stepped up on the outbreak of war. They were given the inestimable advantage over the British broadcasters of a campaign to report which brought as swift a victory as that in Czechoslovakia even though there was actual fighting. This was only the first great shock to military morale among the Allies; in the propaganda war which accompanied it, however, Britain set about creating one of the most successful counter-propaganda campaigns of modern times. It was essentially one of ridicule, and its chief protagonist, a fictional character, 'Lord Haw-Haw', is still remembered by those who heard 'him', and by even more who did not.

British news sent out by the BBC in the earliest days of the war was plagued by censorship and other difficulties when the Ministry of Information was set in place as the interface between the war news and the media. It was only natural for the British public to continue as they had done before the war and comb the air waves for other

[1] On his return to the BBC Guy Burgess became closely involved in this kind of broadcasting, and I shall be examining this in detail in a future volume. Burgess used the phrase 'Bureaucratic Totalitarianism' to describe the system of government which evolved at this time. Whether he invented the phrase or not, it clearly relates to the controversial book by Bruno Rizzi: *The Bureaucratization of the World: The USSR, Bureaucratic Collectivism* (1939 English ed. 1985). In this and the next chapters radio and propaganda, as such, are examined.

English-language broadcasts. They soon found that the German stations were providing vivid and up-to-the-minute reports of great accuracy provided by special teams of reporters who went with the troops right up to the fighting areas.[2] There were also pointed attacks on Britain for entering the war; on the home front sharp contrasts were drawn between the British system of government and the German, particularly over the unemployment question.

These programmes were essentially the same as those begun in April and were put out by the same team, headed by Norman Baillie-Stewart; to most people, who were hearing them for the first time, they were strikingly novel. Among the listeners were some professional journalists who had been sent by the *Daily Express* to a listening post in the country to 'listen in' to what the Germans were saying.[3] The brightest of this group was Jonah Barrington, and it was he who first gave a name to the voice known to the monitors as 'Oxford Accent': Lord Haw-Haw of Zeesen. Even at the time not many people knew that Zeesen was the German overseas transmitting station and that part of the title was soon dropped. Barrington gave him a wife, 'Winnie of Warsaw', also known as Winnie the Whooper, and created other characters, 'Auntie Gush and Uncle Smarmy', names redolent of those given to the popular radio personalities of those days. Only Haw-Haw has survived. In a very short time Barrington had written and published a complete biography of 'Haw-Haw' which had as its preface a brief quotation from Haw-Haw himself:

Dr Johnson had his Boswell. I, thank Adolf, have my Barrington.[4]

When Barrington died nearly fifty years later, his obituary referred to his creation of 'Lord Haw-Haw' as the central achievement of a long life as a popular broadcaster and radio critic

[2] Britain subsequently developed an equivalent group of broadcasters with portable recording apparatus, much used when the tide of war turned in Britain's favour.

[3] The listening post was in the country simply because it had been thought that London would be exposed to saturation bombing as soon as war was declared. The BBC was dispersed from London, as were all vital Government security services. Mostly they returned during the phoney war period, remaining thereafter to see through the Blitz.

[4] The deification of Hitler ('thank Adolf') had its serious side. In March 1937 the Pope had 'warned the Church against the deification of any human being and denounced as idolatrous the Third Reich propaganda in favour of a Race-God'. During the war some 18B detainees held religious services focussing on a deified Adolf Hitler. For these services, which appear to have been taken seriously by those involved, see Public Record Office: HO 214/45. Quoted in Richard Thurlow, *Fascism in Britain: A History, 1918-1945* (1987), p.226.

... celebrated for having bestowed the sobriquet of Lord Haw-Haw on William Joyce, the nasal Axis propagandist in the 1939-45 war ... by calling Joyce Lord Haw-Haw Barrington helped to make the obnoxious broadcaster the laughing stock of two continents.[5]

The strength of the myth is shown even here, for, if there is one thing we can be certain of, it is that the voice called 'Oxford Accent' by the monitors and christened 'Haw-Haw' was not that of William Joyce. The authorities in Britain must have been fully aware of this since they knew that the same voice had been on the air since April and William Joyce was known to have left the country only two days before the Emergency Powers Act 1939 came into operation in August. It was decided to take up the name and develop it into a fully-fledged campaign that swept the country. Naturally this created much speculation as to who 'Haw-Haw' actually was. It was essential if 'Haw-Haw' was to be identified with a living person that no link be made between any political group within Britain, in particular with Sir Oswald Mosley's British Union, whose political line the broadcasts closely followed. The majority of the public listening to the programmes, which was as high as 70 per cent of the listening public at weekends, knew nothing of the details of Mosley's policies, as he had been effectively banned from the media; firm identification of his party with the very shrewd and pointed criticisms of the social system in Britain put out by 'Haw-Haw' would have been a disaster. William Joyce on the other hand was almost unknown to the British public and had hardly any following in Britain; also he was known to be working in some capacity for the German radio. By the time Mosley came to be interrogated, after his detention, the identification of 'Haw-Haw' with Joyce could be confidently made by Norman Birkett and as confidently agreed to by Mosley.[6]

The reality was very different. A radio station in those days required considerable numbers of people to run it. To prepare programmes, write scripts, produce them and carry out the numerous essential jobs that need to be done for a smooth programme, other than simple music shows, to be produced was a complex task. When the Allied forces entered Berlin at the end of the war the British Press were informed that over a hundred English-speaking people, mostly British, had been working for the German English-language radio stations. These included women as well as men, people who had found themselves in Berlin for a variety of reasons when war broke

[5] *Daily Telegraph*, 24 September 1986.
[6] The full transcript of the interrogation has now been released in the Public Record Office, see HO 283. 13-16.

out, or who had made their way there after war had been declared.
Some had even been brought there from prisoner-of-war camps.
Typical of these perhaps, and a source of considerable worry to the
security authorities when they found out about her, was Mrs P.P.
Eckersley, wife of the pioneer BBC Engineer,[7] and the man who had
provided the technical know-how for the Mosley station, in
collaboration with W.E.D. Allen and Oliver Hoare. Originally a
member of the Independent Labour Party, she and her husband had
visited Germany for a holiday in 1935. They saw policies being
implemented to deal with unemployment and other social questions
which were desperately needed in Britain. As she remarked, 'We saw
things being actually done, whereas in England they had only been
talked about.' They had visited Germany every year since, although in
1939 she had gone on her own, taking their son who was going to
school in Germany. In 1938 she had drifted away from her husband
politically, and his devoted adherence to Mosley, as she moved further
to the right and finally joined the Imperial Fascist League.[8] She had
been in Berlin when the war broke out and had stayed initially
because of the sheer difficulty of returning. To this was added the
conviction that the war, 'the Polish business' as she called it, would
soon be over, and the fact that most of her friends there were
American or married to German citizens and not likely to leave.
Internment procedures in Germany were less rigorous than in
Britain,[9] and she had only to report to the police once a week, which
did not force the true nature of her position upon her. When her
money ran out she soon found employment working for the
English-language radio station, first doing some broadcasting herself
and later moving to a desk job that involved going through English
newspapers to extract news and opinion that could be used in
programmes. Perhaps the greatest service she performed for those
running the station was to recruit William Joyce and his wife.

    William Joyce had been warned by a contact in MI5 that he was
about to be arrested under the Emergency Powers' Regulation 18B.[10]

---

[7] See above for an account of P.P. Eckersley and Mosley's radio team, p.120f.

[8] The Imperial Fascist League was founded by a veterinary surgeon, Arnold Leese.
For a full description and history of the party, see Thurlow, op.cit., passim.

[9] A classic example of this is seen in the case of P.G. Wodehouse. All internees in
Germany were released when they reached retirement age and this rule applied in
Wodehouse's case. Wodehouse made a few innocuous broadcasts immediately after
his release, probably without realizing the significance of what he was doing. Then,
given the option of proceeding to a neutral country or staying with friends in the
Hartz mountains, he remained in Germany until the end of the war.

[10] This regulation only applied to those who were known to be in sympathy or
regular contact with a hostile power, namely Germany. Mosley and his colleagues

Instead of going to Ireland, as members of his family had thought most likely, he took advantage of an introduction he believed he had to Goebbels' Propaganda Ministry in Berlin. Unfortunately his contact, who both he and MI5 thought was a German agent, was nothing of the sort, merely a journalist who was dabbling in the espionage field. Joyce found to his horror that he was stranded in Berlin with almost no funds, war had been declared and his approaches to the authorities had got nowhere. One day early in September he and his wife had ended a fruitless day, searching for somewhere to live, having tea at one of the main Berlin hotels, and there, by chance, they were seen by Mrs Eckersley who knew Joyce and had made small financial contributions to his party before the war. On her advice Joyce approached the authorities running the English-language radio station and got employment in a junior capacity carrying out translations. In a short while his actual position as leader of one of the principal National Socialist parties in Britain was recognized and he embarked on his radio career.

Joyce had obtained a first-class degree in English Literature at Bedford College, University of London, and he had subsequently embarked on a Ph.D, at King's College, London. His literary interests and political thought both developed rapidly in Berlin into one of the most sustained outbursts of political polemic in British letters, rivalling the achievements of such masters of the political pamphlet as William Prynne in the seventeenth century.[11] Later in the war Joyce made the mistake of deciding to trade on the British propaganda triumph of Lord Haw-Haw and started a programme in which he himself spoke featuring as the 'real' Lord Haw-Haw. Many listeners in England at the time knew that this was not the voice they had got to know and hate,[12]

had taken great care to have no connection with Germany or the Nazi Party and therefore could not be detained under this regulation. When they were eventually detained it was under the specially drafted Regulation 18B(1a). Joyce was on a very short list of 18B detainees and would have been imprisoned immediately.

[11] William Prynne (1600-1669), one of the most prolific political pamphleteers in an age of pamphleteers. Wood said of him in *Athenae Oxoniensis*. 'I verily believe that if rightly computed, he wrote a sheet for every day of his life reckoning from the day he came to the use of reason and the state of man', vol.ii, p.852, Bliss's edition. Anyone looking through the immense output from Joyce's radio channels would conclude that he equalled this achievement. Like Prynne he wrote in a less than perfect style, on occasion, though from choice rather than inability. Prynne suffered for his polemics, being twice sentenced to have his ears removed by the common hangman. Joyce led a relatively untroubled life until he too met the common hangman nearly three hundred years after Prynne's death.

[12] Although there was intense propaganda pressure to sustain the identification of Joyce with the original Haw-Haw, the public were not always fooled. See 'Debased Lord Haw-Haw' by F.H. Loxley, *Daily Telegraph*, 30 September 1986.

but the fiction had now become fact, a fact that was to take Joyce to the gallows.

Joyce's scripts, especially those written for the clandestine stations, were so convincing that they created a particular problem for the counter-propagandists at the Ministry of Information. This was the seemingly unstoppable spread of rumours which were given a spurious authenticity by being attributed to 'Lord Haw-Haw'. The old tag 'I read it in the papers' had long been replaced by 'I heard it on the radio'. This now became 'Haw-Haw said'. The department which dealt with these so-called 'Haw-Haw rumours' was the appropriately named 'Anti-Lie Bureau' of the Ministry of Information. The purpose of this bureau was originally to counteract supposed German propaganda lies with the truth. More often they found themselves in the position of giving the lie to rumours which were in fact true. Joyce and the other script writers soon realized that information from spies was unnecessary when writing for the average member of the British public. It was quite sufficient to tell them things directly related to their own environment, things happening around them, for everything else to be carried along with it, including demoralizing half truths and embarrassing political facts. The sources of the 'rumours' most used were those that Mrs Eckersley and her colleagues worked from that inexhaustible quarry, the British newspapers. It is clear from evidence given in interrogations after the war that Joyce had access to the full range of the British Press within twenty-four hours of publication. Britain had German and other enemy papers in the same time; the planes which carried them arrived at specially arranged points at neutral airports, usually in Spain and Sweden, where waiting porters rapidly exchanged the bundles of newspapers from one plane to the other.

Anyone who now reads the wartime British press, censored though it was by a variety of means, can soon see how the most 'authentic' rumours could be broadcast within hours of the things referred to actually happening.

To make the matter absolutely clear, two examples, found in papers in the Public Record Office, one a typical 'Haw-Haw rumour', the other more serious, are given here.[13] The first was a statement reported to the MOI that 'Lord Haw-Haw' had said that a woman had recently closed her nursing home in Beaumont Street, London and moved to Bracknell because the air-raids on London had made her business impossible. This was denied by the MOI's Anti-Lie

[13] There is a Haw-Haw rumours file in the Public Record Office: INF 1/265. This contains a great deal of unsorted material, from which the present account is largely drawn.

Bureau, as were all such rumours; but an internal enquiry that followed further insistence that the rumour was true established that the broadcast had in fact taken place and was based on an advertisement in the *Times* personal column the previous day.[14]

The second example was at the time of the 'parachute' scare. Just before the planned invasion of Britain a number of German spies were parachuted into the country with radio sets. Rumours of their arrival spread rapidly, aided by reports on the German English radio. The Anti-Lie Bureau counteracted these by spreading stories likely to ridicule the reports, usually along the lines of men disguised as nuns with heavy boots being seen descending by parachute, or of a parachute having been found in a field of corn with nobody attached to it, and no tracks leading away from it.[15] These stories are still remembered and repeated today. More direct rumours also cropped up. One, for example, actually reported the capture of one of the parachutists. On 26 September the secretary of the Beckenham branch of the Ministry of Information's local Committee wrote to the Anti-Lie Bureau about a report that a parachutist had landed at Denton, Northampton and been captured shortly after. The Anti-Lie Bureau replied with its usual lie that no parachutists had landed and that there was no truth in the rumour. On 11 October the secretary replied in some confusion, saying that the report was apparently true as a Civil Defence circular had been issued locally to act as guidance in future cases. He went on:

> This notice stated that the German parachutist was found in a ditch near Denton, five miles east of Northampton, three weeks ago. He was arrested at 5.30 p.m. having apparently been dropped during the previous night, and had in his possession a loaded six-chamber revolver, a wireless transmitter, £200 in notes (old and new) and a forged identity card, giving a Birmingham address. It is also stated that the man spoke perfect English and on being interrogated he said that his instructions were to go to Stratford-on-Avon, where he lived before the war, to mingle with friends and transmit any news which might be of importance to the enemy.[16]

This very circumstantial account would have made anyone think that a parachute had indeed landed. And they would have been right, for exactly this incident had occurred. The name of the parachutist was

[14] Public Record Office: INF I/265.

[15] This story was always slightly suspected by countrymen: anyone trying to follow tracks in a field of corn with a breeze playing can loose his own tracks as easily as someone else's. The story was repeated in print as recently as 1979. The question of how the parachute opened and fell without anyone in it was also left unanswered.

[16] Public Record Office: INF 1/265.

Gösta Caroli, a Swedish citizen; he later went on to become one of the famous double-agents who fed information to the Germans under British control, surviving the war and dying in Sweden in 1975.[17]

Clearly the Anti-Lie Bureau could not use one of their standard lies in this case and so they resorted instead to covert threat, writing on 25 October:

> Thank you for your letter of 11 October. I am afraid I have been rather a long time in answering it, and I now have to give you an unsatisfactory reply. I have made a good many enquiries but it does not seem possible that I can get any further in the matter without the name and number of the member of the Home Guard who gave the original information.[18]

Hardly surprisingly this brought the correspondence to a close.

The whole matter of rumour and the activities of the Anti-Lie Bureau would have remained merely an embarrassing episode in British history, of limited importance and of significance only as an example of the sort of thing that could happen even within a democratic society when faced with a situation of total war. But unfortunately the tinge of totalitarianism became stronger when it was decided, on the model of similar legislation in Nazi Germany, to prosecute people who spread these rumours. It is difficult, at first, to see how a prosecution of someone for the spreading of a 'Haw-Haw rumour' could be carried out, and on what possible evidence a Court would be able to convict, especially when it is borne in mind that many of these rumours were known to be true and were only denied for reasons of security and morale. The method used was to arrest someone who had without doubt been spreading a rumour and attributing it to Lord Haw-Haw. The BBC was then approached and asked if the Monitors had taken down any similar 'rumour' at the time. If the answer was negative a prosecution took place at which the BBC gave evidence.

From the first the BBC officers involved were anxious about the reliability of the evidence they were giving. Writing to the MOI on 28 May 1940 Mr R. Burns, Director of the Monitoring Service, drew attention to the problem:

Prosecution at Bath

> Confirming our conversation yesterday I am just placing on record that I attended at Bath Police Court on May 26 and gave evidence in the

[17] For an account of the actual incident with full information, see Nigel West [pseud: Rupert Allason], *MI5* (1983 ed.), p.233f.

[18] Public Record Office: INF 1/265.

case where a senior man in the Bath Fire-Watching Organization named Carle was convicted of spreading a rumour that Lord Haw-Haw had said that certain places in Bath would be bombed ... Although I think my evidence helped, I believe he would have been convicted even without it. It was a particularly difficult case for me to give evidence in owing to the rather vague nature of the rumour.

In certain cases of this kind one could give very definite evidence and in order that your regional offices may be able to make the fullest use of what we are able to do, I repeat below certain facts which I think should be known widely if we are to be of real help in the matter. There are two aspects: (1) the checking of rumours at the earliest possible moment, and (2) prosecution if the rumour can be traced to an individual.[19]

He went on to try to explain exactly when evidence could be given, making the point

the BBC Monitoring Service maintains 100 per cent coverage of all broadcasts in English directed to this country from Germany and German occupied territory.

It is obvious from their papers in the Public Record Office that the MOI Anti-Lie Bureau misunderstood the situation. It was thought that the monitors kept a record of *all* radio broadcasts from Germany, with little understanding of the impossibility of any monitoring service achieving this, let alone covering clandestine or pirate stations which might change their frequencies often. Mr Marriott[20] of the BBC, writing to Lindsay Wellington at the MOI, drew attention to this:

To judge from an enquiry addressed by Miss Hornby of 'Anti-Lies'[21] to Wakeham yesterday, there seems to be some misconception of our coverage of German broadcasts in English. The matter has a bearing on the whole question of so-called 'Haw-Haw' rumours.[22]

He went on to draw attention to the fact that many English-language broadcasts to places other than Britain were never monitored but could easily be picked up on radios in Britain. He ended:

[19] Ibid.

[20] Richard Marriott was the founder and head of the wartime BBC monitoring service. He wrote an account of the service in *Association of Broadcasting Staff Bulletin* for August 1960.

[21] By 'Anti-lies' is meant the Anti-Lie Bureau. It was appropriate that this organization for spreading lies under the guise of answering them should have been located in the Ministry of Information's building at Senate House, which was the model for George Orwell's Ministry of Truth in his *Nineteen Eighty-Four* (1949).

[22] Public Record Office: INF 1/265.

No monitoring service in the world, if it had ten thousand monitors, could state with certainty that any given statement had or had not been made unless it knew the wavelength on which it was reported to have been made.

The public outcry about these proceedings was considerable, and a number of people who had been convicted and sentenced subsequently had their convictions quashed. The sentences were in most cases minor, and never on the scale of those exacted in Germany where, in theory, the death penalty could be asked for the most serious offences.[23]

The whole episode illustrates both the strength of the invasion scare, which also caused the suppression of the British Union and other political groups, and the difficulty of using supposedly reliable expert witnesses when the basis of their evidence was not understood. There is no doubt that the majority of those convicted, denounced by neighbours and colleagues in vicious campaigns of rumour and innuendo that would have been easily recognized by religious bigots of earlier centuries, were entirely innocent of anything other than unwisely repeating what they had heard on their radios in their own homes.

Besides the campaign of ridicule, there was a more conventional counter-attack in the normal BBC programmes. The first serious attempt was a weekly broadcast by an anonymous commentator who answered some of the more scurrilous truths that had been noticed in the German English-language broadcasts and which had been the subject of letters to members of Parliament and the BBC's correspondence unit. After much thought by the Ministry of Information and the BBC it was decided to have a series written by Norman Birkett. The question of anonymity was an important one since Birkett was also the Chairman of the Committee that was hearing appeals by interned enemy aliens against their detention. No doubt his experience of close cross-examination of people from a wide variety of political backgrounds to determine whether they were genuine refugees or 'Fifth Column' Nazi agents gave him an impressive grounding in just the sort of questions that 'Haw-Haw' asked. Unfortunately his authoritative views failed to convince the

---

[23] I have not been able to establish whether the death penalty was ever enacted for this offence; special tribunals were to be set up to deal with such cases, but they had still not been established by the end of the phoney war. Contrary to the impression given by propagandists in Britain, it was never an offence in Germany, before the war, to listen to foreign broadcasting as such, and BBC programmes were printed in the German national press.

BBC's audience, and very shortly he was replaced by somone whose opinions were further to the left, J.B. Priestley.[24]

The series with which Priestley was ever after associated, *Postscripts*, was one in which he was at first merely a contributor, and not the first choice of speaker. However, once he began to deal with questions of immediate concern in his earthy rural voice, belying his Cambridge education, his ratings with the audience rose so rapidly that he made the series his own. He was indeed a very successful answer to the National Socialist propaganda being written by Joyce and the others. At times the resemblance between his views and those of the German radio was almost too close; a regional security officer wrote to his superiors that ordinary people in the country had great difficulty in distinguishing between propaganda of the 'right', National Socialist, and 'left', since both advocated curing social problems by revolution and both criticized the capitalist system on very similar grounds.[25] Priestley's views were occasionally quoted verbatim on German radio, and these examples were unfailingly noted by the secret Monitoring Intelligence Unit and reported to the Minister of Information who drew Churchill's attention to them.[26]

In one notorious broadcast he gave a graphic account of how an attempted tour around England in wartime was hindered by the fact that all hotels in the countryside that were at all reasonable were filled by wealthy refugees from London who were living off the fat of the land while poorer people were suffering the Blitz. The broadcast could have been written by Joyce, or the comrades of the British Communist Party in King Street; Duff Cooper so objected to passages in it that he personally removed the more revolutionary statements when it went to the Ministry for censorship. So 'political' was Priestley's line that attempts were made to use it and get him to put into his talk propaganda elements which the Government wished to see broadcast,

[24] J B. Priestley remains one of the few literary figures of the period whose reputation was inextricably bound up with his political opinions. Immensely successful during the war, he passed almost into obscurity in later years, still holding closely to opinions of the left. During the war itself he was involved with Common Wealth, a party founded by Sir Richard Acland. At the very end of his life there was some revival of interest in his work when his *English Journey* was re-interpreted in a visual form through television by Beryl Bainbridge.

[25] Public Record Office: INF 1/319. In a weekly intelligence report for 6 December 1939.

[26] Others who were frequently mentioned were George Bernard Shaw (occasionally entire speeches and articles were broadcast) Lloyd George and the military historian, B.H. Liddell-Hart. Liddell-Hart was actually notified of every occasion his name or his books were referred to in broadcasts in case there was some military significance in their use.

as a *quid pro quo* for the latitude he was being given. In America a series of speeches by ex-President Hoover against the Allied blockade of Europe, which was making innocent people suffer, caused annoyance to the MOI and the Government. Priestley was asked to insert some material that would help to counteract this. At first he agreed and altered his script to incorporate the required material but, for reasons which were obscure at the time, the programme never went out.[27]

Equally obscure was Priestley's later 'banning' by the BBC, his removal from the air by 'the authorities'. Great attempts were made by Priestley and papers that supported him, such as the *News Chronicle* to make this a *cause célèbre*. The reality was somewhat different. Priestley had become one of the greatest media celebrities of the day; he demanded fees that reflected his status, and while the BBC paid its radio broadcasters of those days well, it could not easily match the figures he could get from the popular press. For a series of six episodes, of half an hour each, Priestley would be paid roughly the average annual earnings of a skilled male worker of the time. This, in the end, was more than the BBC could stand. In addition it was obvious that they were struggling, perhaps for the first time, with a media personality who actually used it in the modern way, creating his public image through it, and then holding the media to ransom.

Priestley was finally caught in a manoeuvre that he had successfully carried out before. He had at first wished to cease appearing for a while, partly on financial grounds. He had then come back, but the Ministry of Information meanwhile had become worried about the tone his broadcasts were taking, especially after the threat of invasion was past. His contract was renewed, but only provisionally for a series of six talks. Priestley had assumed that this small number referred to the rate of payment at which his talks were being commissioned, and that after six talks fresh arrangements at a new fee would be made. Instead, at the end of the final talk, he was told the series would not be renewed. He immediately went to the press, and the myth of his 'banning' was born.

Priestley had, in fact, been beaten at his own game, a game very few were playing at the time, that of Media Politics. Of the radio personalities of the day who fought the same battle only one, W.J. Brown, also a *Postscripts* broadcaster, beat the BBC and the authorities. Having been induced to go to America on tour after a successful radio series, Brown returned to discover, as Priestley did, that his series was not being renewed. He saw that a by-election was

[27] BBC Written Archives Centre: J.B. Priestley contributor file. The file is extensive and gives much information about Priestley as a writer and a politician.

shortly to be fought, registered as an Independent candidate within days of the deadline, and was duly elected entirely on the strength of his radio personality.

This kind of political power in the media only developed during the war itself; before the war, in the period dealt with in this volume the battle had been carried on underground. This was all that was possible for either side when the British public had been shielded from the political conflict taking place on the continent by a combination of censorship in the media, the 'conspiracy of silence' at the BBC,[28] the control exerted by the Government over the press, and the fact that the Government in power was a 'National' one, latterly heavily weighted towards the Conservatives. The war brought propaganda and politics to a public that had never heard them before in the form, as we have seen, of a virulent alliance between the far right, heard in the writings of Joyce over the German radio, and the far left, the Communist Party and fringe groups travelling with them. Priestley, and another powerful pre-war radio speaker with a Cambridge background, John Hilton, went over entirely new ground for the listening public with impunity for months at a time.

These and other political arguments that raged on the home front during the phoney war were dealt with in *Realpolitik* terms by dismissing the common demand of the left and right, a People's Peace, and urging defiance of Hitler's Germany. Nor were the fundamental grievances, the basis of the political struggle, neglected by the authorities. They set up a commission headed by Lord Beveridge, whose name was always associated with the report it produced.[29] The battle over the implications of this report was fought on the home front in the latter part of the war, and on into the post-war years after the period with which this book deals. But the roots of that battle were in the propaganda wars that raged over the radio beneath the smoke-screen of 'Haw-Haw' counter-propaganda and the efforts of the MOI, its Anti-Lie Bureau and other departments all engaged in wartime equivalents of the pre-war 'conspiracy of silence'.

If the political war being carried on in Britain was largely an underground one and undescribed, the secret radio war waged by Britain against the Axis powers during the 'phoney war' was kept from the British public even more carefully. Like the pre-war activities of the JBC it remains unknown to this day. Much has been written about the BBC's broadcasts to Germany, and of the later 'black' or

[28] See above, p.41f.
[29] William Henry Beveridge, Lord Beveridge (1879-1963). First Chairman of the Employment Exchanges Committee; Director of Labour Exchanges 1909-16; Ministry of Food 1916-19, where he was largely responsible for rationing.

clandestine stations which were run by Sefton Delmer from Woburn Abbey which began in late 1940.[30] What took place before this station was set up is still largely a mystery. The JBC carried on with its pre-war activities, but on a much increased scale. Its overt side provided more and more programmes for South American and other neutral countries in the world, Europe included. The activities of its covert side are perhaps one of the most closely guarded secrets of wartime propaganda still kept within the archives of MI6.

It is worthwhile first to point to a classic example of bureaucratic muddle in the propaganda to enemy countries which has not been noticed before but which makes the position of the various elements in the propaganda set-up clear. This was on the subject of propaganda to Italy. When Britain declared war on Germany she did so in the context of last-minute Italian attempts to provide a peaceful solution to the Polish question, as she had done at the time of Munich. This time Italy failed, but she did not declare war on Britain. Neither did Britain declare war on her, despite the existence of the Axis pacts. Mussolini made it clear that Italy was remaining neutral. Unfortunately for British propaganda to Italy at this crucial time, Italy had been classified by the British authorities as an enemy power. Propaganda to her therefore should have come from Electra House.[31] The Ministry of Information was only supposed to deal with propaganda to neutral countries, which Italy was, but here also it had been assumed that Italy would be an enemy power, and there was no Italian section. To complete the picture, Electra House had decided that its well-staffed Italian section could not deal with Italy until she came into the war. The result was that no propaganda whatsoever went to Italy. As the civil servant dealing with Italian affairs wrote at the time

> It is almost incredible that such a state of affairs should have been allowed to come about and the existing position should not for a moment be allowed to continue. No wonder there have been difficulties

[30] See above, p.109n7 and below, p.192.

[31] After the Munich crisis Chamberlain had asked Campbell Stuart to set up an organization that was to deal with publicity (i.e. propaganda) in enemy countries. This followed the debacle of the BBC's attempted broadcasts to Germany. Electra House, on the Victoria Embankment in London, was the headquarters building of one of the largest cable and telegraph organizations. It was also the offices of the Imperial Communications Advisory Committee, of which Campbell Stuart was Chairman. All communications from Campbell Stuart, acting in his secret capacity, were sent on ordinary Imperial Communications Advisory Committee notepaper, marked 'secret'. For example, see Public Record Office: FO 395/647C; P2288/105/150. Campbell Stuart was considered an authority on propaganda (but

over Italy lately, difficulties which have caused Sir Percy Lorraine such distress ...[32]

Attempts were made at the Ministry of Information to deal with the problem, and Lord Macmillan wrote a placatory letter[33] to the Foreign Office saying that matters were being dealt with. In fact they were not, and Orme Sargent and others there became increasingly worried. Unquestionably the failure to deal with the Italian position was a major blunder in British policy. Reports from Italy all spoke of a swinging away from Germany, of a feeling growing after the signature by Germany of the pact with Moscow that the Italian/Nazi Axis would soon be replaced by a Soviet/Nazi one, and that this would be a far happier situation for Italy. The Catholic Church had suffered extensively under the Nazis, and the invasion of Poland by Germany had meant that the same could be expected there; worse, the Russian invasion of the greater part of that devoutly Catholic country could only foreshadow appalling tragedy for the Church – a tragedy that was to be shared by the churches in all the Baltic states.[34]

The Foreign Office struggles to get Italy dealt with in a more positive way point to a serious difference of opinion between them and other factions in the Government, echoing, no doubt, the aftermath of the Italian intervention in the Spanish Civil War and the very word 'Fascism', which had been fixed on by all shades of left-wing opinion as the final word of condemnation passed on all creeds not exactly in line with the Comintern view of the world. It would have meant the continuation of Chamberlain's pre-war policy of appeasement, as against that of hatred of Italy and Mussolini which characterized Eden's view.

In the complete absence of any official propaganda about Italy, the authorities both Italian in Britain and British in Italy were reduced to clutching at straws. A speech by Winston Churchill contained some references to Italy which normally would have passed without remark but in the charged atmosphere of late 1939 were commented on in

---

not security!) by virtue of his role in World War I. See Campbell Stuart, *Secrets of Crewe House: The Story of a Famous Campaign* (1920).

[32] Public Record Office: FO 371/23787; R8053/1/22. 21 September 1939.

[33] The letters from Macmillan are in the Public Record Office: FO 371/23787; R8259/1/22.

[34] One of the most significant effects of the alliance between Britain and Russia later in the war was to remove the fate of the Baltic states from public consciousness, although they pointed directly to the likely reality of post-war Europe. The fate of Czechoslovakia is remembered in great detail, and frequently; that of Lithuania, Latvia and Estonia is entirely forgotten.

Rome and London. Sir Noel Charles[35] in Rome sent a telegram mentioning that the broadcast had been the subject of an article by Gayda[36] in the *Giornale d'Italia* on 13 November, which was minuted:

> Mr Winston Churchill's actual words in his broadcast of 12 November as reported in *The Times* were 'Italy which he had feared would be drawn from her historic partnership with Britain and France ... a partnership which will become increasingly fruitful, has adopted a wide [sic:wise?] policy of peace' (this was reported in the *Guardian* as 'has adopted a policy of strict neutrality'). These words were not well chosen and Lord Perth [Ministry of Information] rang me this morning to enquire whether there was nothing we could do to curb Mr Churchill. I replied that so far I was aware we had never been consulted but that if we had been this sentence would never have appeared.[37]

It is clear that Churchill, like Vansittart a Germanophobe, was also willing to look kindly on Italy, and that this was liked in the Foreign Office but not in the Cabinet. Orme Sargent then minuted the telegram:

> I must exonerate Mr Churchill. He *did* show me the draft of his broadcast and gave me the opportunity of suggesting various omissions and alterations which he accepted. I must however plead guilty to having acquiesced in the passage about Italy as whole ... I confess that I did not appreciate the true heinousness of his apparently most friendly references to Anglo-Italian relations ... The Italian Ambassador in conversation with Sir A. Cadogan criticized the whole tone of the broadcast but said nothing about this passage.[38]

Signior Bastiani, the Italian Ambassador, had indeed gone to see Cadogan to say how shocked he was by the tone of the broadcast, but, as Sargent implied, he had been by no means as negative as might be expected. In addition to his general comments, he made a remark about the Bürgerbräukeller bomb plot against Hitler a few days before which Cadogan quoted:

---

[35] Sir Noel Charles (1891-1975). Entered the Diplomatic Service in 1919; Counsellor and then Minister at Rome 1937-1940, where he had the difficult task of re-establishing relations in the aftermath of sanctions. During the war he was Ambassador to Brazil, but he returned to Italy in 1944, when he re-performed the same difficult task, re-establishing relations in the aftermath of the war.

[36] Eugenio Gayda, Mussolini's Propaganda Minister.

[37] Public Record Office: FO 371/23787; R10116/1/22.

[38] Ibid.

He thought that the effect of the failure of the bomb plot would be to start further internal drives in Germany, rather than necessarily to launch an irrevocable offensive against England, but he could not say how things would turn.[39]

There is something slightly enigmatic in this remark. It was the standard line of German propaganda that this plot had been masterminded by the British Secret Service, working through Otto Strasser. Britain rejected this charge then, and has done so to the present day, and this view is well-nigh universally held. The remark by Bastiani suggests that he too automatically assumed that it was in some way a British plot, and Cadogan did not make any comment on his apparent assumption, or ask if that is what it was. The whole question of the Bürgerbräukeller bomb plot, and the 'Venlo Incident' after it, when two British Secret Service agents were seized by the Gestapo and dragged into Germany, remains a tantalizing mystery in which broadcasting was much involved.[40] As this also closely involves the hitherto unknown activities of the secret British German-language broadcasting stations, and the activities of Otto Strasser, it is worth pursuing here, as far as the limited information available will allow.

For the first months of the war British propaganda made considerable distinction between the German people and their leaders. This distinction was based on a false reading by Britain and her allies of the stability of the German regime. The Polish ambassador in Berlin was convinced that within a few weeks of the outbreak of war Polish troops would be in the heart of Germany. His Government was sure that the actual commencement of hostilities would create a revolution in Germany, probably lead by dissident Army Officers. The British authorities seem to have believed this as well but, whereas the Polish Government was soon disabused of the idea in the catastrophic three-week campaign which resulted in its extinction, the British went on believing it.

The Secret Service were among the main supporters of the theory of a dissident group in the Army and, relying on similar sources to Vansittart, they went on trying to make contact with the leaders of

[39] Public Record Office: FO 371/23787; R10188/1/22.
[40] Stuart Hibberd remarked in his autobiography: 'On 23 November I had to read nearly three pages about the Venlo incident ... in view of the importance attached to this piece of news I should like to have read it over beforehand, but on important occasions such as this last minute phone calls are often made to the Government Department concerned. In this case it was the Foreign Office and I had to read it all at sight.' *This – Is London* (1950), p.180. An uncharacteristic observation for Hibberd, one of the best-known announcers of his day. He no doubt resented the part he was made to play in this news manipulation, extending even to the Home Service.

this supposed group. By October they seemed to have succeeded. The security service agents in Holland had made definite contact, and had got as far as getting a radio to one of these groups and setting up regular communications with them. The overthrow of Hitler by an army putsch seemed a real possibility.

The 'Venlo Incident' was the culmination of these activities. The junior German officers with whom the British had been dealing had at last arranged to bring forward a senior General from the Wehrmacht to commence serious talks. After some delays two British agents arrived at the frontier town of Venlo but, instead of meeting a German General, found themselves overpowered and taken into Germany, where they remained until the end of the war. The radio contact, which had been the factor above all that had led them to take the matter seriously, was entirely run by the German Secret Service. Both sides were later to play this game, but 'Venlo' was one of the earliest and most successful examples of its use.[41] If there were any dissident German officers, as the bomb plot in 1944 and later research has suggested, the British Secret Service had failed to get into contact with them. However, the entire incident was raised to one of much greater significance by the events of the previous day. A bomb plot against Hitler had actually taken place, obviously well-prepared, and not surprisingly the German Government was convinced that it was planned to coincide with the meeting arranged at Venlo, particularly as the original meeting planned for that day had been postponed for twenty-four hours.

The complicity of the British Secret Service was widely believed at the time, although all subsequent evidence appeared to discount the possibility, and this included the transcripts of interrogations of the man who planted the bomb. However, there was one factor which has not so far been examined and which points to the actual possibility of some wider knowledge of the plot than that of a single man working on his own.[42] This was the existence of a radio propaganda broadcast

[41] Britain's subsequent use of this technique has been described in detail by one of those involved: J.C. Masterman, *The Double-Cross System in the War of 1939-1945* (1972). The book is also of interest in being one of the first books published supposedly in the face of Government disapproval (it was actually first published in America). The technique has been used frequently since for books on the Security Services, where no official history is ever to be written but it is felt that public interest is such that some broad unattributable outline of their activities should exist.

[42] The plot was attributed to one man, a carpenter, Johann Georg Elser (1903-45), just as the Reichstag fire was said to have been caused by a single man acting alone. In the case of the bomb plot the possibility that a single person was responsible seems, with hindsight, remote. Sigismund Payne Best included in his book on the Venlo Incident an account of a correspondence he had with Elser who was in the same

on a supposed German Freedom Station, or *Freiheitsender*, urging people to support those who had attempted to assassinate Hitler.

When Best and Stevens,[43] the British agents, arrived at Venlo they did so to the accompaniment, on the same day, of broadcasts on a radio station urging those who sympathized with the bomb plotters to rise and overthrow the Hitler regime. It would obviously have been impossible for a simple carpenter, however clever, to have arranged a *Freiheitsender* himself, or to have contacted a Freedom group with information of his bombing attempt without some further links being made between himself and the underground movement running the station. Who, then, organized these broadcasts?

Two obvious candidates were identified in an extraordinary publication apparently put out by the Communist Party in London shortly after the incident took place. Written anonymously, it was called *Freedom Calling: The Story of the Secret German Radio* and was widely circulated in London, a copy reaching Hugh Dalton, who asked for enquiries to be made.[44] The pamphlet referred specifically to the broadcasts which had been made at the time of Venlo and the bomb plot, and went to considerable lengths to show that these had been made not by the 'original' Freedom Station, which they claimed to be theirs, but by a 'Fifth Column' station operated by Goebbels to draw into the open unwary sympathizers with the opposition to Hitler. Dalton remarked in his letter to the Foreign Office:

> I hear, on what seems to be good authority, that the Freedom Station is in fact run by quite a different crew, and that the manoeuvres of Henry Mann and Co. are designed partly to attract funds and public notice, and partly to provoke denials of their story.[45]

---

concentration camp. A graphic, and self-evidently false, account is given of the bomb plot – allegedly a deliberate attempt by Hitler to kill rebellious colleagues at the meeting in the Bürgerbräukeller. Since Payne Best's book was written with the full cooperation of the Security Services it can only be assumed that this ludicrous story was added with their approval. Why it should have been necessary to insert such disinformation is an open question. S. Payne Best, *The Venlo Incident* (1950), p.130f.

[43] Sigismund Payne Best and Richard H. Stevens. For an orthodox account of the incident, see Nigel West [pseud: Rupert Allason], *MI6* (1985 ed., p.130f.).

[44] Public Record Office, FO 371/23058; C20850/1645/18, contains a copy of this publication. Its author was described as 'the representative in Great Britain of the Freedom Station'. I have not been able to establish who this was; the book contained information about people in Britain who had broadcast from the station's London office to Germany before the war, including Victor Gollancz and Noel Baker. It seems likely that this was yet another activity of the JBC.

[45] Public Record Office: FO 371/23058; C20850/645/18.

In a report by Campbell Stuart to Gladwyn Jebb at the Foreign Office the identity of this 'different crew' was apparently revealed:

> I understand from a report on the German Freedom station which I received early in December [it was to this that Dalton referred] that there are two stations operating in France on three wavelengths. They are directed by Willi Münzenburg and are said to be in receipt of financial support from the French Government. I cannot vouch for the exact veracity of this report, but I believe it to be substantialy true.[46]

The Communist Party were particularly angry about Münzenburg's activities as he had been one of their best propaganda agents and had subsequently deserted them. It is likely that the purpose of their pamphlet was to disavow Münzenburg and transfer the identity of the *Freiheitsender* to their own group; the suggestion that Goebbels ran it would have been simply a mischievous red herring. No station of this kind was ever run by the German propaganda departments, as far as is now known, and it would have been an extraordinary thing to have established a station for this event alone. Indeed this type of station seems to have been shunned by all countries; even the British Black broadcasting station at Woburn appears to have drawn the line at broadcasting English-language broadcasts for Britain purporting to be run by the British Union or their sympathizers. And the Communist Party in London would have known of the *Freiheitsender* since the JBC were apparently involved with it, and Guy Burgess ran that part of its activities.[47]

It is conceivable that the *Freiheitsender* broadcasting at the time of Venlo was Münzenburg's, but there were other possibilities. Indirect evidence is provided by the BBC Monitoring Service. This monitored secret stations, but *not* those which were run by Britain herself. At the time of the Venlo incident the monitors made no report on the *Freiheitsender*. The BBC Engineer's report accompanying the Monitors' report remarked that the station known as the *Freiheitsender* was very weak and that no coherent message had been made out. It then went on to say that the BBC news had carried a manifesto from the station although the monitors had not been able to hear it. They did not ask or answer the question where the BBC got the manifesto from, but it can only have been from sources close to the station itself. If the monitors could not hear the station it is very unlikely that any

---

[46] Ibid. Campbell Stuart made no reference to the alleged station's offices in Britain and no comment on the origins of the publication itself, which would have established the truth of the matter without difficulty.

[47] For Burgess's activities, see Index.

other listener could have. Münzenburg's stations were satisfactorily monitored by the BBC, and so it would seem that there was indeed a 'Freedom Station' in operation aside from those already identified, which was known to the British, and it could well have been this broadcasting after the Bürgerbräukeller bombing.

The other central claim of the Nazi propaganda was that the actual arrangements for the bombing had been made by Otto Strasser. It has been assumed that this also was a complete fiction, and no link has been made between Strasser and the British authorities at this time. There were, however, very strong links indeed. They were through Vansittart and his private information service, run by Col. M.G. Christie. Writing to the Foreign Secretary in October 1939, Vansittart warmly endorsed a suggestion that a committee be set up of exiled Germans and British experts on German politics. He had received from Christie some while before an account of suitable people known to him, and in his letter he recommended four men for the German posts on the committee. These were Hermann Rauschning, Otto Strasser, Baron Putlitz and Herr Halterman.[48] Vansittart remarked:

> It is no use getting unlimited numbers of Germans together ... it will only lead to a lot of chatter. The right way to utilize Germans in this country is contained on p.2. of Christie's letter. On that, he and I, Putlitz and our own intelligence service are all agreed ...[49]

Christie's report on Strasser was a glowing one that mentioned, in passing, that he was working for Christie at the time in Geneva. It is worth quoting as, by Vansittart's remark, it was an opinion shared by most people in the Intelligence Service:

> *Dr Otto Strasser*: The ex-propagandist of the Nazi Party; knows Hitler and all the party leaders intimately. Quarrelled with Hitler and left, or rather was expelled from, the Nazi party in 1928/9! Hitler caused Gregor Strasser, elder brother to Otto, to be murdered in 1934 because he feared his (Gregor's) rivalry and hold on the party. Otto Strasser built up an organization in Germany that has worried Hitler severely,

[48] The first two were well-known public figures at the time, Rauschning because of a stream of publications purporting to give a detailed account of Hitler's private conversations with him, and Otto Strasser because of the activities of his 'Black Front' and his books, published in England, such as *Hitler and I* (1940). Baron Putlitz was a German Diplomat who was spying for Britain and also, it seems, for Russia. He defected to East Germany after the war and published his memoirs, *The Putlitz Dossier* (1957). For an account of his likely role in affairs, see Anthony Glees, *The Secrets of the Service* (1987) passim. Halterman was a Social Democrat in London.

[49] Vansittart's letter enclosing Christie's report is in the Public Record Office: FO 371/23057; C18260/1645/18.

and still has its tentacles into highest Nazi Party circles. Strasser went to Czechoslovakia in 1933 when Hitler came to power, but has carried on his fight to undermine the Führer and his gang ever since. Strasser came greatly under the moderating influence of President Masaryk when in Czechoslovakia, and wrote a book staunchly supporting Masaryk's conceptions of democracy in Europe. Otto Strasser would be a tower of strength and of the greatest value as an active member of an advisory committee both for short and long-range policies. He is creative, original, has great energy and drive; knows every low-down Nazi trick, and has a following in the party even today. I have known him intimately in past years ... he is no saint; has passed through varying stages of radicalism, but his bitter feeling towards Hitler, the murderer of his brother, his unique knowledge of Nazism's vulnerable spots and the fact, as my friends assure me, that Masaryk's influence and his own decent family life have leavened him, constitutes him, in our opinion, a person of infinite value to an advisory committee. He is at present in Switzerland helping my little band of German friends to supply accurate information from within Germany. He has told me through friends that he would gladly come over and work for England.[50]

Unfortunately the exact date of the original memorandum cannot be determined but clearly it was well before the bomb plot. At the time Vansittart wrote Strasser had already moved from Switzerland to France and was under the impression that he was to go to England shortly as a member of a German National Council, which looked upon itself as the nucleus of a future German government. But when William Strang[51] at the Foreign Office conveyed this information to Cadogan, on 20 December, he received the reply:

It is the first I have heard of a 'German National Council' which, so far as I know has received no sort of official recognition from us.

To which Lord Halifax added:

I have never heard of any question of official recognition for anything like a 'German National Council'.[52]

---

[50] Ibid.
[51] William Strang (1893-1978). He entered the Foreign Office 1919 and after a brief spell in Moscow, 1930-33, returned to the Foreign Office as Head of the League of Nations Section until 1937; at the time of this note he was Head of the Central Section. He first made his name with his handling of the Metro-Vickers trial in Moscow. During the war he was very pro-Russian. See his *Home and Abroad* (1956).
[52] Public Record Office: FO 371/23057; C18260/1645/18.

And indeed Strasser's star had waned. From the time of the bomb plot onwards even Vansittart turned against him, clearly implying that his reputation had been bound up with it and Venlo in some way. By his own account he was moved to Portugal and then, via the West Indies, to Canada with the help of the British authorities.[53]

The only British Secret Service agent who seems to have been completely sceptical of Strasser was Claude Dansey, who had set up a secondary intelligence service when it had been realized that the normal MI6 group, to which Stevens belonged, had been discovered by the Germans. Commenting on the German National Council he remarked:

> Dr *Rauschning*'s group in London and *Strasser*'s statement to M. *Zaleski*: I learnt from Dr. *Spiecker* a few months ago that he had been invited by *Rauschning* to come over to London and join some sort of National Council of German Refugees established in London. He told me that he had replied that he would have nothing to do with them because he did not believe in their ideas or their methods. He added that in his view these men's real quarrel with the Nazis was that they did not hold the positions in Germany today that they thought they merited.[54]

About Strasser he was even more damning:

> As you know, in the last four years I have had a great many dealings with the German refugees. My quarrel with most of them is that their quarrel with Hitler is that he sits in the chair they want. In this connection the following which is good evidence and from a reliable Swiss is worth noting. Last July the famous *Otto Strasser* held a meeting in his house ... *Strasser* had been inveighing against France and England, particularly the latter, because they would not instantly declare war on Hitler. My informant challenged him to answer 'Yes' or 'No' to the following question: 'Are you yourself prepared to go and take up arms and fight against Germany with the British and French?'

[53] His own account is contained in letters written by him to Douglas Reed that were intercepted by the Postal Censorship, which opened and examined all mail entering and leaving Britain during the war. The activities of this department, known as MC3 and MC5, with the cooperation of MI7 until its suppression in the early part of the war, were among the most secret of the Secret departments, although they were labour-intensive, with thousands of operatives involved. The contents of all letters of interest were transcribed in full. Examples may be seen in the Public Record Office: FO 371/23040 et al.

[54] Claude Dansey's report, like all communications from the Secret Intelligence Service, was written on unheaded paper without any mark of provenance, but its identity is established beyond doubt by an inscription by Cadogan: 'These are Dansey's comments on my talk with Gillies.' It can be found in the Public Record Office: FO 371/24420; C897/796/18.

No direct reply was forthcoming, but in the end when pressed by the Swiss present to give some reply, the famous *Otto Strasser*, so dearly beloved of certain people in England replied, 'I believe in the unity of a Greater Germany, therefore I could not fight against my nation.'[55]

If Strasser did indeed have a following in the German army, then they were not prepared to act, and he had no way of influencing them. The *Freheitsender* was thought by the BBC's Engineers to be located in Switzerland, and one of the record-player transmitters of the kind produced by the JBC was later found there in a raid by the Swiss Security Services;[56] it is at least conceivable that this was the station that broadcast at the time of bomb plot. Certainly the station's manifesto somehow got into the BBC's hands some time before the station launched it, early enough to be read out on the day it happened, when no actual station could be heard. This at least is the circumstantial case for the view that Otto Strasser and some part of the British Secret Service were involved; though it was not the MI6 known to Cadogan or Strang, but the 'ghost' security service set up by Vansittart,[57] possibly acting in collaboration with the JBC.

The final solution to this problem, whether the bomb plot, like the successful assassination of Heydrich,[58] was backed by the British Government, will only be known if the relevant British archives are opened. What is clear is that, far from being a wild propaganda story, the idea of the involvement of Strasser and, through Christie, Vansittart, the JBC, and the British Intelligence Service, is distinctly plausible.

This brief mention of the Joint Broadcasting Committee in our efforts to unravel the background to the broadcasts about the Bürgerbräukeller bomb plot gives only a slight idea of its wartime activities. These were extensive on both the 'white' and clandestine side and continued until the service they provided was absorbed into the BBC's transcription service in 1941, some while after the death of Hilda Matheson, its founder and director. By the time the take-over actually took place the clandestine side had been run down almost

---

[55] Ibid.

[56] For an account of this discovery, see Nigel West [pseud: Rupert Allason], *Unreliable Witness: Espionage Myths of World War II* (1986 ed.), p.74.

[57] A remarkable fact about the 'private' secret service developed by Vansittart before the war was that it was widely known about in Germany and elsewhere. Christie was specifically named as a member of the 'British Intelligence Service' in a book published in Britain and America in the summer of 1939: Fritz Max Cahen: *Men Against Hitler* (1939) p.198. There was thus ample opportunity for infiltration both by the left, men such as Zu Putlitz, and presumably also from the right.

[58] For Heydrich, see Günther Deschner, *Heydrich: The Pursuit of Total Power* (1981).

completely. There was, however, one aspect of its activities which MI6 and later SOE could not duplicate, and this was the actual production of records of propaganda material for dropping behind enemy lines, as opposed to those possibly used by Strasser and others in Switzerland. It is not known to this day which brave patriots had the equipment to play these records, or who ran the underground secret stations that must have existed for them to be needed.

There is no mention of this side of the propaganda war in the later activities of the SOE in any of the published works. The circumstances in which the BBC found that they were doing work for SOE were somewhat amusing.[59] For a brief period after the outbreak of war the JBC's activities had been disrupted by a move to the country, but they were soon re-established and developed rapidly, particularly in South America. The BBC became aware of the JBC's growing size and were worried that their monopoly was in a sense being broken. In theory, the difference between programmes broadcast from Britain to South America and programmes sent out to South America for broadcasting *there* might not seem great, but the skills required were very different, especially when it was records that were being sent and not scripts. Also, there were a large number of stations in South America, and the JBC had been far more successful in finding these and getting them to accept material than the BBC.[60]

The BBC were so worried that they finally succeeded in getting agreement to a complete take-over of the JBC. But it was only a few days before this event that the MOI wrote to the BBC to explain, in embarrassed terms, that the BBC would have to deal with the Security Services directly over some aspects of the JBC's work:

Dear Dunkerley,
The 'Under-cover Boys' came to see me a few days ago about preserving the facility formerly granted them by the J.B.C. for making gramophone records. It was always the intention of this Ministry to

[59] The reasons for believing that the SOE *was* the organization here are that the names of those involved, Lionel Hale and Captain Sheridan, are mentioned in the official history of the SOE written by M.R.D. Foot.

[60] The lists of stations contacted by the JBC in the South America were passed over to the BBC when it was absorbed into the London Transcription Service, along with some remnants of the JBC's files. A further, not negligible, reason for thinking that the JBC was an entirely independent organization, rather than part of MI6, came to light when the JBC staff were transferred to the BBC, for none of them had been given any security clearance. There are no papers for the Joint Broadcasting Committee in the Public Record Office, although its 'white' side operated as an ordinary Government department and corresponded with foreign governments on that basis.

preserve them that facility as long as possible after the transfer, and I understand that the type of material they record is not in itself of a secret nature; it is merely that the method of distribution is not communicated to anybody, nor the purposes for which the records are used. I see no reason, therefore, why the actual making of the records should not be as easily arranged as before.

I have suggested to Captain Sheridan that he should get in touch with you.[61]

A few days later the Security Services made direct contact with the BBC and an agreement was worked out between them:

Dear Dunkerley,
    You and I had a telephone conversation about the J.B.C. further to my meeting with Mr Stephens earlier this week, and we seem to be agreed on the important points.
    The first of these points is that we shall retain the right, which we had when the J.B.C. was administered only by the Ministry of Information, to make use of the facilities of the J.B.C. for the production of records.
    The second is that negotiations between us on the production of these records shall be directly between yourselves and us without any other intervention.
    There are one or two other points which remain to be cleared up, among them questions of material for records, speakers, and cost. When I have had a talk with Miss Hodgson about these I should be very glad if we could meet again.
    With many thanks for your co-operation,
                                        Yours sincerely,
                                        Lionel Hale[62]

Perhaps the closest we can get to the activities of the Security Services at this time, and the JBC before that, is contained in a memorandum sent within the BBC when the question of material prepared for the Allied Governments in exile in London was being considered. It is reprinted here in full for the light it casts on the most obscure of the wartime propaganda exercises:

                                                        5th April, 1941

Stokes, who is getting down to work on the J.B.C. question has had a preliminary discussion with the J.B.C. people about material they have in the past supplied to Allied Governments. I give below Stokes'

---

[61] BBC Written Archives Centre: E2/374/6.
[62] Ibid. Miss Hodgson was the JBC's secretary.

comment on this matter. The grant to which he refers was an allocation from S.I.S. [MI6] funds which was discontinued some time ago.

'The J.B.C. has in the past supplied Allied Governments in this country with recordings of special material. These records have been supplied to foreign nationals in this country, and also sent to foreign communities in South America. This work was not financed by the M.O.I., and they are not interested in it apparently. It seems that the work was paid for out of a special grant (origin obscure) which the J.B.C. obtained at the beginning of the war, and which was used originally for material to be smuggled into Poland, Czechoslovakia, etc.

'There is still a demand for special foreign stuff, but the J.B.C. cannot provide it unless the Allied Governments who ask for it are able to pay for it themselves. A case in point is a request by the Danish Government for material about the activities of Danes in this country, to be taken to the U.S. by a Danish mission which is going there soon. In this particular case the Danish Government can pay, and the J.B.C. is providing the records.

'There have, in the past, been requests for us [i.e. the BBC] to broadcast in Czech, Polish and other languages to North America, and this had always been resisted. It seems to me that sometime in the future we might provide transcriptions for some North *f* nerican stations. I believe there are several foreign stations in the U.S.; Clinton Baddeley [of the JBC] mentioned a Polish one in Chicago.'

H.J.Dunkerley[63]

The reference here to material to be smuggled into Czechoslovakia indicates one of the controversial aspects of this kind of activity of the JBC. Burgess spoke of his involvement in the manufacture of these records, getting a Sudeten German to do the introduction to a speech by Benes to the Czechoslovak people. What he did not make clear was that the records produced were for use in a secret radio station and that those hearing them in Czechoslovakia would think that they were hearing a station in their own country, and that some underground movement was in contact with Benes. This was the reason for using a Sudeten German as introducer and compere. There were acute dangers in this kind of programme, not least for anyone associated with the secret radio station that played the records over the air. In

[63] BBC Written Archives Centre: E2/374/4. The allusion to foreign communities in South America is no doubt to German, rather than Japanese, communities, as there were never any Japanese speakers in the JBC. The German communities receiving these records were, it seems, led to believe that they came from Germany. The records which they played were largely popular entertainment with a propaganda message skilfully woven into the programme. Later this technique was developed by Sefton Delmer, although he most definitely did not invent it, as has been suggested.

this case there appears to have been a catastrophe when young students involved in the broadcasts were found with records in their possession. A debacle followed which is still among the closely guarded secrets of 'D' Section's activities; it appears to have resulted in the closing down of the Czech universities and been part of the background to the appointment of Heydrich as Protector.[64]

Whether this work by 'D' Section, which took place before SOE was established, also contributed to the re-shaping of the security services that was seen as absolutely essential in 1940 is also secret and will no doubt remain so, even if the long-felt need for an honest Freedom of Information Act is finally met, against the protests of the very un-English breed of bureaucrats that have evolved in Britain during the present century.

So far as is known the Germans did not engage in similar activities. They confined themselves to operations of the kind countered by the Haw-Haw campaigns until, under the guidance of William Joyce, a new brand of secret stations aimed at Britain finally brought the 'phoney' period of the radio war to an end.

[64] There is reference to this debacle in Bruce Lockhart, *Comes the Reckoning* (1947), pp.65, 70, 73. News of a revolt in Czechoslovakia was carried by the BBC in London, as had been the manifesto of the *Freiheitsender*, but this was described by Lockhart as '... grotesquely exaggerated and the London Czechs, who were then in hourly touch with their compatriots in Czechoslovakia, were bitter for had they been consulted by the newspapers [!] they could have contradicted the rumour. The need for closer cooperation was glaring ...' He then went on to describe (p.17) the actual rising of 17 November. Burgess's reference to his getting Benes to do a talk to the Czech people, recounted to Tom Driberg (op.cit., p.56), specifically said: '... records of the talk were to be dropped by air in Czechoslovakia', in the context of his working for the JBC. The obvious conclusion seems to be that this revolt was organized by the Security Services and carried out with the aid of this JBC material.

9. The New British Broadcasting Station Fights for Peace

The radio war entered a new phase in April 1940 with the rapid deployment by Germany of a new type of English-language radio station. These were exactly similar to those used during the Spanish Civil War, but instead of being broadcasts for Spain in Spanish purporting to come from there but actually being sent from Italy,[1] they were stations seeming even to careful listeners to be in Britain. There were three main stations, the New British Broadcasting Station, known as the NBBS, and often called the New BBC; the Workers Challenge, purporting to be run by a determined band of socialist revolutionaries somewhere in industrial Britain; and, in total contrast, a pacifist station, the Christian Peace Movement, whose signature tune 'O God, our Help in Ages Past' especially annoyed the authorities after Dunkirk.[2]

The broadcasters on NBBS were carefully chosen. They did not sound revolutionary in tone; rather the principal announcer spoke with a quiet upper-middle-class accent, that of an honest long-suffering civil servant of the old style who knew that the time had come for change at last.[3] The few recordings that have survived suggest that Professor Mackintosh might have been the speaker,[4] but he was never positively identified by those captured after the war. There was even a hint in the broadcasts that they were in some way official, that a group of senior men had realized that invasion and conquest were inevitable and this radio was to be the voice of the new administration. As an actual possible invasion drew closer this became more and more the identity the NBBS took on. The Workers

[1] For Spanish broadcasts originating in Italy, see above, p.34.

[2] For a script of a typical Christian Peace movement broadcast, see Appendix, below, p.251-2.

[3] Four brief recordings of the New British Broadcasting Station have survived and may be heard at the National Sound Archives: NSA 12550.

[4] Professor Noel Mackintosh. It was Mackintosh who accompanied P.G. Wodehouse to Berlin when he was released from internment and introduced him to the broadcasting authorities. His papers are among those released at the Public Record Office: HO45/25830.

Challenge was spoken by a rough cockney voice and so convincing in its revolutionary tone that even today it would be a serious annoyance to the authorities.[5] It forced practical democracy to its limits, for example, by telling the unemployed not merely to protest to their Member of Parliament in writing or interview, but to get together a group, find out where the MP lived, knock at his door and press their demands face-to-face.[6] The programmes were spiced with obscenities which attracted an audience considerably wider than the working men for whom they were intended.

The pacifist station was perhaps the most insidious of all. The theme song was an old favourite Victorian hymn never omitted at any funeral service and with emotional associations for every family in the land. There were large numbers of genuine pacifists in the country who believed that the war was wrong, and also a number of fringe political groups that used a pacifist front. Some were of native British origin. The Duke of Bedford, at this time the Marquess of Tavistock, ran a party called the British People's Party which professed pacifism as its central aim but, as he candidly revealed in his autobiography, had a far sterner purpose.[7] He produced a stream of seditious pamphlets throughout the war with titles such as *The 'Can't Trust Hitler' Bogey* (1940) and *If I Were Prime Minister* (1942), the latter containing passages of pro-Nazi and anti-semitic writing as virulent as have ever appeared in Britain which would have jailed anyone but the Duke under emergency regulations. There were other pacifists on the left, John Middleton Murry,[8] author of *The Necessity of Pacifism* and *The Necessity of Communism*, prominent among them. Through the Peace Pledge Union he published a series of works in 1940 called 'The Bond

[5] For two typical examples of this programme, perhaps the most powerful of the German 'Black' broadcasts, see Appendix, below, p.246f.

[6] It was one of the paradoxes of the war years that, according to Harold Nicolson, for example, the role played by Members of Parliament diminished markedly. Many were in the armed forces; others found the continual suspension of sittings for a variety of reasons, and the difficulties in transport, a bar to regular attendance. Nicolson said that even his mail-bag dwindled to a shadow of its former size. For the system of radio programmes, and government instructions that encroached on the normal democratic processes, see above, p.173.

[7] For example, the Duke remarked: '... I am afraid I cannot deny the charge of being an extremely militant pacifist! ... The champions of the war discovered that not only was the cranky pro-Nazi pacifist prepared to defend himself: he was even able to deal some very shrewd blows in return (no very difficult task, incidentally, in view of the strength of his case!).' Hastings, Duke of Bedford, *The Years of Transition* (1949), p.180.

[8] John Middleton Murry (1889-1957), founder and editor of *The Adelphi* (1923-48). Murry's early criticism, such as *Dostoevsky* (1916), was highly regarded. His later political work, of the kind mentioned here, has been less attended to.

of Peace', his own contribution being *The Brotherhood of Peace* (1940). Another highly respected group of authors all drawn from the left produced a series of writings for the National Peace Council which included such works as *The Spiritual Basis of Peace* by Ritchie Calder[9] and Norman Bentwich,[10] The debate on pacifist questions had its more serious side, as can be seen for example in the publication by the respected Oxford scholar A.D. Lindsay[11] of *Pacifism as a Principle and Pacifism as a Dogma* which appeared in May 1939, by chance at the same time as the Duke of Windsor's broadcast from Verdun.[12] But the political roots of the movement, far more insidious, were to be found, for example, in C.R. Attlee's 'Peace Indivisible' given at a meeting of the Anglo-Russian Parliamentary Committee in honour of M. Maisky, the Soviet Ambassador to Great Britain.[13] To establish the background of the Christian Peace Movement radio run by the Germans who were throughout this period of the war in alliance with Russia, it is worth quoting from it directly:

> I think to us socialists there is no difficulty whatever in accepting the proposition that peace is indivisible. Our conception of a peaceful world is not a world of warring states, each one of them directed by an egoism which is the idealistic expression of a group of capitalist interests – of a group of warring states that are for a moment of time held in equilibrium. Our conception is of a world of citizen states, co-operating to a common end.

and ending:

> ...I am persuaded that we, in this country, have got to take our share in building up constructive peace, and with our comrades all over the world – our comrades in Russia, our comrades in Scandinavia, our

[9] Ritchie Calder (1906-1982), scientific journalist and broadcaster; made Baron Ritchie-Calder of Balmashenar in 1966. At this period he was writing for the *Daily Herald* (1930-41). He was in the Foreign Office 1941-45.

[10] Norman Bentwich (1883-1971), Attorney General, Government of Palestine, and for twenty years Professor of International Relations at the Hebrew University, Jerusalem. Director of League of Nations High Commission for Refugees 1933-36.

[11] Alexander Dunlop Lindsay (1879-1952), educationalist and academic politician. He was Master of Balliol for twenty-five years, from 1924 to 1949, and on his retirement became the first Principal of Keele University. According to Christopher Hill in *DNB*, this was 'the crowning achievement of Lindsay's career'.

[12] See above, p.161.

[13] The texts of the speeches were published in the Anglo-Russian Parliamentary Committee's '*Peace Indivisible*' (published by the committee June 1936). In *A People's Peace* (1941) Edgar P. Young pointed out that the slightly earlier publication *Labour's Way to Peace* (1935) had been recommended by Attlee in 1940, a further direct link of the kind mentioned here. See Young, op.cit., p.3.

comrades in France, our comrades in New Zealand, our comrades in Czechoslovakia, our comrades everywhere – now is the time to unite our forces and to call upon all the people of the world – and the people of the world who want peace are the vast majority – to realize that peace is indivisible.[14]

The linking of pacifism with the alliance between Russia and Germany, echoed in the earlier speeches of the Labour Party leaders themselves, presented one of the most difficult problems the counter-propaganda departments faced.

The tactic adopted for dealing with these secret stations was the complete reverse of that used towards those which had been dealt with by the 'Lord Haw-Haw' ridicule campaign. They were kept a close secret, and all reference to them in the press or the BBC was strictly forbidden.[15] The authorities at the highest level began to think seriously of jamming all the NBBS and Workers Challenge broadcasts. The security officer who suggested this at one of the regular meetings with the BBC did not succeed in persuading the BBC to co-operate, and it has always been said that the British never jammed enemy broadcasts during the war. While it may be true that they never jammed 'white' enemy broadcasts, the NBBS and Workers Challenge frequently had that honour. Nearly all the NBBS transmissions at the time of the fall of Paris were jammed, and so extensively that the monitors were unable to transcribe anything for days at a time. Who did this jamming is not known.

The NBBS formed the main body of serious propaganda and was recognized as the most serious threat. Churchill appears to have listened to it regularly and gave it the unique tribute of quoting from it in one of his Secret Session speeches in the House of Commons.[16] They managed to produce considerable annoyance in security circles by a graphic account of a row which was said to have taken place at Electra House between Sir Campbell Stuart and Major-General F.G. Beaumont Nesbitt over a leaked document, claiming that the row had developed when Beaumont Nesbitt heard the leak referred to on the NBBS.[17] There is no doubt that the NBBS made use of material

[14] Anglo-Russian Parliamentary Committee, op.cit.: speech by Attlee, p.21.

[15] This is made clear by statements of Norman Birkett when interrogating Sir Oswald Mosley at his 18B(1a) hearing.

[16] See Winston S. Churchill, *Secret Session Speeches* (1946), pp.72-3.

[17] This remarkable incident, a further example of the machinery of censorship becoming visible when the system breaks down, was first noticed by Charles Cruickshank in his pioneering work *The Fourth Arm: Psychological Warfare 1938-45* (1977; OUP ed. 1981) pp.105-6. His preface also contains the candid statement:

captured at Dunkirk and elsewhere in its bulletins, but occasionally its information was extremely sensitive and was not passed by the MI5 vetting organization which checked the BBC's Monitors' reports. An example of this kind of material was the broadcast on 4 September 1940 about negotiations for British acquisition of fifty destroyers from the United States, part of which we print here:

> Quite recently we had occasion to warn you concerning secret negotiations which were taking place between the Cabinet and President Roosevelt. You may remember that at the time we revealed the surrender of a considerable portion of our trans-atlantic Empire to the United States, in consideration of very handsome payments made to Churchill and his colleagues by Mr Bernard Baruch, on behalf of American Jewish Finance and the American Government.
>
> When we made this announcement, we stated that an attempt would be made to disguise the disgraceful nature of these transactions by arranging for the transfer to Britain of fifty antiquated and practically useless destroyers. Of course, at the time, our statement was characterized as untrue, but once more we have proved to be right when the whole propaganda organization of the Government has striven to denounce us as liars.[18]

Apart from the highly objectionable content, the supposed source, the communications between Roosevelt and Churchill, had been the subject of a major secrets trial in April 1940 which had involved just such a leakage: the Tyler Kent and Anna Wolkoff case. The NBBS report clearly pointed to knowledge of the events, in itself a security leak, and with even more serious implications, as we shall see.[19]

A more direct impact on affairs can be seen in the NBBS reports on the Duke of Windsor in October 1940. It had been suggested that the Duke and President Roosevelt might meet. It is not clear what was in the way of such a meeting, but extensive correspondence between Lord Lothian[20] and Cadogan at the Foreign Office took place. This

---

'... no one remembers accurately what happened thirty or more years ago. Therefore I am not indebted for a single fact to anyone other than the authors of contemporary official letters, minutes, memoranda and records of meetings.' A salutary truth worthy of frequent recall in this age of mole-hunters.

[18] The Monitors' report did not appear on this day (see below, p.236n48) but the text of the Intelligence Unit print-out has survived in the Public Record Office: HO 45/25728.

[19] See below, p.236.

[20] Philip Henry Kerr, Eleventh Marquess of Lothian (1882-1940), Secretary of the Rhodes Trust 1925-39, British Ambassador in Washington 1939-40. Originally a member of Milner's Kindergarten and founder editor of *The Round Table*, Kerr was early drawn into the Astor circle, accompanying Nancy Astor and her party on their

was seen by Walter Monkton,[21] who also read the output of the secret Intelligence Unit at the Ministry of Information, which watched the NBBS closely. On 9 October he wrote to Cadogan:

> I have seen the telegrams passing between the [Foreign] Office and Lothian about the suggestion that the Duke and the President might meet in the apparently not too far distant future. The attached extract from a German broadcast in English from the New British Broadcasting Station, sent to me by the Censorship Intelligence Unit [sic], may suggest some confirmation of the office view that even discussion of such a meeting is not without risk. You may have heard from the Secretary of State of the efforts made by some circles in Spain to prevent the Duke from leaving Lisbon. I had and have no doubt that this was because the Germans could make use of his presence, particularly after an expressed intention to go away – in much the same way as they are now using the possibility of his meeting the President.[22]

The NBBS broadcast concerned again shrewdly built up a false picture on the basis of facts which must somehow have been leaked in America or Britain:

> 7.10.40. Peace News. According to reports from the USA President Roosevelt will try to bring about Peace Negotiations between Great Britain and the Axis powers. The three-power alliance has put the USA in a difficult position, as she can neither defend the western hemisphere nor come to the help of Great Britain. The Duke of Windsor may also play a part in this attempt. He is known to have become convinced of the necessity for making peace when he was liaison officer in France. The Government sent him to the Bahamas to get him out of the way, but he accepted the appointment so that he could be within easy access of the USA. He will shortly leave the Bahamas for the USA in order to talk with the President.[23]

The intelligence report which accompanied this said:

---

celebrated visit to the Soviet Union in 1931. Unfortunately he also became associated with a fictional 'Cliveden Set' created by Communist Party propaganda in the late thirties. Claude Cockburn is claimed to have invented this, but its full savour can only be experienced in such publications as *Sidelights on the Cliveden Set* (1938, published by the Communist Party of Great Britain). Cockburn was himself a Communist.

[21] Viscount Monckton of Brenchley (1891-1965). Attorney-General to the Prince of Wales 1932-36; at this time Director-General of the Press and Censorship Bureau. For his life, see Lord Birkenhead, *Walter Monckton* (1969).

[22] Public Record Office: FO 371/24249; A4271/434/45.

[23] Ibid.

The Germans have ... started a *peace-rumour campaign*. Now they are again linking it up with the *Duke of Windsor* and bringing in his announced trip to the USA – which, for that if no other reason, might usefully be put off.[24]

And this is what indeed occurred. The Duchess of Windsor wrote on 20 October:

> And I don't think there is a hope of the US before the spring ... I begin to think we are fated never to go to America. Gt. Britain hates the idea of us going, because you know the Duke is an independent thinker and they don't want him to open his mouth. Also Lothian is controlled by Nancy Astor – as you know, an arch-enemy of ours – and Lothian will advise against coming on account of the press. That will be the excuse ...[25]

Her guess that the Press would be the excuse was quite close to the truth; the actual reason was the radio propaganda of the NBBS.

The policy of keeping all mention of the secret stations out of the press and radio meant that there was little speculation at the time about who the broadcasters might be. It is possible to put together a picture of the group involved in the broadcasts from the few transcripts of the 18B interrogations and papers on renegades captured after the war that have been released in the Public Record Office.[26] One clear fact emerges. The voices that were heard in Britain were not those of the author of the talks which were almost entirely the work of one man: William Joyce. As an occasional speaker on the

---

[24] Ibid.

[25] There was one other factor – the American Presidential elections at this time. All these factors had to be considered, but the fact that the proposed visit had begun to figure in German wireless propaganda was probably the most reliable pointer to the effect of the visit, and the most likely to have prompted action.

[26] The files so far released appear to have been chosen at random; further files, including some relating to William Joyce, are to be released shortly, according to the Home Office, although they will not divulge whose files they are holding for release at some future date. A representative list is as follows, all class HO 45: 25789 E.S. Bowlby, 25792 J.G. Lingshaw, 25794 Ralph Baden Powell (a nephew of the Boy Scout leader), 25798 Walter Purdy, 25806 S. Provost-Booth (a relation by marriage of R.A. Butler), 25811 Pearl Joyce Vardon, 25823 G. Chatterton-Hill (a notorious case: Hill was an elderly doctor unable to leave Germany because of illness who did occasional translation work; the authorities after the war held him under the strictest conditions without adequate food or medicine, and as a result he starved to death), 25826 J.A. Ward, 25833 C.P. Gilbert, 25839 W.J. Murphy. There were many others (see above, p.175). The measure of the success of the 'Lord Haw-Haw' campaign and of Joyce's supposed responsibility for all his broadcasts can be seen in this partial list of actual broadcasters, and the contents of the files cited.

main German English-language stations he never spoke on the secret
channels, since this would have shattered the illusion the German
propagandists were trying to build up, but it is clear without doubt
from the evidence of Mrs Eckersley and others that it was he who sat
down each day and poured out this stream of propaganda in each of
the different styles needed.

As the campaign in Europe developed, the NBBS broadcasts began
to resemble more and more those of an alternative official channel.
The situation in France showed that the radio had been used there to
undermine morale in an exactly similar way. The secret channel 'Le
Voix de la Paix' was so successful that it was actually recommended to
British audiences – those who could speak French – by *Peace News*,[27]
the pacifist paper, which did not realize it was a German station, any
more than did the censor who allowed the text of their
recommendation to go through. The texts that follow are a sequence
selected from the broadcasts that NBBS put out in May 1940. They
were to culminate in final and decisive action by the Government
against those they thought responsible, the British Union and the far
right in league in some way with Joyce in Berlin.

A central and often repeated theme of the NBBS broadcasts at this
time was the need to coordinate all anti-war groups. Besides the
pacifist movements already mentioned, the extreme right and left, in
the form of Mosley's British Union and the Communist Party of Great
Britain, both followed a 'Peace Now' policy. The purpose of the NBBS
broadcast which follows was to precipitate a common Peace Front.

> The time has come when those who really desire peace should not
> remain inactive. The irresponsibility of the Government must be met
> with calmness.
>
>   Those who wish to take part in a movement to stop the war must get
> into touch with any movement to end the war – even if its and their
> aims are not entirely in agreement. There must be an appeal to pacifist
> organisations to unite forces. Such organisations may become illegal. In
> that case membership should be pooled. A shadow organisation could
> be formed immediately. Details, such as lists of members, must be
> carefully concealed. In the case of banning, houses and offices will be
> raided.
>
>   Arrangements must be made to keep in touch with all members as
> public meetings or even large private meetings may be banned. The

---

[27] See *Peace News*, 22 March 1940, p.5. There was also an embarrassing direct link
between the Peace Pledge Union and an equivalent German body which they
innocently thought had similar ideas to their own – it was of course one of Goebbels'
creations.

best system will be to have small groups represented in higher organisations.

It must be borne in mind that no illegal action is contemplated. Before the ban descends, it is necessary to organise for the future.

Our aim is simple. We want an honest, manly peace between the nations of the world before we are reduced to weakness. If the war is fought to the end, it will be a bitter end indeed. The future Versailles, dictated by either Britain or Germany will be the same. Years of distress – and then a new England or a new Germany trying to rise up in her former glory. A peace by negotiation made now would last.

Aged capitalists stand in the way of peace, and will willingly send numbers of men to the vilest death to preserve their own advantages.[28]

The agreement worked out between the Labour Party and the Conservatives which resulted in the new administration under Churchill and Attlee was a serious concern to the Nazis. The most obvious point was that it effectively removed all political opposition, in a formal sense, from the House of Commons.[29] Joyce seized on this in the NBBS broadcasts describing it as the obverse of the coin of National Unity, essential in a nation at war, and a step towards the creation in Britain of the unified control of the totalitarian states. The NBBS presented itself as at the head of a peace group which was to be a possible opposition. Joyce projected into this the role he had seen for himself and his defunct party. As heard in Britain the authorities no doubt feared it would be identified by the listening public with Mosley and British Union.

15 May

Hitler, Mussolini and Stalin together could never have formed a more absolute dictatorship than that under which we live today. It is all the more insidious because it is based on money power. It is futile to pretend that the Labour decision to join the Cabinet was taken over night. The uniformity which manifested itself in the House was by no means spontaneous. Churchill sounded the key note of the new Government, 'nothing but hardship'. Gentlemen receiving not less than £600 per year, and many 20 or 30 times as much, declared that the nation was willing to make further sacrifices. Now suppose that we are not willing to give up any more, or suppose that we cannot – what is the position then? Who is going to represent us? Who will voice our

[28] BBC Written Archives Centre: Summary of World Broadcasts for 7/8 May 1940.
[29] The Party Truce, as it was called, was effectively broken by the creation of the Common Wealth Party, founded by Richard Acland, J.B. Priestley and others. A full idea of what the movement stood for can be seen in, for example, *Common Wealth: First Agenda for the Second Conference Easter 1944* (1944). At the time we write of here the Party Truce was unchallenged.

grievances? Who will place before the Ministers of the Crown the grievances of the people when they become intolerable?

We repeat where is the opposition? If it cannot be found in Parliament it must be found outside Parliament, and so it shall. Now that the Parliamentary opposition has collapsed, the nation as a whole must assume its duties. There will be a new demarcation in our national life. Parliament is synonymous with Government, but as days go by the nation will become synonymous with the opposition. We have reached a new stage in the development of our institutions and masses of our people can only get redress for their grievances by organising public opposition to the political and financial tyranny which must be expected from Churchill and the men he has bought. There is no time to be lost. In the first days proof may not be clear to many people, but once it is found that real dictatorship is present and that there is no constitutional safeguard against it, a new and unprecedented situation will arise. If Parliament will not, or cannot, serve our purpose, we are not going to become its slaves. We shall concern ourselves with our own freedom and not with the liberation of Poles and Finns. At last all these elements representing international finance and corrupt democracy have crystallised themselves, and we now know that the position is between Westminster on the one hand and England on the other.[30]

Since the Government was censoring all mention of the clandestine stations, and thereby hoped to prevent the growth of a whispering campaign about the station's existence which might lead to the creation of a mass audience, they could not publicly announce on any great scale that the stations were actually in Germany, although they were finally driven to this. Their initial reluctance gave the NBBS ample scope to amuse themselves by describing hair-raising escapes from the attentions of Scotland Yard.

16 May

And now a few words to our friends. We have heard that many of our regular listeners desire to get into contact with us with a view to active co-operation in our work for peace. As to getting into contact with us there are obvious difficulties in the way, since we must keep our whereabouts secret. We have our way of keeping in touch with what you are thinking and doing but this contact is indirect and must remain so. We have to do all we can to avoid the attention of Scotland Yard. The absurd theory that we are not an English station at all but a German one, which the Minister of Information solemnly voiced in the House of Commons not long ago, wasn't believed by the minister who made the statement for the joint purpose of excusing his inability to silence us and of putting us off our guard, so that by some ill-considered

[30] BBC Written Archives Centre: Summary of World Broadcasts for 15 May 1940.

statement or action we should expose ourselves to the tender mercies of the police.

We are not falling into the trap. Remember it is not illegal to listen to us, although we are taking a big risk in broadcasting. Form listening and discussion groups of people who have an open mind and are willing to see both sides of the question. The Opposition in Parliament has been bought up by the Government. You and I are now the Opposition and we must see that our country is not allowed finally to plunge into destruction in this gamble to make the world safe for capitalism. Some of our supporters have leaflets printed and distributed advising the public to listen regularly to our transmissions, and giving information as to times and wavelengths. Others have taken shorthand notes of our talks and had them duplicated and issued to those who have been unable to listen. One enterprising group publishes a weekly local news sheet containing summaries of our talks. Now use your imagination and organise round your radio set a unit of the movement for the salvation of this land.[31]

The reference at the end of this talk to the printing of pamphlets about the station was a particular worry to the authorities and was undoubtedly a key element in the decision to pursue the British Union, for the fact had to be faced that posters, stickers and handbills did indeed appear throughout London and the home counties, and in most other major centres of population. The press silence was broken only once in the country as a whole, and then only by Scotland Yard appeals to anyone who knew anything about these posters to provide information.[32] Despite the most thorough search, which continued into the following year, only one of these clandestine presses was ever found, and this not a principal one.[33] It is astonishing that complete presses could be concealed as effectively in the twentieth century as during the Civil Wars three hundred years before, but this was the case. The weekly periodical referred to in the broadcast also existed and was published by Charles Watts who was detained under 18B(1a). The fact that the NBBS – that is, Joyce – knew of its existence is an indication that he maintained contacts of some sort

[31] Ibid., 16-17 May 1940.

[32] See, for example, *Express and Echo* (Exeter, 24 May 1940) p.3: 'Fifth Column Bill Stickers: a display of small posters calling attention to a so-called NBBS is being investigated by Scotland Yard ...'

[33] In October one Roy Day was convicted of publishing a pamphlet, *Uncensored British News Bulletin*. It is presumed that a press was also found. There were other similar cases of the discovery and prosecution of small individual initiatives, but no presses capable of printing posters and stickers in large quantities have ever been identified. Nor have the offices and presses that must have been associated with a periodical such as *Voice of the People*, mentioned below.

with the underground in Britain, for the periodical, called *The Voice of the People and Home Defence Movement*, was only known to few and was never referred to in the media.[34] Despite Watts' detention, the presses that produced his periodical were never found. The Security Services, working under Maxwell Knight, did infiltrate one group that was producing a peace chain-letter, but this was a more amateur effort.[35]

Faced with the possibility of large numbers of parachutists landing in Britain, and with the need for a mass army to deal with an invasion, the authorities decided to create a civilian force on a massive scale which was based loosely on the Territorial Army idea. Eden had been an enthusiastic supporter of this, joining before the war, and he broadcast in May appealing for volunteers for a new force to be called the 'Local Defence Volunteers' (later the Home Guard). This was the closest approach in World War II to the famous appeal from Kitchener in World War I, with its slogan 'Your Country Needs You!' It was, if anything, of greater emotional force, harking back to the great volunteer movements of the previous century but multiplying its force by the universal audience reached by radio. Eden's broadcast brought over a million men to the colours in a few days, a unique achievement and a remarkable example of national solidarity. The NBBS's reply to this was obvious and particularly menacing. For it was quite true that the raising of such a civilian force created the problems always associated with a partisan force, namely that all civilians were then considered as combatants in the terms of the Geneva Convention and other agreements.

> *Parachute Corps gives Germans Free Hand.* It is significant that Eden's first action as War Minister was to announce the formation of Local Defence Corps to watch for parachute troops. It gives us food for thought, when the Government is forced to consider our own fair land as the next battlefield.
>
> It is true I have come across several people who have joined the new defence corps and they seem to be very pleased with themselves. But that is not enough. Complacency can be dangerous. We must not calmly wait for the events of the next few weeks as though we were preparing for a sports festival. We must realise what dangers lie ahead and do our best to avoid them, besides thinking of how to deal with them if they come. We must realise just what this defence corps implies.

[34] I have been unable to find examples of the output of these presses, or this periodical, and know of no bibliographical enquiry into them. If the authorities release the files on these cases, a proper description of at least the examples seized will enable work to be begun and further examples to be identified on typographical evidence – the products of these presses had no printers' marks, for obvious reasons.

[35] See below, p.238f.

I have heard that its members will be armed although they will not actually be in the army. This means that though our security will be increased in one way the civil population is put in an awkward position. The Germans are given a beautiful excuse for bombing any and every town in the country. With the defence corps everywhere – and according to the B.B.C. there are already a million volunteers – no town will be an open town, in the view of international law – at least, in the German view of International Law. We are all in the front line now and as soon as the Nazis reach the Belgian coast the big offensive will probably begin. The war is coming home.[36]

With the possibility of invasion growing daily, the NBBS began to clothe its listening group propaganda in the guise of 'Guidance for Britain if Invaded':

We have been pleased to hear that many listening groups have already been formed. We hope this number will become as large as possible. Remember, it is not illegal to listen to our broadcasts, and no risk is involved in this respect. Those who have not yet started a listening group may welcome some hints on the subject. [We recently had] the pleasure of listening at one of the groups already established. This was attended by a representative of this station. It took place in a house in North-East London. The family living there invites anyone who cares to come to be present at a meeting of the group. This takes place at about half past ten till midnight. The family in question are well-known local Conservatives, but their (guests ?) represent all shades of political opinion. The number attending on any one evening varies from a dozen to twenty, but the actual membership is much higher, because they are not the same members who attend every evening.

At ten thirty, the second broadcast of the New B.B.S. was tuned in, and during it one member, (elected ?) leader of the group, made notes for subsequent discussion. At the end of the broadcast, the leader had compiled a list of about half a dozen questions arising out of the talk. Those he proceeded to put one by one to the group. The members expressed opinions on each of the questions, and a lively discussion ensued.

The next part of the meeting was devoted to the practical problems of increasing membership, and starting other listening groups. It was explained to our representative that there was, in addition to this listening-group, a smaller group (employed ?) on the harder work of compiling and distributing leaflets and notices and for putting up posters.

Another aspect of the matter must be borne in mind. When the invasion comes, the enemy will make every effort to occupy immediately all radio transmitters, or failing this, to destroy them. We

[36] BBC Written Archives Centre: Summary of World Broadcasts for 18 May 1940.

believe that the New B.B.S., which has managed to avoid detection by Scotland Yard for so long, would also manage to keep out of the hands of the invaders, at least until such time as a house-to-house search is made. We shall continue to transmit, if necessary long after the B.B.C. becomes silent, and we shall do our best to ensure that the danger to the civilian population is reduced to a minimum.[37]

At this point the authorities had already decided to act for a number of reasons, not least to ensure that the obvious audience for the NBBS, those mysterious people who had been plastering the walls of London with NBBS posters, placing stickers in telephone kiosks and on lamp posts and anywhere where the public might see them, should be put out of temptation's way.

[37] Ibid., 27 May 1940.

10. Emergency Powers

The clearest possible warning to the British public that invasion was a real possibility, for the first time in centuries, came with the arrest of Sir Oswald Mosley, as leader of the British Union party, together with a number of other well-known figures from it. Mosley's arrest was carried out by the police under the newly enacted Emergency Powers Act regulation 18B(1a). It was the first time a political leader in Britain had been arrested and detained without trial on the grounds that he was the leader of a political party.[1]

The operation to suppress the British Union was extensive, and it involved considerable logistical difficulties at a time when the country was already in a state of turmoil caused by the movement of evacuees and troops. The leaders of the party in London were apprehended without much difficulty. But those in the provinces, by far the larger number, were not fully accounted for by the time Mosley had appeared for interrogation before the 18B(1a) committee under Norman Birkett. When the operation was complete, more than 1500 men and women had been detained. Large numbers were allowed to remain at liberty, on the tacit understanding with the local police that they enlist in the armed forces immediately. A few went underground. Some of the most difficult cases involved those British Union members who were already in uniform but were thought by the Security Services to be particularly dangerous. The most careful instructions were given to ensure that no serving Officer of the British Army was brought to prison in uniform. If they were in uniform when arrested they were to be taken first to their homes and obliged to put on civilian clothing, by force if necessary. Considerable difficulty arose when it was found in practice that the legality of detaining an Officer serving under the Crown who was not liable to Court Martial for any offence known to Army regulations and, indeed, whom it was not intended to prosecute for any offence was not clear. The matter was never resolved satisfactorily, but the Officers involved were detained at Brixton

---

[1] The detention order was in several parts. The first referred to the banned organization British Union; there followed later a section dealing with Mosley's personal reasons for detention, which are examined below.

Prison, from where they made a collective appeal to the War Office against the dishonour which had been brought upon their regiments.[2]

The majority of the senior men in the British Union were detained in Brixton, and these were given reasons for their detention and told that they could make known their objections to detention to the 18B committee if they wished to do so. The grounds were simply that they were, or had been, members of the British Union under the leadership of Mosley. They were also supplied with a copy of the reasons for the detention of Mosley and were astonished to discover that of the personal particulars given the first was his involvement in the setting up of a radio station in collaboration with the German authorities.

> In or about the months of June and July 1938 you entered into close association with persons concerned with the Government of Germany in connection with the erection of a wireless broadcasting station in Germany, to be used by an English company in which you were closely interested.[3]

It was immediately assumed by most of the men detained that the New British Broadcasting Station must be the radio station referred to. This assumption was confirmed when Security Service officers who interviewed the men made repeated efforts to find out who was responsible for the printing and distribution of the stickers and posters advertizing the station that were still being put up around London and the provinces. These interrogations were the favourite topic of conversation, particularly the identity of the Army Officer who conducted the main interviews. The name he gave was not his own, and he was not, in fact, an Army Officer at all but Maxwell Knight, who took particular care to see that his identity was not revealed. At

---

[2] Prominent among these was Lt. Dudley M. Evans, who had been a close associate of Mosley's before the war (see above, p.123) but had later become so alarmed by what he saw in Germany that he had volunteered before war began. The instructions issued for his detention by MI5 read: 'If he is in uniform on arrest, arrangements should be made, if necessary by having him escorted home, to enable him to change as soon as possible into mufti. In no circumstances should he be taken to prison in uniform.' On his arrest Evans remarked that he 'would welcome Court Martial or any other proper trial with Army Officers present'. In view of the political nature of his 'offence' nothing of this kind was permitted, so he and some other officers sent a telegram to the Home Secretary which read: 'Our Military and Service reputations and the honour of our Regiments or RAF establishments are at stake. We feel that the Secretary must agree that the action taken in our detention is contrary to all traditions of the Service and we are aware that this has led to grave apprehension in our service circles.' Details may be found in Public Record Office: HO 45/25727 and related files.

[3] Public Record Office: HO 283/12.

least two of the detainees, Neil Francis-Hawkins,[4] Mosley's right-hand man, and Quintin Joyce,[5] William Joyce's younger brother, knew Knight by name and appearance. For this reason they were kept apart from Mosley and the others throughout their period of detention. Knight's ruses were remarkably effective, and his identity never became known to the men at Brixton. Francis-Hawkins and Joyce never saw Knight in uniform and never subsequently made the connection between the Army Officer in Brixton and the MI5 officer they had known under a number of other guises.

The detention of the British Union members was covered by the British press in a strictly factual way, with no mention of the reasons for the detentions, or the New British Broadcasting Station. Mosley himself was, of course, silenced and with his paper outside his control and very little was heard from the British Union.[6] The political debate continued in another medium with Joyce's next broadcast on the NBBS.

Powers Bill: 'Martial Law'. As a result of the Emergency Powers Defence Bill, a state of martial law now exists in this country. Make no mistake about it. These emergency powers the Government has taken bring out a state of affairs the true name of which is 'Martial Law'. Never before

[4] Neil Francis-Hawkins was Mosley's second in command and there are numerous references to him in the Mosley literature; see for example Thurlow, op.cit., p.185. Thurlow's book is among the first to be written after the files on the 18B detainees were opened. However, although he cites the Francis-Hawkins file, he does not seem to have appreciated the significance of Hawkins' statements about Knight. Francis-Hawkins files may be found in the Public Record Office: HO 45/25700 and related files.

[5] Although William Joyce has been the subject of keen attention, his family have been largely ignored, perhaps fairly, since with one exception they were apolitical. In view of William Joyce's interest in broadcasting the authorities must have been intrigued to discover that, on the outbreak of war, he had two brothers and a sister working for the BBC! His sister returned immediately to Ireland while his two brothers were detained briefly under 18B before joining the Army and seeing through the war honourably in the Middle East and elsewhere. There was another brother working for the Air Ministry, Edwin Quintin Joyce, who was detained and held throughout the war as a major threat to security, despite his youth. His papers and his many appeals may be found in the Public Record Office: HO 45/25690 and related papers.

[6] The British Union paper *Action* was not suppressed at the same time as the British Union, and two more numbers appeared. But the authorities had merely allowed it to continue for a short while so that other British Union men, so far undetected, who approached the paper for information about what was happening, could be detained. After the last issue all who had written for it were detained. On similar grounds Lady Mosley was allowed her freedom for some while after Sir Oswald's detention because the authorities hoped that a shadow organization would evolve around her which could then be suppressed in turn.

has a Government taken similar powers, no matter how difficult the situation. Even the illusion of democracy has been dropped, and Churchill is determined to force the people of Britain to defend him and his kind to their last drop of blood. In the event of an occupation of this country by German troops, the power of our rulers would be broken, and they would be forced to go into exile. What has caused this change of face? Mr Attlee admitted the cause in the first words he spoke when he rose in the House of Commons to give the decision of his capitalist masters. 'I rise to inform the House that the situation is so critical that the Government is compelled to seek special powers'.

The situation is critical indeed. Since the outbreak of war in the West, the Government has kept from us the truth of the enemy's rapid advance towards our island. People have been deluded with stories of work accomplished by the Allied troops and Air Forces.

The Government knew that, had the truth of the German advance been known, while people retained their liberties, there would have been an irresistible move for peace in face of the inevitable. Only in the belief that victory was still possible would the working class accept the sacrifices that it was called upon to make. The Government was aware that before the truth was known, the people had to be stripped of every possibility of protest. They had to be put under a more complete dictatorship than exists in Germany and Russia.

We protest against a war which was begun by finance against the interests of the people, and which must be stopped by immediate negotiation if our nation and western civilization is to be saved.[7]

In reality the authorities were not sure exactly what the relationship between the broadcasting station which Mosley had been planning pre-war and the wartime German English-language stations was. They were glad to avail themselves of the opportunities presented by the mass detention of their prime suspects to find out more, although this was not as straightforward as at first appeared. While it was possible to impose on the more junior members of Mosley's party by interrogating them in prison, Mosley himself and the older members of the party were clearly not to be dealt with in the same way. Fortunately the regulation under which they were detained had provision, exactly similar to those 18B regulations earlier in operation, for the detainees to make objections to their grounds for detention to a committee appointed by the Home Secretary. Although these committees were referred to as appeal committees by the authorities, and by most who appeared before them, they were specifically not referred to as such in the regulations.[8] The most obvious differences

[7] BBC Written Archives Centre: Summary of World Broadcasts, 24 May 1940.

  In a 'Note of Procedure', issued at the 28th Meeting of the Central Conference of Chief Constables on 16 January 1941, clause 1 stated: 'Every person detained under

between the interrogation committees and an ordinary appeal committee or tribunal was on the question of legal representation. The detainee was not allowed any form of legal representation whatsoever. Despite equivocal replies to questions asked in the House of Commons on this matter no lawyer was ever present at an actual meeting of the committee.[9] In only the most exceptional cases were the detainees – they could not be, and were not, referred to as 'accused' because they were not accused of anything – allowed to bring forward evidence, or witnesses, and even then they could not be present when these were examined. They were not supplied with transcripts of their own interrogations either during or after interrogation. This meant that the committees were ideal opportunities for the authorities to find out as much as possible about the British Union and related organizations. The detainees were mostly under the delusion that the committee they faced, as an appeals committee, could order their release. In reality they had no such powers and could only recommend to the Home Secretary that a person be released from detention, and a contrary opinion from MI5 almost always over-rode that recommendation. It was stated clearly that the Committee sat alone and that, while the detainee had no legal representation, he could be assured that the committee was independent of the authorities. This was believed by all, including, it seems, Mosley, but the reality was that the committee always had sitting with it an MI5 officer. In Mosley's case this was F.B. Aikin-Sneath, an officer from F division of MI5.[10]

Regulation 18B has the right of making objections to an Advisory Committee. The procedure is not precisely that of appeal and the report of the Committee takes the form of a recommendation to the Home Secretary whose decision is final.' Clause 4 read: 'There is no specific charge against the objector and the procedure is not like that of a criminal trial. The objector [i.e. the detainee] is not legally represented nor are representatives of MI5 or the police present.' (It is worth noting that the Chief Constables were being deceived here, for MI5 were present during interrogations: see below.) This 'Note of Procedure' may be found in the Public Record Office: MEPO 2/6433.

[9] In view of the specific reference in the police instructions (see above, n.8) that no legal representatives were present, the authorities' denial that this was the case in the House of Commons seems more inexcusable than Ministers' equivocations usually are. There are extensive examples of the facts in the the HO 45 sequence of files at the Public Record Office.

[10] Francis Brian Aikin-Sneath OBE, MI5 officer, later Clerk in Holy Orders. Before the war Aikin-Sneath lectured at Berlin University, having graduated at Christ Church. At this time he was the officer most involved with 18B cases; besides Mosley he dealt with Quintin Joyce and most of the other 'serious cases'. When the 18B cases had finished, he moved over to a department dealing with German political exiles. He is not mentioned in the standard books on MI5 or in

There was a further general biasing of the main committee, and that was in the person of its Chairman, Norman Birkett. Not only had Birkett been hearing objections against detention by large numbers of German and other enemy detainees, which might have prejudiced him, but he also had taken an active anonymous role in the radio propaganda war himself.[11] If Mosley knew this he never raised the question; he seems only to have raised a personal matter with Birkett on the question of freemasonry. Knowing that Birkett was a mason, Mosley made a spirited defence of that institution, although he himself was not one. This can only have been to please Birkett, for all National Socialist parties of whatever hue shared a revulsion from freemasonry which went back to the slanders against both Jews and freemasons contained in *The Protocols of the Elders of Zion*.[12]

Mosley's interrogation began on 2 July 1940, and after extensive discussion of the nature and origin of his party Birkett made a clumsy attempt to elicit information from Mosley about the NBBS:

Birkett: Is there a possibility that many of your supporters, contrary to your own view, were acting in a subterranean manner to assist Germany?

Mosley: None whatever.

Birkett: Take a small thing to start with. You have probably seen some of these sticky-back labels stuck up and down the place. Take the New British Broadcasting Corporation [sic].

Mosley: I have heard a lot of that while I have been in goal. That I understand advertizes a German wireless station.

Birkett: Yes.

Mosley: It seems to me to be an absolutely half-witted activity, considering the German wireless stations have been advertized in our whole press.

Birkett: That one has not.

Mosley: How can anyone not a half-wit think he is helping Germany by putting up a sticky-back label mentioning a German wireless station when you have only to look in *The Times*.

Anthony Glees, *Exile Politics during the Second World War* (1982), though some of his memoranda are cited anonymously in the latter. For an attempt he made before the war to establish an independent British School in Berlin, free of Nazi influence, see Public Record Office: FO 395/633; P12/12/150. He died in 1972.

[11] See above, p.182. Birkett was known as 'Onlooker' and insisted on his anonymity, obliging the BBC to go to extraordinary lengths to conceal who he was. Even the studio staff only knew him as Mr X.

[12] For *The Protocols of the Elders of Zion*, see, for example, Thurlow, op.cit., where it is referred to (p.24) as 'the emergent bible of European anti-semitism'. For the dominant role of freemasonry in the British Security Services, see Peter Wright, *Spycatcher* (1987) [not published in Great Britain], pp.30, 187.

Birkett: It is not in *The Times*. It has never been published, this so-called New British Broadcasting Corporation.[13]

Later in the same day Birkett asked more direct questions about possible links between the British Union and William Joyce, much to Mosley's annoyance, as Joyce had left the British Union under circumstances of great rancour after a dispute about funds supplied to the British Union via Joyce.

Birkett: On this point there is just one other matter I will ask you before we adjourn. Suppose it were established that some of your leaders were in communication with 'Lord Haw-Haw', would that be a matter of surprise to you?

Mosley: Now in communication, or before the war?

Birkett: No – since the war.

Mosley: I should think that outrageous.

Birkett: It would be a great surprise to you?

Mosley: I should think it would.

Birkett: It would be a matter which had been carefully concealed from you if it occurred?

Mosley: Good heavens, yes! I should say utterly impossible.

Birkett: Or that efforts were being made through an intermediary to get in touch with him?

Mosley: I should consider it the gravest thing I ever heard of.

Birkett: If any of your leaders were known to have tried to congratulate 'Lord Haw-Haw' upon the success of his broadcasts, that would equally be a great surprise to you?

Mosley: It would certainly, apart altogether from national issues. If anyone in my movement either before the war was in touch with that man [Birkett had previously identified him with William Joyce] to assist him or congratulate him, he would be slung out, anyone who knows the story of that man …

Birkett: After the war?

Mosley: Then of course it is a perfect outrage to me as well as to the nation – to me personally.[14]

Immediately after Mosley's arrest the NBBS put out a series of broadcasts to explain how they were able to continue to send out their programmes when obviously nearly all of their supporters were being arrested. At first they took the obvious line, saying that they had indeed just escaped detection and that some of their members had been arrested.

---

[13] Public Record Office: HO 283/13.
[14] Ibid.

We hope that listeners will be able to locate us on the new wavelength. Owing to interest taken in us by Scotland Yard we have had to change our quarters. Now we hope we have escaped the ring closing around us. We are holding the opening ceremony by cocking snooks at Scotland Yard, the BBC, Uncle Winston Churchill and all. Only with difficulty did we avoid capture to coincide with the arrests of Ramsay and Mosley yesterday, but even if we were sent to Brixton the work of the NBBS would continue as there are other people and other transmitters ready to carry on. The only danger would be that if we had to make the change at the usual hour of transmission we would be off the air for one evening this week.

Five of our collaborators have been arrested, including two representatives of the Institute of British Opinion. In spite of this we promise that the service of uncensored information will be continued. Our principal connections remain intact. In addition to our direct collaborators, several of those who cooperated by distributing leaflets and posters and passing round printed copies of our talks have also been arrested. We express regret to their dependants and renew thanks to those still carrying on.

Liberties taken from the people are never returned. Restrictions of the last war remain today. We fight against the Government and we are proud to know that through our efforts the freedom taken from the British people will be given back.

(Monitor's note: NBBS on its new wavelength of 25.08 m. was jammed tonight but 50.63 m. was audible.)[15]

In order to guard against the possibility of 'other transmitters' existing and, for example, some portable relay station actually being set up, the authorities decided that they had no alternative but to ban all car radios in Britain. The reason for this drastic step was never made public, but it was clear that any transmitter fitted to a car could be made indistinguishable from a car radio to anyone but an expert, and that suitable aerials could have been located at various sites beforehand. The only solution was to ban any form of radio apparatus in a motor car.[16]

The Institute of British Opinion was an opinion poll which the NBBS purported to be running in Britain. The NBBS added an additional touch of authenticity by saying that they had previously

---

[15] BBC Written Archives Centre: Summary of World Broadcasts, 25 May 1940.

[16] For transmitters in cars, see above, p.110. The ban was imposed under the Emergency Powers Regulation 8(2a) on 27 May 1940. It was removed after a Parliamentary Question by Captain Plugge on 25 February 1944. See Hansard 397, col.982 and col.1118.

worked for Captain Plugge's International Broadcasting, an accusation which so worried him that he asked a parliamentary question on the subject, pointing out to his former employees, if they existed, that they were committing treason by working for the Germans.[17]

Throughout the period of Mosley's detention before his interrogation the NBBS kept up a barrage of programmes and returned frequently to the difficulties they were experiencing, placing great emphasis on the reliability of their news broadcasts as opposed to the 'censored' BBC. At some point they became aware that the NBBS was being jammed and referred to the efforts they were making to get over the problem which, in common with all stations that were bothered with jamming, they failed to do:

> We have sources of information which the Government dreads because we know the truth and will reveal it. We have helpers in the ministries and in important positions throughout the country. We represent the chief, almost the only effective opposition to the Government. We have become the leaders of a great and powerful movement for peace and every short wave wireless set is our local headquarters. Now the Government, desperate for some means of defeating us and retaining its vicious power, has attempted to jam our transmissions by means of a special apparatus so that those who tune in to the broadcast cannot distinguish our words. So far this has been to a great extent ineffective, and I want to assure you that it will fail in the future. We shall see to it that our transmissions take place every evening at the regular time and if you don't hear our signature tune exactly on this wavelength then you will hear it on another.[18]

The theme of the short-wave wireless set being a Fifth Column headquarters was repeated again and again. On 15 June the NBBS warned people:

> Rumours are rife throughout the land. Soon, they say, France will make a separate peace with Germany and Italy and leave England to fight alone. England, it is said, would make no great effort to oppose such a settlement. Most people believe that Weygand himself never expected the hastily improvised line to hold.[19]

It went on to repeat the need to spread disaffection:

[17] See Hansard 351, col. 968.
[18] BBC Written Archives Centre: Summary of World Broadcasts, 12 June 1940.
[19] Ibid., 15 June 1940.

Remember that your wireless set is the local headquarters of the movement to stop the war and to save England from destruction. You have certain responsibilities, not to this station but to the country, it's no good leaving it to the others ... The great thing is that the truth should be spread throughout the country. The Government exists on falsehood and misrepresentation. We shall defeat it and bring peace by studying the truth.

The BBC had already been warned by the authorities that the dangers of Fifth Column activity might be real and were in the main not those of infiltration but of outright attack. Armoured cars were provided for key BBC personnel, and broadcasting stations were given additional protection from attack by shutters and barbed wire in the country, and armed guards positioned at key points in the buildings in cities. These risks and the seriousness with which they were taken can be seen from a minute sent to the Director General of the Ministry of Information on 7 June 1940, headed 'Risk of Fifth Columnist Action at the BBC'. The Deputy Secretary of the policy committee of the MOI wrote:

> ...after Mr Wellington and I had discussed the matter last night Lord Swinton, Chairman of the Committee for enquiring into Fifth Column activities in this country, spoke to me on another matter and I mentioned the BBC position. He entirely endorses the view which I understand from Mr Wellington that Sir Allan Powell is taking, namely that every possible step should be taken to ensure the security of Broadcasting House against Fifth Columnist activities, even at the risk of some loss of efficiency in the broadcasting services – temporarily one would hope ... Incidentally, Lord Swinton asked me to come and see him to discuss (i) the other security measures which my BBC Security Measures Committee has been considering and of which a note is before you and also (ii) the arrangements which we are proposing for the security of this building.[20]

The most serious problem facing the BBC from the NBBS was that it would indeed take over, or try to, if an invasion force landed. If once the invaders got access to a transmitter on the mainland, the signal strength and wavelengths would make the programme indistinguishable from a BBC regional station.

The most practical step taken was to alter entirely the image of the men who read the actual news broadcasts. Before the war these had been taught to speak with the most perfect accents, using pronunciation and diction which was agreed by a special committee.

[20] Public Record Office: INF 1/333.

Unfortunately the recommendations of this committee were all published and extensively circulated, and the fact had to be faced that the Germans could copy them very effectively. The answer was to announce, for the first time, the name of the newscaster.[21] After a brief period the public would come to recognize the voices of these men and substitution would become difficult, if not impossible. The result, not foreseen, was to change entirely the way the public related to the BBC. For the first time the modern media-personality emerged and the previously neutral voices were transformed into celebrities.

The first serious alarm about an invasion envisaged the event, called 'The Day of Crisis', as taking place at the beginning of June. The BBC worked out a programme of broadcasts to be used which conveyed a great sense of alertness. The true state of preparedness is seen in the fact that it was not until a Board Meeting on 19 July that the BBC decided what engineers should do if they found themselves in enemy occupied territory.[22]

The scheme of broadcasts was confined to special talks at the times usually occupied by the main News Bulletins:

Thursday May 30th		Mr Malcolm Macdonald on Evacuation (arranged)
Friday May 31st	9 p.m.	Mr A. Greenwood on 'Economic Pressure in Germany' (Apparently the script of this has been approved by the P.M.)[23] This will be most useful from the Home Morale point of view if it is made clear that the Germans are probably much worse off than we know.
	6 p.m.	A member of the Services to give an account of the heroic conduct of evacuation. As a contrast to General Mason

[21] The idea had originated in Holland where the Fifth Column was thought — wrongly, as it transpired after the war — to have been well-nigh universal.

[22] They were to disable their transmitters by removing essential parts and concealing them. After two weeks they were to resume normal operations under whichever administration was then in power.

[23] Shortly after Churchill became Prime Minister he introduced a rigorous system of censorship of ministerial broadcasts. Ministers in the War Cabinet were free to broadcast what they pleased. All other ministers had their scripts personally approved by Churchill. The system was kept a closely guarded secret and has remained secret until now. However, the BBC producers had to be informed that they could not ask a Minister to do a broadcast without prior permission and, more important, had to refer to the Cabinet Office all requests from Ministers to do talks. See below, p.241. Those interested in pursuing this controversial topic may wish to look at files for R.A. Butler and Nicolson at the BBC Written Archives Centre, in conjunction with related files in the Public Record Office INF 1 series.

		Macfarlane he should be a sailor and, if possible, a rating or Warrant Officer.
Saturday June 1st	9 p.m.	Postscript: another talk by a member of the Services.

It is not possible to plan to the day beyond Saturday, as the crisis may have taken place by then, or may be delayed for several days.

Day of Crisis		News broadcast by the Prime Minister as soon as possible, *or*, if the House is sitting, broadcast by Mr Duff Cooper directly after P.M.'s announcement.
	9 p.m.	Speech by Prime Minister, repeating news and passing on to the theme 'To Your Posts'; followed by General Ironside (who may be introduced by Mr Duff Cooper), giving an account of our Home Defences.
Second Day	6 p.m.	The Queen, speaking specifically to women – sympathy and encouragement. Followed by similar (shorter) broadcast in French to French women.
	9 p.m.	Mr Duff Cooper, telling civilians what to do and announcing further talks of practical advice; followed by Mr Bevin, on what Labour can do.
Third Day	6 p.m.	Address by Secretary of State for War taking up point, which should be mentioned in Prime Minister's Speech, that we intend returning to France and building up a great Army to help our Allies.
	9 p.m.	Monsieur Reynaud (in English) Prime Minister (in French) on allied determination to stand together to beat Germany.[24]

The NBBS did not begin seriously to talk of invasion until later in June. Their broadcast on 28 June extended the game of bluff by beginning to talk to alleged agents in Britain in a nonsensical code, followed by ever more urgent requests to bring about a revolution.

Invasion: NBBS Plans

We must face the necessity of making arrangement for the eventuality of invasion. Thing have become pretty chaotic in recent days, but when invasion and panic come, the circumstances in which we work will be

[24] Public Record Office: INF 1/878.

even more difficult. We must organize so that there is no break in our efforts to restore peace. As long as possible we shall continue to broadcast. The worst problem will be refugees. Of the millions in France, thousands died by the wayside. Millions of our people may be driven like cattle into Scotland and Wales, but their fate will be even more terrible, as there is no friendly Switzerland or Spain to receive them. We must do all we can to alleviate their suffering. Those who work with us must maintain connection, if you go with the refugees, you should have a portable short-wave set with you. Invasion may be long and bloody, or short and without much suffering. We must all strive for the immediate stoppage of hostilities.

For the sake of efficiency, I have evolved instructions for use during invasion, but they will begin to work immediately. Listeners are divided into two classes: Listening groups known to me, and in touch with representatives of the station. Their leaders have been handed a number of typewritten sheets, giving instructions and a code. Explanations have also been given them orally. These are Group A. Group B comprises all other listeners who are not known to me. They will only be given instructions through the microphone. Group B is divided into regions and referred to accordingly. Their instructions cannot be so explicit as those given in code to Group A. You must prepare a plan of action in your locality.

Instructions for Today. Here are instructions for the next 24 hours:

Group A – I call the following localities according to letters you will find in blue pencil at the top right hand corner of the first page of the code book – AFN, AFO, DRD will operate special plan 17. Locality AFL will operate plan 17 in region five only ... When invasion is distant only by a matter of hours we find ourselves in the hands of men who are to all intents and purposes criminal lunatics.

It will be no use asking them to go. They must be hurled bodily out of Downing Street, and made to pay for the immense and indeed irreparable wrong which they have done to our country. They must not escape. They must drink to the very dregs the cup of disaster which they have prepared for us. When our country is in enemy possession it would be rather late to start dealing with them, so we had better start now.[25]

This seems to have been too much for the Government to stand and, at the beginning of July they actually launched a direct attack on the NBBS which produced an immediate reply on 2 July:

[25] BBC Written Archives Centre: Summary of World Broadcasts, 28/9 June 1940.

The Ministry of Information, and its fateful voice, the BBC, considered it appropriate yesterday to deliver a particularly absurd attack on the New British Broadcasting Station. The Government, it seems, is very angry because we have presumed to give you advice for your own good. The opening gambit of the attack was quite naturally to accuse us of being a German Station. With this irresponsible falsehood, we have dealt before, and we don't mean to waste words in refuting it now. Anybody who dares to tell the people the truth is at once branded as an enemy by the corrupt dictatorship which contaminates the land today.[26]

The detention of British Union members throughout this period continued unabated and would appear to have been justified if seen from the standpoint of a security official worried that at any time some contact might be established between the broadcasters and a political movement in Britain. And there were some worrying incidents around Britain which pointed to possible developments in the situation, for example the assault by some British Union men at Branscombe in Devon on a LDV recruiting officer.[27]

In an NBBS broadcast protesting against the detention of Admiral Sir Barry Domville and Captain Ramsay[28] a vigorous attack was made on the German and Austrian refugees who were living in Britain:

Anybody who tries to reveal and expose the corruption and incompetence of the Churchill despotism is, of course, a German, or at least an employee of Dr Goebbels, and if some thoroughly unsavoury Jewish adventurer comes to England on a mission of espionage, as many have done, to promote the work of the fifth column on behalf of the enemy he is treated as an English patriot of impeccable integrity.[29]

Whether this attack and other similar moves in the propaganda war were the decisive influence will not be known until all records are

---

[26] Ibid., 2 July.

[27] An account of this incident may be found in *Express and Echo* (Exeter, 19 June 1940): 'LDV Section Leader assaulted by Fascist sympathisers that he had provoked.'

[28] Sir Barry Domville and Archibald H. Maule Ramsay were both sympathetic to the far right and detained under 18B(1a). There is an extensive account of their activities in Thurlow, op.cit. Ramsay was a Member of Parliament and is often said to have been the only Member in Britain to have been detained; but two other Members in Northern Ireland were also detained. These may not have been included in official lists because Northern Ireland was treated by the Security authorities as a foreign country – all mail to mainland Britain was censored, for example.

[29] BBC Written Archives Centre: Summary of World Broadcasts, 21 June 1940.

released,[30] but three days later the Home Secretary, Sir John Anderson, announced in the House of Commons that all aliens were being interned. This was the beginning of one of the sorriest chapters in modern British history, involving the reintroduction of transportation to Canada and Australia.[31] There is no doubt that this measure was taken in a time of panic. Reading the radio broadcasts, all purporting to be coming from Fifth Column sympathizers within Britain and with a large underground audience, not least of which were the privileged groups, including Members of Parliament, who were allowed to read the BBC monitors' transcripts of these broadcasts, the panic largely produced by them can be understood.

The most extreme measure taken by the Government that would have affected British citizens was that under the Emergency Powers Act introduced on 10 July, creating special courts which would operate in areas within military jurisdiction; that is, in areas threatened with immediate occupation by the enemy. As initially planned the Court would have consisted of a Judge, referred to as the President, assisted by two Justices of the Peace. There would have been no jury and no appeal against sentence which could include summary execution for any offence, including the spreading of rumour, looting and other offences which might entail a strengthening of the law where necessary. This the House of Commons would not countenance even under the most stringent emergency. It was agreed to allow appeal against the death sentence in the Act as passed on 1 August. But the situation generally had so changed by then that on 23 July Churchill announced that sentences passed on people for defeatist talk,

[30] For a particularly determined, but only partially successful, attempt to wrest closed records from the Home Office, see Peter and Leni Gillman, *'Collar the Lot!'* (1980), p.xii. Their success was not achieved by the present writer. An interview was granted to him over a year after an initial request. It was conducted amicably, and he was informed that certain papers relating to the detention of William Joyce and others were to be released, indeed had already been released, by the department concerned. However, the paperwork involved in release and deposit at the Public Record Office meant that he could not actually see them. After a delay of some months these papers, although released, were still not available for inspection and this book was sent to press as a further delay of publication on this sole ground was considered unjustifiable. The Public Record Office have not at the time of writing received these papers.

[31] For an account of these deportations, see Gillman, op.cit. One ship, the *Arandora Star*, was sunk with great loss of life among the deported detainees. Far from there being any distinction between Jewish refugees and Fascist sympathizers, the opportunity was taken by MI5 to round up all known Fascists and send them off to Canada, many on this ill-fated ship. The officer involved was Guy Liddell who included the then managers of the Ritz and the Savoy in his list. See Public Record Office: FO 371/25192; W8633/8023/49, cited in Gillman, p.315.

including the spreading of 'Haw-Haw rumours', would be reviewed.

The NBBS radio campaign began to lose contact with reality at the same time; on 15 July, for example, they claimed that 67 people had been sentenced to death for sabotage and Fifth Column activity and that 573 workers had been arrested for refusing to work overtime. On 19 July Hitler addressed the Reichstag and included in his speech his offer of Peace to Britain. On 22 July, while the NBBS was broadcasting that two hundred people had been arrested for distributing uncensored versions of Hitler's speech, Lord Halifax, the Foreign Secretary, broadcast the British Government's rejection of the offer. This marked the end of Joyce's NBBS 'invasion' propaganda campaign. All broadcasts to supposed Fifth Columnists in spurious codes were dropped in favour of new broadcasts from the 'Workers Challenge Station' and a fresh campaign was built around the slogan 'A People's Peace' which was to culminate early in 1941 in a massive 'People's Convention' held in London and run by the Communist Party of Great Britain.[32]

By chance 22 July was also the day of the last of Mosley's appearances before Norman Birkett. The reality of the Fifth Column threat, such as it was, had been looked at as closely as Birkett, one of the finest legal brains in the country, could manage. Mosley's radio projects before the war had been examined carefully. He had been asked about his finances, and about W.E.D. Allen's involvement in all his projects. Oliver Hoare's name had been mentioned, but not the project that he and Eckersley had put forward to the British Government; Mosley had made no admission other than his knowledge of Hoare's involvement with Allen's business ventures. The connection which Birkett had hinted at between one of Mosley's senior men and 'Lord Haw-Haw' had proved an embarrassing case of mistaken identity. A man called Richard Findlay[33] had been found to be in contact with Germany and

[32] What might be called the manifesto of the People's Convention was D.N. Pritt, *Forward to a People's Government* (1940). The links with Russia were made very clear in another pamphlet published by the People's Convention Committee: Commander Edgar P. Young, RN, *A People's Peace* (1941), p.7: '... the policy of the Soviet Government, clearly stated by Molotov on 31 October 1939, makes it highly probable that the USSR would feel itself bound to intervene diplomatically (and in certain circumstances would go even further) in order to assist the ending of the war and the making of a satisfactory peace.' The revolution which Pritt and others thought would result from the Convention did not take place. It was obviously very worthwhile for the German propagandists to tie in with this campaign, for, had there been a revolution and a People's Government established in Britain, the war would inevitably have come to an end. The failure of this archetypal 'National Committee' in Britain did not deter the Soviets from establishing similar committees among German and other exiles in Moscow.

[33] Richard Findlay was detained under 18B(1a), but his papers have not been released. He became Camp Leader at Peveril Detention Camp, and some

William Joyce via Jugoslavia. He had also been in frequent communication with Mosley, or rather he had often written to Mosley. Unfortunately for MI5 and the committee, this was not the man they thought to be the British Union's Director of Public Relations, who was actually someone else entirely, a man called A.G. Findlay. Mosley was clearly amused by the confusion and gave a lucid account of how he came to know of Richard Findlay – a man, he said, who had left the British Union in order to go and fight an election campaign as an anti-Baldwin Conservative on behalf of Randolph Churchill.[34] Mosley had never himself met Findlay, who wrote to him continuously in an attempt to regain his membership of the British Union. Findlay had accompanied George Pitt-Rivers[35] on a tour of the continent and, like him, had extreme right-wing, pro-German views that lead to his internment. A.G. Findlay, on the other hand, had never made any contact with Germany or Joyce. All other attempts to establish that there was any connection between Mosley's radio station and the broadcasts put out by the NBBS similarly failed. Towards the end of his interrogation Mosley essayed a direct attack on MI5. He had first been annoyed when, having with great difficulty got permission for Neil Francis-Hawkins to go to his house in Chester Square where the British Union's papers were, he discovered that the Security authorities had also been there and removed documents that Francis-Hawkins had found.[36] When he put this to Norman Birkett there was considerable embarrassment; Birkett finally said that the men involved had been police at the premises to search for the printing presses that had been making the NBBS stickers which were still being circulated. Mosley then moved on to more serious matters, for it had emerged during the interrogation that the committee had not been told about his earlier radio business ventures by MI5, but only about the contracts with Germany and Hitler's Propaganda Minister Goebbels. Birkett said candidly: .

---

correspondence of his in that capacity has surfaced in a related file at the Public Record Office: HO 214/67 (reference owed to Thurlow, op.cit., p.222, n.88).

[34] I have been unable to elucidate Mosley's reference here.

[35] Before the war Pitt-Rivers (grandson of the founder of the Pitt-Rivers Museum) had submitted a formal report to the Foreign Office of the atrocities committed against the Sudeten Germans in Czechoslovakia, on behalf of a scientific body. In retrospect its bias is obvious, but at the time only a shrewd Foreign Office official would have been able to detect it. See FO371/20591; W19090/9549/41.

[36] For further discussion of this and letters of complaint written by Mosley at the time, see the Mosley papers in HO45 class.

Birkett: Speaking for myself I do not think they [MI5] had any papers
               relating to Sark or anything else, because apparently it was
               new to everybody.

Mosley: I very much hope they had the Sark contract. This was in the
               safe of a bank; they went through it; I then removed them all to
               my private house, and they took them all away.

Birkett: If those investigating this case knew of the German contract, a
               Belgian contract and a Sark contract, it was their duty to inform
               us of the Belgian and Sark contract as well. All I can say is that
               this committee heard about the Sark contract for the first time
               when you mentioned it. I agree that if they [MI5] knew of it it
               was their duty to put that before the committee as well.

Mosley: If you had seen the Sark contract fifteen months before, your
               impression of the whole thing would have been different. In
               other words if they [i.e. MI5] had those papers, which I am
               sure they have, that evidence was, to put it mildy, a little
               cooked, and therefore it is legitimate for me to enquire whether
               other pieces of evidence have been presented in the same
               partial manner to the committee.

Birket: In your interest I may say that in putting the points we have on
               evidence to you there is nothing, so to speak, which this
               committee has kept back.

Mosley: Thank you very much ...[37]

By chance Aikin-Sneath was not sitting with the committee at this
session, as he had to be at another court. When he read Mosley's
attacks on MI5 and, implicitly, on himself he wrote to the secretary of
the committee firmly repeating that nothing had been held back from
them and that the accusations of rigged evidence were groundless.

   This cannot have been true, although it may well have been that
Aikin-Sneath was not himself in possession of all the facts. The figure
at the centre of these investigations working under Brigadier A.S.
Hawker, was Maxwell Knight. Knight has been referred to more than
once in the course of this narrative, but it was only during the
interrogations for 18B suspects that it became clear to anyone reading
the papers how his interest and knowledge of the British Union and
other Fascist parties developed. Unlike earlier espionage stories of
World War I, this is of genuine political interest for, in the radio
propaganda wars, the extent of the validity of the claims of the scare
campaigns run by Joyce and the NBBS were a vital part of the
Government's intelligence. In deciding to intern large numbers of
aliens the Government was following a path first laid down in World
War I and followed all over the world whenever there were great

[37] HO283.16.

movements of alien people to cope with. But the suppression of a political party was something entirely new in British life. Knight's covert activities and, later, the activities of other members of the Security Services, such as Philby and Burgess, were themselves of major political significance.[38]

Knight, as we have seen, was somehow known to Quintin Joyce, William Joyce's younger brother. The committee who inadvertently came across this fact did not pursue the matter further but, with Knight's passion for anonymity and security, it was a fact that needed explaining. The solution to the problem was given by Neil Francis-Hawkins. On the last day of his interrogation he decided to launch an attack on Knight, who had made some attempt to get in contact with him while he was in prison. He revealed that he had known Knight for many years, since before the British Union had been founded. It was almost a domestic connection, for one of Knight's agents had married Francis-Hawkins's sister and had then used the connection to spy on him, to his fury. Francis-Hawkins had been a member of the original British Fascist party founded by Miss Lintorn-Orman;[39] there he had first met Knight, who joined at about the same date and was acting as the party's research officer. It was a particularly stirring time as the first serious attacks on them by the Communist party were being organized. The party's meetings were often broken up, and fights were common. At one of these knives had been used and a young supporter of the party had sustained a savage injury to his face. This was William Joyce, and Knight's connection with him probably also began then.

In the biography of Joyce written with the co-operation of his family after the war[40] there were two incidents cited connecting Joyce with MI5. In the first Joyce mentioned that he had been asked by MI5 to go to Germany and join the National Socialists there later to act as a source of information or, as we should say today, a mole. He had declined to go, preferring to remain as Mosley's director of

---

[38] It is to be hoped, for this reason alone, that the present blanket closure of *all* files relating to the Security Services will be relaxed, enabling even some general authentic political history of Britain at this period to be written.

[39] Miss Rotha Lintorn-Orman (1895-1935), founder of the British Fascisti in 1923. In World War I she had volunteered for an ambulance and twice been awarded the Croix de Charité for her work in Salonica. Despite the thoroughly British nature of her organization she seems to have had some contact with James Strachey Barnes' International Centre for Fascist Studies, being like Barnes a great admirer of Mussolini. There is an illustration of her in Colin Cross, *The Fascists in Britain* (1961). Until the appearance of Thurlow, op.cit., Cross's book was the standard text on the subject and is still of considerable value.

[40] J.A. Cole, *Lord Haw-Haw: The Full Story of William Joyce* (new ed. 1987).

propaganda, an office which he took over from C.E.M. Joad.[41] Later he broke with Mosley and formed his own party which had much closer avowed links with Germany than Mosley's. When the original 18B orders were issued, Joyce, unlike Mosley, was on a list for immediate detention. The second contact with MI5 was in a warning phone call from someone in MI5, late at night, two days before the actual order to implement 18B was carried out. The warning enabled Joyce to escape the country.

Joyce's biographer makes no attempt to establish who this MI5 contact was. But it seems more than likely from Quintin Joyce's interrogation that it was Knight. Quintin Joyce's account of his brother's last days in England corresponds closely with other accounts, but contains additional information about a number of matters all of which pointed to the fact that he was both very young and politically naive. He was quite unaware that Knight was an unusual person to know. On the contrary, when he was first interned he sent Knight all his papers, which he thought would refute the charges brought against him – papers which were never returned. Had Knight contacted *him*, the matter would have been in some doubt, but there can have been no other way in which this younger member of the Joyce family could have known about Knight and his position in the Security Services than through his older brother. He had never had anything to do with Mosley or any other Fascist party and only began to take an interest in politics after the founding of the National Socialist League by his brother and John Beckett.[42]

Further confirmation of Knight's connection with Joyce came indirectly during Knight's most important and successful case of the war years, the trial for spying of Tyler Kent and Anna Wolkoff.[43]

[41] C.E.M. Joad had in fact been Director of Propaganda in Mosley's original New Party. During the war he gained wide popularity from his part in the BBC Brains Trust, where he succeeded in getting home the rudiments of a philosophical attitude by his continual repetition of the phrase 'It all depends what you mean by ...'. The British Union rank and file regarded him as a traitor, and a film of the Brains Trust put on in the East End during the war had to be withdrawn after his appearance was greeted with violent abuse. Converted to Christianity during the war, his public career ended in ignominy after his conviction for a minor offence, a victim of twentieth-century puritanism.

[42] For John Beckett, and his seizing of the mace in the House of Commons, see above, p.11n7.

[43] There are many accounts of this famous trial, but they differ, largely because, once again on a vitally important political matter, the British authorities have declined to release any of the papers on the case, and have no intention of doing so for reasons that remain unknown. Gillman, op.cit., p.116, remarks: 'An examination of the Kent/Wolkoff affair leads to the unpalatable conclusion that it was part of a political conspiracy at the heart of power in Britain.' There are extensive references in

Knight's main agent was a young woman called Joan Miller. At the beginning of the war she had applied to enter the war office on the recommendation of a society friend, unaware that she was applying to work in MI5, on the administration side. When her application was read, it was seen that she gave as her reference 'the Dame of Sark'. Knight seems to have realized immediately that this must mean either that she was in sympathy with the right-wing political views of the group around some members of the family[44] or, more likely, that she knew nothing about this or Mosley's business relationships over the setting up of his transmitting stations and was merely a family friend. What was clear was that she would be an ideal person to infiltrate the Right Club,[45] as the people she knew would all be drawn from people in that world and would point to a sympathy with their aims. Knight became very close to her during the war, getting her a flat in the same block, Dolphin Square, in which he and, incidentally, Sir Oswald Mosley, also lived. He later moved into a house with her, and it was assumed that they were having an affair of some kind. Joan Miller's posthumously published autobiography makes this doubtful, but it does not explain why Knight should have kept so close to her, or do anything to dispel what was a nagging worry to Knight, that she may, in fact, however peripherally, have had some sympathy with those in the Right Club.

At the time of the Wolkoff case Joan Miller was used to get Anna Wolkoff, with whom she had established friendly relations, to send material to William Joyce in Berlin. The actual material that her alleged associate Tyler Kent had unquestionably taken from the American Embassy were telegrams between Roosevelt and Churchill which pointed to a clandestine attempt to bring America into the war and to make other deals. It was known that Kent had shown this material to Anna Wolkoff and then to Captain Ramsay. There was, however, no proof that she was in contact directly with the enemy. By using Joan Miller, Knight obtained clear confirmation of this, or what seemed to be clear confirmation. In fact it was nothing of the sort. The method chosen to entrap Anna Wolkoff was to attempt

---

Thurlow, op.cit. But both these accounts, and all others, were written before the publication of the posthumous memoirs of a central figure in the case: Joan Miller, *One Girl's War* (1987), [not published in Great Britain].

[44] The fact that Joan Miller remarks about the Sark connection in the first lines of her autobiography perhaps indicates that she had become aware of this aspect of things. For the connection between Mosley and Sark, see above, p.122f.

[45] There is an account of the Right Club in Thurlow, op.cit., passim.

to make use of her boasted ability to use the Italian Diplomatic bag.[46] Joan Miller approached her with an introduction to a friend who, it was said, wished to get into contact with William Joyce with vital material. Anna Wolkoff agreed and was introduced to Knight, apparently using one of his many aliases, who produced a packet for Joyce, with a covering letter. Joyce was to acknowledge receipt of the letter by referring to Carlyle in one of his broadcasts which, eventually, he did. Anna Wolkoff seems even to have added a small note of her own, written on an MI5 typewriter in Joan Miller's flat. It then became obvious that she did not have access to the Italian Diplomatic bag, as she claimed, or any way of getting this combined message to Joyce. Whereupon Miller introduced her to another MI5 mole in the Right Club who definitely had access to a bag, though not the Italian one. The packet and letter were duly sent off and Joyce received them. Anna Wolkoff was proved guilty.

The question that was never asked at the time and has not been asked subsequently is why Anna Wolkoff should have wished to communicate with William Joyce or have been thought able to? Was it suggested that this was the way to communicate vitally important secrets, such as the Tyler Kent letters, to the Germans? It is obvious now that a foreign radio propagandist who had barely got to know his German masters would be the last person to whom a genuine spy would have entrusted such vital material. Plainly Anna Wolkoff was not involved in these matters at all. The person who wished to be in contact with Joyce was Knight, and he succeeded, through circles of which Joyce must have been fully aware, those around Captain Ramsay. Did Knight even send him copies of the Churchill-Roosevelt correspondence? Photographs of the letters taken at the time were never accounted for, and Joyce's scripts included what was undoubtedly leaked information about the fifty ships exchanged with Britain, as we have seen.[47] This would also explain why the reports on the broadcasts referring to this were, uniquely, entirely suppressed; The monitors' report for that day was simply removed rather than censored in the usual way and production difficulties were given as the reason for its non-appearance.[48] Although the arrests of Kent and

[46] There was nothing particularly sinister in this boast. It was a commonplace at the time for people wishing to give themselves social status in certain circles to claim to have access to a bag. Indeed it is not unknown today.

[47] See above, p.205.

[48] As mentioned above, the Intelligence Unit print-out of the suppressed edition of the monitors' reports has survived and may be seen in the Public Record Office: HO 45/25728. The relevant issue may genuinely have been prevented by 'technical difficulties' such as a raid. In any case the survival of the relevant document

Wolkoff took place in May they were not to appear in court until later in the year, and were not actually sentenced until 7 November 1940. From the dock Anna Wolkoff had threatened to kill Joan Miller for her part in what had happened; however it is clear from Miller's book that she did not fully understand her part in the charade which lead up to the conviction and was herself convinced of Wolkoff's guilt. Knight only told her part of the story and began by saying that the Kent papers had already been discovered in the papers of the German Embassy in Italy[49] making what she was doing seem less devious. That the fact that Anna Wolkoff was shown *not* to have had access to the Italian Diplomatic bag destroyed the case against her, aside from the incident created by agents provocateurs, seems not to have dawned on her.

The trial as a whole thus shows the extreme lengths the authorities were prepared to go to establish a connection, of whatever kind, between Joyce and the broadcasts and the political movements within Britain. As the clash between the British Union and the LDV turned out in the end to be no more than minor incidents such as that at Branscombe, so the NBBS groups, when found, were only the smallest groups barely more effective than an individual acting on his own.

While the trial of Wolkoff and Kent was proceeding Knight had a typical NBBS case coming to fruition. After the cancellation of the 'Invasion Scare' programmes another full-scale peace campaign had been launched on NBBS and a central idea of this had been the sending of chain letters. All were brief and contained the typical sentence:

Join the Peace Chain! Rather bury the hatchet now than bury the bodies later. If you want the war to stop copy this out including this sentence, and send it or deliver it without your name to six other persons. By doing so you will help to bring peace and prosperity back to Britain.[50]

---

establishes the facts about these broadcasts. The interpretation given here would be more than enough to explain the Government's failure to release all related papers.

[49] Anthony Masters alludes to the German Ambassador in Rome having read the Churchill-Roosevelt correspondence, cited also by Thurlow, op.cit., p.194, mentioning the Government Code and Cipher School intercepts. This seems very unlikely. It may have been a cover story, subsequently embroidered, to link in with the supposed fact that Anna Wolkoff had access to the Italian diplomatic bag. In fact she hadn't, but the cover story remains, a necessary fiction perpetuated as fact after the necessity had passed. Anthony Masters, *The Man Who Was M* (1984).

[50] Quoted in virtually every NBBS broadcast at this time, and recorded in the BBC's monitors' reports, the Summary of World Broadcasts.

Astonishing though it may seem to us today in an age of mass mailing and sophisticated public relations this naive message was actually copied out and sent by numbers of people. Knight had succeeded in getting one of his agents into such a group, centred on an ex-colonial Civil Servant, Aubrey Lees.[51] Knight's report to Brigadier Harker has survived and is printed here as an example of Knight's and MI5's actual working methods.

> A meeting was held on Sunday, November 10th, at Molly Stanford's flat at 45 Queen's Gate Gardens. Present were: Molly Stanford, Aubrey Lees, Aubrey Lees' wife/fiancée/or girl friend and one other man.
>
> The purpose of the meeting was to discuss means of organizing aid for internees of Fascist or Right Wing persuasion. About a dozen persons are stated to have indicated their willingness to help in such an organization. Among them are: Mrs Maule Ramsay, Mr Shaw, M.P., Mr Pickthorne, M.P., and the members of Captain Ramsay's group in the House of Commons, Aubrey Lees, Molly Stanford and General J.F.C. Fuller.
>
> The plan was that money should be collected from those willing to help and be sent to various prisons in rotation. The sums were to be sent through Lady Mosley's sister so that it would then appear as purely private gifts of money. The sums would be administered in the respective prisons by internees chosen by the outside Organization; one of these internees is to be Lady Mosley.
>
> An alternative plan was discussed by which the Governors of the Prisons would be approached and asked if they would allow sums of money to be spent for the benefit of selected internees. It is not yet decided which plan is to be adopted.
>
> The meeting then turned vehemently to discuss the Wolkoff case and it was agreed that Anna Wolkoff had been framed up by the Jews and Freemasons. Anna was regarded in the light of a patriot who had done her duty gloriously and it appears that she expects to be out of gaol by the end of a year since Hitler is expected to have successfully invaded us by then and will immediately release her.
>
> In the meantime, the meeting propose to advise Mme Wolkoff to turn 18a Roland Gardens into a boarding house and to recommend their friends to stay there and help Anna's mother in her distress. If this plan is carried into effect, Mme Wolkoff's house would become a haunt of

[51] Aubrey Lees had been a colonial official in Palestine. He claimed to have been removed from his post without warning after attempting to report an incident in which a suspected Arab terrorist was shot in his hospital bed by British soldiers. His views were far to the right, but he had never actually belonged to the British Union or any other organization. This rendered his detention invalid, to the acute embarrassment of MI5 when he revealed the fact to the committee interrogating him. His papers have been released in the Public Record Office: HO 283/45 and HO 45/25728.

Fascist and Right Wing sympathizers.

After much political discussion the meeting adjourned to Aubrey Lees' flat whose address our observer does not know owing to the fact that the company went there after black-out time. It lies, however, south of Gloucester Road Tube Station.

There Aubrey Lees expounded his plan for a new form of propaganda hostile to the war effort of Great Britain. This propaganda is to take the form of a chain-letter advocating Peace exactly on the lines of that suggestion given out over the N.B.B.S. In fact Aubrey Lees produced a chain letter which was identical in every particular with the suggested letter dictated over the N.B.B.S. when the suggestion of a chain letter was proposed. This had been taken down by Lees himself from the N.B.B.S. broadcast and he openly admitted the fact.

Lees further proposed advertizing the N.B.B.S. in such a chain letter but Molly Stanford opposed this, saying that anyone who touched anything to do with the N.B.B.S. now-a-days was laying themselves open to a sentence of five years. Whether or not it will actually be advertized has not yet been decided.

The chain-letter is to be produced on a 'jelly-slate' and each member of the Group is to write either a word or a sentence at a time so that it can not be attributed to any one person. A further meeting is being arranged to produce it.

Contact is being maintained.[52]

It is interesting to notice that one of those involved, Molly Stanford, had realized that the NBBS was viewed with particular severity by the authorities. Indeed the actual report submitted by Brigadier Harker to the Home Office recommending that Lees and Stanford be detained spelt out the security services' view of the station:

It is submitted that:

(a)   Any person who engages in the distribution of a chain letter advocating peace is open to suspicion unless it is clear that he is guided by genuine pacifist motives.

(b)   If the motive can be shown to be one originating from the influence of persons hostile to this country there is a presumption of disloyalty.

(c)   Any person who seeks to disseminate any matter however innocent broadcast by the New British Broadcasting Station is prima facie disloyal.

(d)   Any person who seeks to advertize the New British Broadcasting Station with the knowledge that it is a German propaganda station is undoubtedly disloyal.[53]

[52] Public Record Office: HO 45/25728.
[53] Ibid.

The pettiness of such cases, when compared with the claims made for the numbers of its followers made by NBBS, shows that Knight was either being relatively unsuccessful, or that the NBBS claims were ludicrously exaggerated. Probably both were true, but there was another element in the situation. Knight was relatively unusual in MI5 in being as determined an enemy of Communism as he was of Fascism. Indeed he might well be seen as having sympathies with the right, although from his earliest days with the British Fascists he had been working for the Security Services and not out of personal conviction. It was a fact of life in the MI5 of the time that the pressure to detain those pacifists and anti-war protesters who were on the left, even members of the Communist Party, was almost non-existent, despite the Soviet-German Pact which had caused Poland's invasion and World War II. Whether this was due to pressures of *haute politique* from Cabinet level, with a view to getting Russia over to the allies' cause as soon as possible, or from some inbred sympathy with the Communist cause that had developed within MI5 during the thirties, especially at the time of the Spanish civil war, can only be established if the relevant records still exist and are made available for scholarly research, an unlikely event in modern Britain. It is certain that almost no left-wing supporters were detained under 18B(1a) at a time when their colleagues in the British Union were being interned wholesale. The result of this immunity was that, throughout the Blitz that followed the Battle of Britain, at a time when British morale was most threatened, a major peace campaign ran on unhindered. Broadcasts from the NBBS, the Workers Challenge and the Christian Peace Movement stations continued through the period, but the political response was not on the right amongst Aubrey Lees' and similar groups, but on the left. Had the authorities looked *there* they would have found a thriving movement whose roots went back as far as Attlee's 'Peace Indivisible' address to Maisky in 1936.

At a slightly lower level than Cabinet *haute politique*, on 11 July R.A. Butler, then Under-Secretary of State at the Foreign Office, had made a statement on Anglo-Russian policy in a written reply to a parliamentary question

> The policy of H.M. Government has been and remains to improve and strengthen the relations between this country and the USSR. Success in this policy has appeared more likely since March of this year, when the USSR made a friendly approach to H.M. Government and proposed the resumption of trade negotiations. This move on their part constituted a welcome departure from the unfriendly attitude which the Soviet government had adopted since the breakdown of the political negotiations in August of last year.

H.M. Government at once responded to this approach by the Soviet Government, and it is to be hoped that the discussions on which H.M. Ambassador in Moscow is at present engaged may finally remove any danger which may have been apprehended that the Soviet Government would work either economically or militarily against Britain in the interests of Germany ... I trust that this statement will dispel any false and mischievous impressions which German propaganda has sought to create.[54]

And it was this policy which no doubt formed the background of MI5's benevolent treatment of those numerous supporters of the 'people's peace' campaign.

The country's main strength at the time was unquestionably Churchill. It has been said that he viewed propaganda with disfavour and was particularly suspicious of the BBC and broadcasting. While it is true that he attempted unsuccessfully to bring the BBC more directly under Government control,[55] he was fully conscious of the importance of broadcasting and used it himself extensively. In the absence of satisfactory control of the BBC, he evolved a system whereby he himself censored all broadcasts by Ministers who were not actually members of the War Cabinet. Scripts by Ministers were sent to the Ministry of Information in the normal way, but were then taken in greatest secrecy direct to Churchill who gave them his imprimatur. This was not always granted. On one occasion he banned a talk by Harold Nicolson because he had suggested, at a crucial time, that the nation must be careful of ever getting to the position where a House of Commons would address the Prime

[54] Hansard, Vol. 362 cols. 1358-9. Herbert Morrison, addressing the Central Conference of Chief Constables on 16 January 1941, four days after the People's Convention had begun, made the remarkable statement: '... a member of the Labour Party, even one with extremist views, was not necessarily a Communist; and it did not always follow that a man was dangerous because he had dabbled in Communism at one time or another. Chief Constables should therefore exercise discretion in accepting reports of Communist sympathy or activity when these reports originated from sources which might not be well informed as to the various grades of political opinions on the left' (MEPO 2/6433). Whether this also was an expression of *haute politique* or simply a desire to prevent Labour Party comrades being locked up for advocating peace with Germany is not clear.

[55] Churchill's memorandum to the Minister of Information requesting that he establish more effective control over the BBC is in the Public Record Office: INF 1/869. The attempt failed after some two years' procrastination by the BBC and the appointment of liaison officers between the BBC and MOI for Home and Overseas affairs, who speedily became absorbed into the BBC staff structure. Control over the *content* of broadcasts, as opposed to the BBC itself, was soon established by censorship. For an illustration of a document with the BBC's censor's stamps on it, one for policy and one for security, see W.J. West (ed.) *Orwell: The War Broadcasts* (1985).

Minister with cries of 'Heil Churchill!'. On another, in 1941, he banned a talk by R.A. Butler, within twenty-four hours of the broadcast, on the grounds, it would seem, of its excessive defeatism, immediately afterwards moving him to the post of President of the Board of Education (the banned broadcast had referred to education as being one of the only sure hopes for the survival of our civilization).

Churchill's awareness of the value of radio propaganda was not confined to the famous speeches to the people of Britain. In October he broadcasted to France with the specific purpose of counteracting German radio propaganda, exhorting them to look to Britain rather than Germany:

> Do not imagine, as the German-controlled wireless tells you, that we English think to take your ships and Colonies. We seek to beat the life and soul out of Hitler and Hitlerism. That alone, that all the time, that to the end. We do not covet anything from any nation except their respect.[56]

Barely a week after Churchill had made this broadcast wide publicity was given to one by the American Ambassador to Britain, Joseph Kennedy, who had recently returned to America. In a lengthy broadcast he made his position as a leading exponent of American neutrality as surely as he could.

> All during my first year in England I felt strongly that if England got into war, in the long run it would be most unfortunate for the interests of our people ... After my experiences of the past year I am more convinced than ever that America should stay out of the war. The American people are overwhelmingly in favour of avoiding war and at the same time giving all aid short of war to Britain ... From the day I went to St James's until this minute I have never given to one single individual in the world any hope whatsoever that at any stage or under any conditions could the United States be drawn into the war ...[57]

Perhaps with this clear statement of American neutrality Churchill began himself to think in terms of reaching an agreement, not with the Axis itself, but with one part of it, Italy. In a remarkable broadcast to Italy on 23 December he launched an appeal to the Italian people couched in the most personal terms:

> Whoever imagined until the last few melancholy years that the British and Italian nations would be trying to destroy one another? We have

[56] As reported in the national press.
[57] As reported in *Keesing's Archives*, p.4344.

always been such friends. We were the champions of the Italian *Risorgimento*. We were the partisans of Garibaldi, the admirers of Mazzini and Cavour. All the great movements towards the unity of the Italian nation which lighted the nineteenth century were aided and hailed by the British parliament and public ... We have never been your foes until now. In the last war against the barbarous Huns we were your comrades. For 15 years after that war we were your friends. Although the institutions which you adopted after that war were not akin to ours, and diverged, as we think, from the Sovereign impulses which had commanded the unity of Italy we could still walk together in peace and goodwill. Many thousands of your people dwelt with ours in England; many thousands of our people dwelt with you in Italy. We liked each other, we got on well together. There were reciprocal services, there was amity, there was esteem.

And now we are at war; now we are condemned to work each other's ruin. Your aviators have tried to cast their bombs on London; our armies are tearing and will tear your African Empire to shreds and tatters ...[58]

Churchill went on to make a savage attack on Mussolini, whom he held responsible for all that had happened. The broadcast is interesting not only because of its content, which shows Churchill trying to remove Italy from German influence as aggressively as others were trying to sever Russia from her slightly less binding relationship with Germany. It is also a classic example of the radio propaganda technique of trying to create a revolt within a country, just as the Germans were trying to create revolt in Britain. And the parallel was even more specific, for Italy had been putting on a series of broadcasts during the Blitz in English which had been written and spoken by Barnes.[59] Indeed, apart from the attack on Mussolini Churchill's broadcast might have been written by Barnes. The reference to Fascism now universally regarded as the origin of all the difficulties and tensions of the inter-war years and later as, without naming it, 'institutions which you adopted after that war ... not akin to ours' is particularly striking. Whether Churchill knew, when making a reference to Garibaldi, that the General Garibaldi then living had come to England to plead the same cause and had been refused the microphone by the BBC, we shall probably never know; it seems unlikely.[60] But, at the end of one of the most eventful decades of British history, that Britain's greatest leader could join in a radio war that would have been impossible at the beginning of it showed the

[58] As reported in the national press.
[59] See above, p.48.
[60] For the Garibaldi incident, see above p.85f.

unique impact of radio and the new technology. That Churchill should find himself advocating a policy that was virtually identical with that advocated for most of the previous decade by Chamberlain, a policy which had got him the label of 'appeaser', a policy rejected by Churchill's later colleague Anthony Eden in favour of Britain's first radio war, shows the new media's extraordinary power in revealing the truth.

An American news broadcast at the very end of the year graphically portrayed Churchill's real view of the peace campaign in Britain, whatever his view of our relations with Italy:

December 30, 1940: Early today Prime Minister Winston Churchill walked down one street and up another, climbing over smouldering wreckage and wading through puddles of water. As the Prime Minister passed down the street, a woman called out to him, 'What about Peace, Mr Churchill?' In characteristic fashion he turned, walked straight up to the woman, looked at her a moment, then said: 'Peace? When we've beaten them.'[61]

[61] Lowell Thomas, op.cit., p.157.

Appendix

The three scripts printed here are taken from the BBC's daily monitors' reports which were recorded, transcribed, edited and printed within a matter of hours of being broadcast. They formed one of the most useful sources of 'inside' information available during the war on the way the war was actually going. Some six hundred copies were printed and sent to Government departments, the BBC, Fleet Street newspapers and other important news distribution centres. It was secret, despite the relatively large print run; for example the copies supplied to the House of Commons were kept under lock and key. This has lead some commentators to suppose that the text printed was uncensored. Facts that have come to light in recent years have established that this was not the case, though the exact extent of the editing, and by whom it was done, is not clear. The original typescripts taken down from the recordings are now in the Imperial War Museum, with the exception of at least some of the clandestine broadcasts, which unfortunately include the scripts printed here. There is some indication of the nature of the censorship in one of the texts printed in Churchill's secret session war speeches, but the texts here contain such savage attacks on Churchill that it would seem very unlikely that such censorship was in operation in 1940. As we have seen earlier, there was a Ministry of Information Intelligence Unit which received important information from the monitors by wire, and the officers who selected this information may have been those who did the censorship.[1] There was one well-known case of a breakdown in the system when an incident alleged to have taken place at Electra House was allowed through into the daily summary. In the inquest on this affair the Monitors defended themselves by pointing out that the text had been passed by MI5.[2] Whether this was a general term for the men who applied the censor stops and selected material for the Intelligence Unit, or was a correct identification of the men doing the work, it has not been possible to find out. There is no mention of any category of the security services carrying out this kind of work in the

[1] See above, p.206 for an example of their work.
[2] See above, p.204.

various books on that organization that have appeared in recent years.

There is one further, perhaps more far-fetched possibility, and that is that the reports may have been used to spread 'black' propaganda of the kind invented by R.H.S. Crossman[3] and the men who worked for him. These took the form of false rumours, known as 'Sibs', from the Latin *sibilare*, 'to hiss, or whisper', and were spread by a variety of ingenious methods, of which inclusion in the monitors' reports could conceivably have been one. However, the texts here are consistent with many others produced by the Workers Challenge station, and any intrusion would appear to be only of a matter of detail, a particular story, not affecting the general tone and content, which is unmistakably that of William Joyce. They are printed here as an example, the first published, of what people listened to night after night in the Radio War.

Workers Challenge Station: Medium Wave: In English for England
20.14 BST: 11.7.40

Workers Challenge. Here is Workers Challenge calling, the movement for revolutionary action against the bosses and war-mongers. They're talking about invasion now, and so far as we can see the Nazis will soon be on top of us if we don't make peace. Well, as we said yesterday, we don't want capitalism or imperialism in any shape or form. We're sick of both. Lots of the people we meet say 'Yes, it's either peace or invasion now' and I suppose they're not far wrong in saying that. But the point we want to make clear is that a capitalist peace is no damn good to the workers. We all know what a Nazi invasion would mean. It looks at first as if we're between the devil and the deep blue sea. But it isn't so bad as all that. We don't know how much longer it will be before the Nazis come, but we've got some time, even if it is only a few days, and in that time we've got to do all we can to overthrow the capitalist government and to set up a state for the working masses. Then if we have to defend it from the German attacker we know we've got something worth fighting for. But are you going to believe that if we do kick the Nazis out, Churchill and his gang are going to give us a real socialist state, a real government for the people, real economics for the proletariat? My friends, if you believe anything like that, go and see a few doctors. Get them to sign a nice little certificate and go into a pretty private residential hotel for the rest of your natural life. You'll find plenty of people of your way of thinking there, even if their manners do seem a bit queer. Don't be so simple-minded as to suppose that we're

[3] For Crossman's activities at this time, see above p.27f.

fighting this war for anything but the bosses. Of course, now that they want to take every young craftsman, every woman and child and every wire-haired terrier and train them as soldiers to fight the Jerries, they would promise anything. They'll promise that after the war we'll live in the Savoy and be waited on in the mornings by flunkies carrying cups of chocolate, bottles of brandy, a copy of *The Times*, to say nothing of a big bath towel, but we've heard all that muck before. When the capitalists get into a tight corner, they would promise anything to get out of it. Yes, you could probably even get a ...? of marzipan if you wanted it. But when the time comes to pay – ay, that's a different thing. That will be the time for economy, for retrenchment, for great sacrifices. They are going to abolish the slums – no, not exactly. They will leave that to the nice kind German Air Force and then, when our wretched homes are bombed to hell Winston Churchill will come round with a beaming smile all over his ugly dial, and say 'There you are, you see. I've solved the slum problem at last.' And if we happen to lose this war and our sticks of furniture and any little personal possessions we have, the Archbishop of Canterbury will come along and say 'Blessed are the poor, for theirs is the Kingdom of Heaven.' Yes, and then a bloody big German bomber will come along and send us to the Kingdom of Heaven, just to make sure His Grace isn't wrong. Still, let's try tonight to avoid thinking too much about the future. I knew it's very dark and dismal, but we all need something to cheer us up. Let's think about the present and a nice lively demonstration instead. Organise a real working-class meeting, a march, a demonstration; get the banners out. Churchill means hunger and war. Down with Churchill. Up with the workers' Britain. No bloodshed for capitalism. Let the bosses fight for their own profit. Kick 'em out of Westminster into the Thames. Hold a demonstration of that kind just to let the capitalist Government see that we don't want hunger and war. No doubt that would be well attended by the police. Well, just remember they are only men like yourselves. If you show any weakness, they've got you; they'll take you off the streets and put you in jug. But if you face up to 'em you'll probably find some snivelling old chief constable who (fought) in the Crimean war, saying 'Oh dear, how terrible. The rank and file is getting out of hand. This is preposterous. Don't do anything to disturb the peace sergeant. It might be bad for us.' You must forgive us if we seem to know the ...? mentality of the world, but the whole question is this: So long as they think the workers are weak they trample on them. But the very moment they think the workers are strong, good Lord, why, butter wouldn't melt in their dear little mouths.

They're really just like most people, after the pay envelope at the end of the week. So don't take them too seriously. What you've got to realise is this; anything that's worth doing is worth doing now, before this invasion, if it really does come. If the workers of Britain today rise in their millions, and put an end to the capitalist tyranny, then the real peace is before them, whether they make a mess of it or whether they don't. We may not all have been to Eton and Oxford, but we have a preference for digging our own graves, not trenches, but graves, and we'd sooner go into a grave of our own digging than one which the bosses have dug for us. The ground rent on the latter might be too high, and the place might be a little damp. In other words, whatever the peace of this country may turn out to be, it is up to us to have our turn. If we make some mistakes, well, we stand or fall by them, but we don't see why the fate of fifty million people should be settled by a handful of capitalist monkeys bowing and scraping at Buckingham Palace, or perhaps setting sail for Canada, when we're left in the lurch. The only system that we want is decent work, decent pay, decent houses, peace and control of our own affairs. Those are the things we want, and how do you think we are going to get them? By sitting back and waiting for capitalist Churchill and imperialist Hitler to decide who is going to rule and boss the country? Where the hell do we come in? The answer to this unparliamentary question is we either come in now, or we don't come in at all. Now is our chance to seize power. Workers of Britain, go out into the streets in your hundreds and thousands to demonstrate, by force if necessary, against Churchill, hunger and war. Think of what the crowd will have to say in Downing Street. Stand at the door and give the bosses notice to quit. Don't make any mistake about it, workers. It's neither Hitler nor Churchill that is master in Britain today. It's you, the workers, if you've got the guts to fight for your rights and carry forward the workers' challenge.

Workers Challenge Station: Medium Wave: In English for England: 21.10 BST. 25.7.40

Workers Challenge. Workers Challenge calling all workers of Britain and Northern Ireland on a wavelength of 213 metres every night at ten past eight, ten past nine and ten past ten.

Here is Workers Challenge calling. Workers Challenge against hunger and war. Churchill means hunger and war. Don't he just. How much he means it was shown by that fat, bloated, self-satisfied bladder of lies, Kingsley Wood, when he opened his new budget yesterday. It was bad enough that there's a gap of more than 2,000,000,000 pounds, but he wasn't satisfied with that, the greedy bastard. Those of you that have ever read Dickens remember how Oliver Twist asked for more. But this blighter asks for more even before he gets his first helping. And who's supposed to give him more? The workers, every time. Lousy Churchill turned down Hitler's offers of peace through that long streak of vestry-crawling futility, Halifax, and good Lord, to judge by the way it was done, you'd think that the Cabinet had a pleasant surprise for the nation. Was it pleasant?

And the workers will have to pay a penny more for their pint of beer, and tobacco's up threehalfpence an ounce. Of course, they put it on to the workers every time. What bloody right have we got to a pint of beer! We're only the proletariat. If we feel thirsty after a day's hard work we can peep through the curtain at some fat boss guzzling his champagne at 25 bob a bottle and playing with some lady friends [as] he wouldn't quite do in public. Well, then if we feel thirsty we can just watch him take another swill and then go home and tell the wife 'I'm a hero, I am. I haven't had my pint tonight because Churchill trusts me to win the war.'

And as for tobacco, well, damn it all, sir, a man that don't smoke cigars is just an outsider. They may cost a couple of bob each, but then they were meant for human beings, not for workers. Of course, if we do a good day's work we like a packet of Woodbines to help us on, but you see, that's a luxury and in wartime the workers mustn't expect luxuries. They must be reserved for the pot-bellied geniuses who stick in their offices thinking hard how to cheat the workers out of another penny. Oh, it's a wonderful game, and of course, a visit to the flicks is going to cost us more. But then these films weren't meant for workers really. They might demoralise us. After all, why should we want to go to the pictures and waste money? Buy the 'Daily Mirror' instead. You'll probably find a big picture of Churchill in it. So instead of going to the films you can sit down at home for two hours without fags and beer and look at Churchill's face. Yes, look at the bugger, and keep on looking at him, and you'll have as good a two hours' worth of entertainment as the Gaumont giddios could give you. Look at him. Keep him before you as the hero who's leading you from behind to invasion. Study his dirty dial in every detail because you won't see it much longer. It won't be there.

Well, that's one piece of advice we can give our listeners and instead of beer try a little water. Water is good for you. It builds bonny babies and gets you used to the prison diet which our dear Prime Minister is planning for you. About tobacco, well, we're not so sure. We are afraid you will have to do without it. But you can always breathe in and out and imagine it's smoke, because you see, this bloody country is free. There's nothing to stop you breathing unless one of Churchill's military courts get hold of you and sentences you to death.

And then another thing that shows the kindness of the bosses is that they are going to deduct money from our wages every week to fight their bloody capitalist war. That's nice, isn't it. Do you remember a little while ago, when prices began to rise, and the Labour leaders, God damn them, were in opposition? 'Oh', they said, 'You mustn't let prices rise without increasing wages. We'll never stand for that'. And they never did stand for it either until the whole bloody lot got safe inside the Cabinet. And now, instead of raising our wages, to keep pace with prices, they're taking something off. So we've got to deal not only with the fall in real wages, but with the deductions as well. Now there is a challenge to the workers the like of which they've never seen before.

Just remember that the rich have got away with it. Most of them have put their money in Canada or the United States already, and if their incomes are compared with ours, what they have to pay is a mere fleabite, poor darlings. When they have paid their taxes some of them won't have more than 30 or 40 thousand a year left. Some of them, like Nuffield and Rothermere, may not have more than a few hundred thousand or a million a year left. Isn't it a shame. Don't our hearts bleed for them as we think of them trying to live on their little bit of bread and cheese and fumbling in their pockets to see if they can find an extra penny for a pint of beer? Yes, we've got a challenge now. The workers' challenge. And it's going to take definite form. We've been telling you to organise for the fight. We've been warning you to prepare for the onslaught that the capitalists would make on you. And now it's coming.

Here is a policy for you in three points. First, no deductions from the weekly wages. Second, no extra tax on beer. Third, no extra tax on tobacco. Here is the material for a first-class campaign, and by 'Campaign' we don't make mean making speeches or holding indignation meetings though they're valuable too. The one way to gain these three points is for every worker in the country to down tools until they're granted. Leave your factories. Leave your mines. Leave your workshops. And just stand firm. Show the government and the bosses. No deductions from wages, no penny on the pint, and no threehalfpence on the ounce. Don't be timid or halfhearted about it. Come out all at once like men, and in three hours time the bloody government will have to give way. And when you've shown the capitalist dictators that you can get your own way once, you'll do it again and again. Those lousy capitalists are only a miserable gang of blasters relying on the coppers whom the workers could eat alive if they wanted. As to the troops, they're not in it. They are not going to fire on the working-class because they belong to the class themselves. Any monkey work with them will mean that Churchill and his gang are put against the nearest wall and shot. That is to say, they'll have to drink the medicine that they have prescribed for the workers. So there's no need to worry about the troops, and believe me, in that connection, there are lousy things happening all over the country today, and if you knew what they were, you'd be very surprised. We are not going to say any more about this, but the government knows that selected groups of workers are already taking action to secure the workers' state. Believe me, Churchill and his thugs have the wind up proper, and they know that behind the workers' challenge there's an organisation that matters. So this is just the right moment to give Churchill and his gang the push. Set to work on these three points: no deductions from wages; no penny on the pint; and no threehalfpence on tobacco. And join the struggle now. Don't argue. Just walk out, and the bosses will soon call you back again with tears in their eyes. That'll be just the first taste of what's coming to them. Don't wait for invasion. Act now. Workers of Britain, rise and claim your own. Then there will be no invasion and no bloody capitalist government either. That is the workers' challenge. On with the first three points of your programme and show that you, the workers, can be the real masters of the country. Forward with the workers' challenge.

Workers Challenge will again be calling all workers of Britain and Northern Ireland on a wavelength of 213 metres tomorrow evening at ten past eight, ten past nine and ten past ten.

Christian Peace Movement: 31.76 m.: In English for England: 19.45 BST: 21.8.40: (Y.U.1).

Germany's Peace Offers Refused

(O God our Help in Ages Past: one verse sung by choir.) This is the Christian Peace Movement, calling all Britons to the true Christian life, and to work for peace. You will hear our services daily at 7.45 p.m. and at 8.45 p.m. on a wavelength of 31.76 metres.

Judge not that ye be not judged, and with what judgement ye judge ye shall be judged, and with what measure ye mete, it shall be measured to you again. From this warning it is clear that Christ does not expect us to judge others. Judge not, that ye be not judged. Beware of judging, and of judging too hardly. The severity with which you deal with others will recoil upon your own head. For when it is time for you to be judged, you shall be judged. Severely. For with what judgement ye judge, and with what measure ye mete, it shall be measured to you again.

This command we should bear in mind when we blame Germany for causing the war. Are we not as much to blame as she is? (Inaudible passage here.) Why did we refuse Germany's peace offer last October? Why did we again ignore her peace proposals last month? Do we really want to carry on the war? Are we so enthusiastic as all that about it? Is it necessary? Those of us who have lost relations or friends in the forces know all too well the sorrow of being parted, that suspense of hearing nothing for weeks, perhaps months, and of not knowing whether they are alive or dead.

When war was declared on Germany last September, the majority of Christians took it for granted that they could do nothing in the matter. It seemed to many that we had to fight, and that there was nothing to do but grin and bear it. What is the Christian attitude? Of course, it would be completely untrue to say that the people in England have any enthusiasm for war. It is, indeed, amazing that the men who started the war have been allowed to carry out their wicked designs unchecked. Why is a nation so easily misled? Generally, because its people have not paid sufficient attention to the word of God, and therefore trouble not to carry out His command. People who ask themselves, 'Is this war a righteous war?' and if everything is going as well for us as we have been told, get a shock.

Ignorance of the Public

But by now there must be many who have awakened to the truth of Christianity, or who have no doubt as to the injustice or undesirability of this second great war. Have you ever stopped to consider the awful significance of the war? Are you worried about the future prospects of the Christian point of view? In spite of many attempts during and after the great war to enlighten the people of this country as to its true causes, the majority, because of that Government propaganda, remained in ignorance of the real state of affairs. It was not until the tragic truth became clear at the end of the war, that the nation realised how far it had been led away from the principles of Christianity.

Once again the Government has misled us into a dreadful war, the result of which many of you have yet to see. How can we pretend to achieve anything good by committing fearful slaughter? ... Before another million of our men are sacrificed, let us ask ourselves: 'What does this war mean to me? What am I being asked to fight for? And what will the result be? Can I, as a Christian, support the war?' The answer is simple. You cannot. It is important to bear in mind that we are told about the last war of 1914-1918 that no obstacle to a universal reign of peace in Europe should survive and that the supreme aim of the Government was to put an end to war. To usher in a new age of democracy and peace; to remove from all nations the intolerable burden of armaments; to lead the people to a better Christian life.

Did they succeed in any of these aims? We were told that never in the history of the world have governments engaged in war been inspired by such noble and unselfish purposes as now. Remember how we were deceived last time, while facing the greatest of all sacrifices – sacrifices that seemed to be absolutely useless. You are now being misled again, into thinking that war can bring you peace and save your religion. War is not Christianity. God's will is peace. Remember Christ's words: 'Blessed are the peacemakers, for they shall be called the Children of God.' Pray for peace. Work for peace. Demand peace.

You have been listening to the Christian Peace Movement, calling all Britons to live a true Christian life and to work for peace. You will hear our services daily at 7.45 p.m. and 8.45 p.m. on a wavelength of 31.76 metres. (O God our Help in Ages Past: one verse sung by choir.) (Transmission repeated at 20.45.)

Bibliography

A tradition has grown up in recent years for the bibliography attached to works of modern history to be, in fact, a general reading list in the field. This bibliography is simply an *index librorum*: a list of books that have been cited in the text, with the numbers after each entry referring to the pages of this book where the work in question is cited. A bibliography of works in the most important neglected area, contemporary printed sources, would alone fill this entire volume were it to be of use.

Action, 9, 90, 217

Max K. Alder, *A Socialist Remembers*, unpublished ms, 77

W. E. D. Allen (and Kim Philby), *David Allens: The History of a Family Firm* (1957), 120, 122; for other works listed see 122n41

Christopher Andrew, *The Secret Service* (1986), 131

The Anglo-Russian Parliamentary Committee, '*Peace Indivisible*' (1936), 203

Anonymous, *Freedom Calling: The Story of the Secret German Radio* (n.d., *c*. 1940), 191

Anonymous, *The Origin and Development of the League of Nations Union* (n.d., *c*. 1931, published by the Boswell Printing and Publishing Company), 84

Anonymous, *Sidelights on the Cliveden Set* (1938, published by the Communist Party of Great Britain), 206

Association of [BBC] Broadcasting Staff Bulletin, 181

C. R. Attlee, '*Peace Indivisible*', see The Anglo-Russian Parliamentary Committee

Oliver Baldwin, *Oasis* (1936), 9

Stanley Baldwin, *This Torch of Freedom* (1937 ed.), 12

Lionel Barber, see John Lawrenson and Lionel Barber

James Strachey Barnes, *Fascism* (1931), 15

    Half a Life (1933), 48

    Half a Life Left (1937), 92

Jonah Barrington, *Lord Haw-Haw of Zeesen* (1939), x, 174

Vernon Bartlett, *The Brighter Side of Chaos* (1925), 24

Norman Bentwich, *Wanderer in War* (1946), 157; see also Ritchie Calder and Norman Bentwich

J. D. Bernal, *Marx and Science* (1952), 59

Lord Birkenhead, *Walter Monckton* (1969), 206

The Blackshirt, x

Robert Blake, *Disraeli* (1966), 144

Anthony Cave Brown and Charles B. MacDonald, *On a Field of Red: The Communist International and the Coming of World War II* (1981), 109

R.H. Bruce Lockhart, *Comes the Reckoning* (1947), 131, 145, 200

Burke's Peerage, 20

Sir Alexander Cadogan, *The Diaries of Sir Alexander Cadogan O.M. 1938-1945*, edited by David Dilks (1971), 147, 152, 159, 163-4, 166

F. M. Cahen, *Men Against Hitler* (1939), 196

Ritchie Calder and Norman Bentwich, *The Spiritual Basis of Peace* (1940), 203

John Charmley, *Duff Cooper* (1986), 145

Harwood L. Childs and John B. Whitton, *Propaganda by Short Wave* (1943), 34, 67

Randolph S. Churchill, *Winston S. Churchill* vols. 1-2 (1966-7), 9

Winston S. Churchill, *Secret Session Speeches* (1946), 204; see also Randolph S. Churchill; Martin Gilbert; Warren F. Kimball; Arrigo Pettacco

J. A. Cole, *Lord Haw-Haw: The Full Story of William Joyce* (new ed. 1987), 233
Ian G. Colvin, *Vansittart in Office* (1965), 134, 144
　The Chamberlain Cabinet (1971), 134
Colin Cross, *The Fascists in Britain* (1961), 233
Common Wealth, *First Agenda for the Second Conference, Easter 1944* (1944), 209
Charles Cruickshank, *The Fourth Arm: Psychological Warfare 1938-45* (1977 OUP ed. 1981), 204-5
Viscount D'Abernon, *The Eighteenth Decisive Battle of the World, Warsaw 1920* (1931), 154
Daily Express, 109, 174
Daily Herald, 203
Daily Telegraph, 175, 177
Roy Day (ed.), *Uncensored British News Bulletin* [no copy found *c.* 1940], 211
Sefton Delmer, *Black Boomerang* (1962), 69, 109
Günther Deschner, *Heydrich: The Pursuit of Total Power* (1981), 196
Dictionary of National Biography (DNB), 11, 12
Tom Driberg, *Guy Burgess: A Portrait with Background* (1956), 47, 116, 121, 200
David Dutton, *Austen Chamberlain: Gentleman in Politics* (1985), 13
P. P. Eckersley, *The Power Behind the Microphone* (1941), 120
Roger Eckersley, *The BBC and All That* (1946), 120
Les Edwards, *Scrim, Radio Rebel in Retrospect* (1971), 2
Egyptian Mail, 93
Lord Elton, *The Life of James Ramsay MacDonald* (1939), 11
　It Occurs to Me (1938), 46
S. Engel, *League Reform: An Analysis of Official Proposals 1936-39* (1940), 18
Evening Standard, 35, 46
Express and Echo (Exeter), 211, 228
Fascist News, 20
David Fisher, see Anthony Read and David Fisher
James Fox, *White Mischief* (1982), 127
Simon Freeman, see Barrie Penrose and Simon Freeman
Gazeta Polska, 156
Geneva Studies, 18, 34, 165
W. R. P. George, *Lloyd George Backbencher* (1983), 13
Martin Gilbert, *Winston S. Churchill* vols. 3- (1971-), 9
Peter and Leni Gillman, *'Collar the Lot!'* (1980), 229
Giornale d'Italia, 188
W. E. Gladstone Murray, *Canada's Place in Civilisation* (1946), 15
Anthony Glees, *The Secrets of the Service: British Intelligence and Communist Subversion 1939-51* (1987),
　53, 58, 61, 109, 119, 193, 221
Thomas Grandin, *The Political Use of Radio* (1939), 34, 165
F. L. Habel, *'Hello Everybody!': A Voice of Friendship: Short Waves over the World* (1936), 71
Louis Hagen (ed.), *The Schellenburg Memoirs* (1956), 167
Lord Halifax, *Fulness of Days* (1957), 112
Julian Hall, *Radio Power* (1978), 95
Hansard, 104, 105, 158, 222, 223, 241
J. Harvey (ed.), *The Diplomatic Diaries of Oliver Harvey 1937-40* (1970), 164
Hastings, Duke of Bedford, *The 'Can't Trust Hitler' Bogey* (1940), 202
　If I Were Prime Minister (1942), 202
　The Years of Transition (1949), 202
Arthur Henderson, *Labour's Way to Peace* (1935), 203
Sir Nevile Henderson, *Failure of a Mission: Berlin 1937-1939* (1940), 135, 168
Stuart Hibberd, *This – Is London* (1950), 189
John A. Hobson, *The Modern State* (1931), 16
Anthony Howard, *RAB: The Life of R. A. Butler* (1987), 125
Ellic Howe, *The Black Game* (1982), 119
International Affairs, 131
David Irving, *The War Path: Hitler's Germany 1933-39* (1978 Papermac ed. 1983), 76, 133, 150, 152,
　159

H. V. Kaltenborn, *I Broadcast the Crisis* (1938), 136, 138, 141
Keesing's Archives, 155, 242
Ian Kershaw, *Popular Opinion and Political Dissent in the Third Reich: Bavaria 1933-45* (1983), 77
Warren F. Kimball (ed.), *Churchill and Roosevelt: The Complete Correspondence* (3 vols. 1954), 9
Kokusai Bunka Shinkokai (The Society for International Cultural Relations), *Prospectus and Scheme* (1934), 149
Richard Lamb, *The Ghosts of Peace 1935-1945* (1987), 106
Neville Laski, *Jewish Rights and Jewish Wrongs* (1939), 152
John Lawrenson and Lionel Barber, *The Price of Truth* (1985 revised ed. 1986), 26
Sir Reginald Leeper, *When Greek Meets Greek* (1950), 25
Eugene Lennhoff, *The Last Five Hours of Austria* (1938), 75, 76
A. D. Lindsay, *Pacifism as a Principle and Pacifism as a Dogma* (1939), 203
The Listener, 82
David Lloyd George, *The Truth about the Peace Treaties* (1938), 13, 131
Charles B. MacDonald, see Anthony Cave Brown and Charles B. MacDonald
Richard D. Mandell, *The Nazi Olympics* (1971), 70
Gerard Mansell, *Let Truth be Told* (1982), 22, 70, 99, 101
David Marquand, *Ramsay MacDonald* (1977), 11
Gordon Martel (ed.), *'The Origins of the Second World War' Reconsidered* (1986), 155
J. C. Masterman, *The Double-Cross System in the War of 1939-1945* (1972), 190
Anthony Masters, *The Man Who Was M: The Life of Maxwell Knight* (1984), 237
Hilda Matheson, *Broadcasting* (1933), 116
Joan Miller, *One Girl's War* (1987) [not published in Great Britain], 235
A. A. Milne, *Peace with Honour* (1934), 144
Kenneth O. Morgan, *David Lloyd George* (1981), 13
Nicholas Mosley, *Rules of the Games: Sir Oswald Mosley and Lady Cynthia Mosley 1896-1933* (1982), 9
    Beyond the Pale: Sir Oswald Mosley and Family 1933-1980 (1983), 9, 121
Sir Oswald Mosley, *My Life* (1968), 9
John Middleton Murry, *The Necessity of Pacifism* (1937), 202
    The Necessity of Communism (1952), 202
    Dostoevsky (1916), 202
    The Brotherhood of Peace (1940), 203
New York Daily News, 9
News Chronicle, 133, 134, 135, 184
Harold Nicolson, *Diaries and Letters 1930-39* (1966), 48
    Politics in the Train (1936), 55
Francis R. Nicosia, *The Third Reich and the Palestine Question* (1985), 156
Edna Nixon, *John Hilton: The Story of his Life* (1946), 37
J. Noakes and G. Pridham, *Nazism 1919-1945*: vol. 2 *State Economy and Society 1933-39* (1984), 73
Sir Lancelot Oliphant, *Ambassador in Bonds* (1946), 23
George Orwell, *The War Broadcasts* (1985), 48, 56, 59, 94, 241
    The War Commentaries (1986), 94
    Nineteen Eighty-Four (1949), 181
S. Payne Best, *The Venlo Incident* (1950), 88, 190-1
Peace News, 208
Penguin New Writing, 61
Barrie Penrose and Simon Freeman, *Conspiracy of Silence: The Secret Life of Anthony Blunt* (1986), 47
Terence Pepper, *Howard Coster's Celebrity Portraits* (1985), viii
Lord Perth (as Sir Eric Drummond), *The League of Nations* (1933), 165
Arrigo Pettacco, *Dear Benito, Caro Winston: verità e misteri del carteggio Churchill-Mussolini* (1985), 9
Kim Philby, see W. E. D. Allen and Kim Philby
The Plebs League, *Fascism: Its History and Significance* (1924), 40
G. Pridham, see J. Noakes and G. Pridham
D. N. Pritt, *Forward to a People's Government* (1940), 230
David Pryce-Jones, *Unity Mitford: A Quest* (1976), 123
Baron Putlitz, *The Putlitz Dossier* (1957), 193
Radio Pictorial, 21, 111

Index